GREATER LOVE

A Directory of Chaplains of the
British Army, Australian, Canadian, East African,
New Zealand and South African Forces
and Ministers of Religion,
who gave their lives in the period
1914 - 1922.

Jesus, confirm my heart's desire
To work, and speak, and think for thee;
Ready for all thy perfect will,
My acts of faith and love repeat,
Till death thy endless mercies seal,
And make the sacrifice complete.

Charles Wesley 1707 - 1788

Published by Printability Publishing Ltd.
on behalf of Revd. David T. Youngson © 2008.

Design and Typography by Ibis Design.

Printed by Atkinson Print Ltd.
10/11 Lower Church Street,
Hartlepool TS24 7DJ
Tel: 01429 267849 Fax: 01429 865416

e-mail: printability@atkinsonprint.co.uk
www..atkinsonprint.co.uk

ISBN 1 872239 53 6

INTRODUCTION

The research for this book began some three years ago arising from a casual enquiry about one Priest, Fr. Matthew Burdess. It became clear that many "men of the cloth" had died during and as a result of the First World War.

Encouraged by David Blake, Curator of the Museum of Army Chaplaincy, I began to look through my library of World War One events. Being blind, I was supported by my wife Eileen, my sons Graeme and Andrew, Tony Watkins and Nancy Milburn - Bates. An in-depth study was undertaken.

I am particularly grateful to The Revd. Dr. Peter Howson, for his advice and research into this subject and Peter Rudd for Graphics and Photographs.

Those who are recorded in this book are men, young and old, of firm faith and intellect, who in the words of others, "made the supreme sacrifice". The world is glad to have known them but, the poorer for losing them.

As the task developed, it became for me a very personal spiritual journey. These people were no longer data to be processed, or names on memorials. They came to life with their pain and sacrifice. All I could do was to offer that pain and sacrifice to God and He gave me Peace to continue.

Many people and agencies have supplied information and, more importantly, encouragement to produce this Directory. They are listed in the Acknowledgements.

There is no doubt that somewhere there is a lot more information about these men. I hope that what has been written will encourage others to look further so that their sacrifice will never be forgotten.

Although he does not meet the criteria for this book, it is worth recording that the oldest serving Army Chaplain was The Revd. James Shaw, a Presbyterian minister with the Indian Ecclesiastical Establishment in Quetta. He was called up for Chaplaincy service early in 1918 at the advanced age of 73 and was demobilised on the 15th February 1919.

It seems to me that some of the words written by Sir Edward Elgar at the end of The Dream of Gerontius are appropriate.

" This is the best of me;
for the rest, I ate, and drank, and slept,
loved and hated like another;
This if anything is worthy of your memory"

Revd. David T Youngson
August 2007

David Youngson is Blind and the Author of,
The Search for a Scottish Soldier
Privately published for his family 1993
The Cleveland Way - A guide for the Visually Impaired
Published by the North Yorks National Park 1998
Stockton's longest serving Rector
Published 2005

PREFACE

There is a Plaque in the Chapel at the Armed Forces Chaplaincy Centre, Amport House, which refers to the 172 Chaplains who died. It was originally in the Royal Army Chaplains' Memorial Chapel at Bagshot Park.

It reads:

FOR REMEMBRANCE
1914-18

ONE HUNDRED AND SEVENTY TWO CHAPLAINS OF ALL THE CHURCHES
GAVE THEIR LIVES.
THEIR NAMES ARE INSCRIBED IN THE SANCTUARY OF THE
ROYAL GARRISON CHURCH OF ALL SAINTS, ALDERSHOT.

HEREBY PERCEIVE
WE THE LOVE OF GOD
BECAUSE HE LAID DOWN
HIS LIFE FOR US:
AND WE OUGHT TO LAY
DOWN OUR LIVES FOR
THE BRETHREN.

A second plaque reads:

IN THANKSGIVING FOR THE GALLANT AND DEVOTED SERVICE
IN PEACE AND WAR
OF THE CHAPLAINS OF THE TERRITORIAL FORCE
1907-1921
AND OF THE TERRITORIAL ARMY
1922-1967

WE WALKED IN THE HOUSE OF GOD
AS FRIENDS.

The Memorial in The Royal Garrison Church of All Saints Aldershot commemorates the Army Chaplains who died during the First World War. This is the only Memorial that lists names. It was designed without references to denomination, decorations or date and place of death. Dedicated at a special service held on the 31st October 1923 it carries the inscription, ***"This memorial commemorates the chaplains of all churches".*** Not all the names on the memorial were of serving chaplains, and not all serving chaplains who died during the war were included.

This book is an attempt, in some measure, to produce a comprehensive appreciation of clergy who died during the First World War and others who, for one reason or another, have been remembered or appear in official records up to 1922.

In 2004 Mrs. Jenny Harrison compiled a document, drawing together the names of chaplain casualties from the Commonwealth War Graves Commission lists and *Officers who died... 1914 - 1918* compiled by S. D. and D. B. Jarvis.

In an article published in the *Journal of the Society for Army Historical Research,* the Revd. Dr. Peter J. Howson set out to analyse the circumstances of the deaths among chaplains. Included were those whose deaths occurred after 1920 and were on the Aldershot Memorial.

Drawing together these sources and including the Forces now designated Commonwealth casualties listed by the Commonwealth War Graves Commission, a total of 257 entries are recorded in the Directory. The information for the Australian and New Zealand Chaplains has been found by my son Andrew who lives in Melbourne and from a Directory of Anglican Clergy who were based in New Zealand. While they are not complete they, like the Canadian and African Chaplains listed, give some idea of how clergy from several denominations within the Commonwealth responded.

From the early stages of my research it was clear that an ecumenical and objective approach would be essential to determine the precise nature of what evolved in terms of Army Chaplaincy during the First World War. Several of the publications referred to in this Directory clearly showed a denominational bias and I resolved not to be persuaded one way or the other. In presenting the data I have tried not to express personal opinions. The reader will draw their own conclusions.

Having been brought up in The Church of Scotland and the Presbyterian Church of England I had some idea of these particular denominations. As a National Training Officer of The Boys' Brigade I also had a certain amount of knowledge of the structures of the non conformist churches. During my National service I became an Anglican by conviction and conversion, being helped considerably by Bernard Harrison, a student at Mirfield, and Graham Pattison a student at Kelham. The three of us were eventually ordained priests.

CHAPLAINS TO THE FORCES

It is not my intention to write a pocket history of Army Chaplaincy but a few historical facts are recorded to give some idea as to the situation at the outbreak of the First World War.

The need for spiritual support to the Forces was something which both those in command and church leaders had recognised over a considerable length of time.

The Army Chaplains' Department was formed in 1796, with a Chaplain General. ('Royal' conferred on 22nd February1919). Presbyterians were appointed from 1858 and Wesleyan ministers served as acting chaplains because their church would not allow them to take Commissions. The Revd. Thomas J. Thorpe, listed below, is an example of a ministry to the Forces outside the Army Chaplains' Department. Missionaries of the Church Missionary Society and the China Inland Mission were involved on a somewhat ad hoc basis to Garrisons where there was no appointed Chaplain. The creation of the Indian Army and the Indian Ecclesiastical Establishment produced a chaplaincy service. Some chaplains mentioned in the Directory had their roots in these structures before becoming Army Chaplains.

The Royal Navy also had a long history of Chaplains at sea and shore establishments. The Boer and South African Wars saw an increase of need, much of which was provided by the church in South Africa. At home local clergy were being encouraged to perform chaplaincy duties to territorial units. However there appeared to be a distinct lack of clergy from denominations outside the Church of England and Roman Catholic churches.

The history of Chaplains clearly shows that ecclesiastical and political considerations were taken into account and placed alongside military requirements.

In his article Peter Howson wrote,

"In August 1914 the establishment of the Army Chaplains' Department (AChD) was made up of 117 regular Church of England, Roman Catholic and Presbyterian chaplains. Some 40 'Temporary' Chaplains were also employed".

At the outbreak of the First World War the Chaplain General was The Right Revd. John Taylor Smith, who had been in post since 1901. He claimed, "Justness and scrupulous fairness" in the selection of Chaplains. He came under severe criticism not only from Anglican Chaplains and Clergy, but also the other Christian denominations. The main thrust of the criticism coming from within the ranks of Anglican clergy in that he was biased against "high churchman" when recruiting Temporary Chaplains. A careful look at the Theological Colleges in the Index and the record of my own college below would tend to indicate that as the war progressed, "churchmanship" ceased to be an issue. It also appeared that Anglican Chaplains received higher ranks than those from other denominations. The issue surrounding Fr. Peter Grobel is detailed in his entry.

Bishop John Taylor Smith did however win a certain amount of credit in taking a firm line with the Archbishop of Canterbury against the conscription of Clergy as combatants.

It is important to understand that Chaplains drawn from the Church of England embraced what are now The Church of Ireland, The Church of Wales and the Episcopal Church of Scotland. There were also Anglican Clergy working overseas who were appointed by the Army Chaplains' Department, whilst others became Chaplains with what is now described as Commonwealth Forces. Some Church of England Clergy on short term contracts, with Incumbency status, continued their "living" and returned to England from time to time to officiate in their parishes. Curates having served their Title, tended to become a Temporary Chaplain to the Forces in the expectation that they would be offered a post at the end of the hostilities.

When the Royal Air Force was established on the 1st April 1918, several Naval and Army Chaplains were transferred to become Chaplains to the R.A.F. Many had been attached to units of The Royal Flying Corps. The R.A.F. Chaplaincy was not set up until after the hostilities had ended. There is one Chaplain Casualty recorded by the C.W.G.C. as being an R.A.F. Chaplain. The Revd. Frederick William Ashton is shown in RAChD Records as being commissioned into the Army but he is not listed as having died or transferred.

Several ministers enlisted as officers and performed chaplaincy duties. Some later became Chaplains. It has been verbally implied from Congregational sources that non conformist ministers offering themselves as Chaplains were pressurised to accept Anglican Orders. However I have been unable to find any documentary evidence to this effect despite this view being volubly expressed to me by a relative of a Y.M.C.A. Chaplain casualty in the course of my research.

The start of the war saw the granting of commissions to Wesleyans. A Memorial in Wesley's Chapel, London reads;

"In Loving Memory of the 26,581 Wesleyan's who gave their lives in the Great War and in gratitude to the 285,000 who also served".

The response by men and women of Christian belief to serve was overwhelming. With such a variety of doctrinal understanding and forms of ministry both lay and ordained, a certain amount of confusion, difficulties and "territorial fencing" was inevitable.

An almost immediate formation of a United Navy and Army Board to represent the needs of smaller denominations was set up. The title was adopted on the 14th of January 1915. As indicated there was a certain amount of "territorial fencing" resulting in ministers of the Presbyterian Church and several branches of Methodism not being included.

A statement in 1915 declared that,

"The Baptist Union of Great Britain and Ireland and the Congregational Union of England and Wales act together in securing the appointment of Army and Navy officiating ministers. A further agreement, sanctioned by the War Office, has now been come to under which we act also on behalf of the Primitive Methodists and the United Methodists".

The authorities, having been persuaded of the need for Chaplains to serve those men who were not from the main stream denominations, recruited clergy. As the war continued Clergy from all denominations were offered short term contracts. (See The Revd. W. M. Onslow Carleton)

The Lists of the United Board ministers who performed Chaplaincy duties, mainly on the home front, for 1915 and 1916 show a tremendous response for this ministry. To illustrate the response this list appears as an appendix. It should be noted that many listed survived the War.

Various titles were adopted in the early stages of the war. Chaplains to the Territorial Forces (C.T.F.) were listed with their units. They served on a different contract to Temporary Chaplains (T.C.F). The Church of Scotland had a pre-existing Chaplaincy Service.

The Roman Catholic Chaplains are well documented in **The Cross on the Sword** by Johnstone and Hagerty.

There was virtually no recognisable training for new Chaplains until 1916. Chaplains were posted to units at home and in the theatres of war. A certain amount of care was exercised to meet the needs of men but this was not always possible. Some inter denominational co-operation took place as will be shown. Types of ministry were varied. Chaplains were seen as Commissioned Officers and some enjoyed "comforts" that front line troops dreamt of. It is worth while reading the diary extracts of the Revd. Rupert Inglis (Internet - Inglis Family). He presents a vivid picture of the life and work of a chaplain behind the lines and on the Front.

Correspondence between Fr. Peter Grobel and several other Roman Catholic colleagues and Cardinal Bourne highlight some of the "difficulties" being experienced between front line Chaplains and their superiors. A failure to understand the real needs is a charge that can be laid on those ecclesiastical dignitaries having a "pastoral oversight".

The official records are bland statements of fact and give little clue as to what occurred. This is particularly so with those who are simply listed as having died. Witnesses to events and other sources create a much clearer picture and have to be read alongside the records. The Revd. Gerald James Lester and The Revd. Cecil Radcliffe Martyn are recorded as having died. But records in Hatfield College Durham show Lester, "he was fatally wounded, and died in France". Martyn is listed "having been wounded, died of pneumonia". His death occurred in a Military Hospital in Belfast.

The death of the Revd. Rupert Inglis is another typical example. In a letter written by the Revd. Neville Talbot to his widow the statement of fact is recorded. However his diary entries give a much greater insight into the mind, courage and cause of death of this brave man.

Additional information on those listed as having 'Died', is shown against the particular entry. Despite all, men of faith conducted themselves with dignity and courage. Such deeds of valour are instanced throughout the Directory.

The Salvation Army was also involved. In his Thesis, **The Salvation Army's Actions and Attitudes in Wartime 1899-1945** - Albert Shaw Clifton argues that "Initially there was a certain amount of disagreement over women Salvationists working with Army Ambulance Units". The International HQ of the Salvations Army felt that the Government was hidebound and short sighted.

The War Office adopted a somewhat ambivalent attitude over recognition of Salvation Army Officers as Ministers of Religion being exempt from conscription. It was argued that every Salvationist serving in the Armed Forces, regardless of rank, was a Chaplain. The Salvation Army maintained that "hundreds of Salvationist servicemen functioned as unofficial Chaplains and the Women Officers in France exercised unusually effective spiritual soul winning ministries".

It is worthwhile noting that the Commonwealth Forces and the USA had 41 Salvationist Chaplains serving the Allied Forces by mid 1917.

Recognition of the Salvation Army as a religious denomination for the purpose of attestation by servicemen, the public participation in Salvation Army religious activities of servicemen in uniform, and the appointment of British Salvation Army Officers as official Chaplains to the Forces was sought. Several concessions were obtained but it was not until April 1918, and after much public debate, four Salvation Army Officers "were made official Chaplains to the King's Army". They were Major Powley, Commandant Otter, Adjutant England and Captain Purkis. They were dedicated by Bramwell Booth at the Westminster Central Hall on the 9th April 1918. Lieutenant Col, Charles Knott was later appointed Chaplain. The only casualty was Walter Harry Powley who appears in the Army List of 1918 and died on the 23rd February 1919. An interesting account of Salvationist "Chaplains" is to be found in *Sportsmen Parsons in Peace and War page 259ff.* Mrs. Stuart Menzies

The scope of my research has produced much more information than I ever envisaged. The names of most are to be found nationwide in churches, colleges and on local memorials. Several specific Memorials have been mentioned. Two of particular interest are in Beverley Minster showing the names of three from different denominations (Finn, Trevor and Wilks) and in All Saints' Church, Woodlands, near Doncaster, where the first Incumbent and his Curate appear. (Ranking and Gibbs)

A brief mention must be made of Talbot House at Poperinghe Belgium. It was set up by The Revd. Philip Thomas Byard Clayton known to his friends as "Tubby". He was an Army Chaplain during the First World War from 1915 serving in France and Flanders. He opened a soldier's rest house behind the Allied lines at Gasthuisstraat, Poperinge in the autumn of 1915 assisted by a fellow Chaplain, The Revd. Neville Talbot. The house was subsequently named Talbot House after the death of Lieutenant Gilbert Walter Lyttelton Talbot of the 7th Battalion Rifle Brigade who died on the 30th July 1915 aged 23.

Talbot House was known in signalers jargon as Toc H and became a unique place of fellowship and sanctuary from the fighting for all ranks with a Chapel at the top of the house (Hop Loft). Although it was similar to those which the Y.M.C.A. and other voluntary organisations had set up elsewhere, it had something unique, which flowed from the character of Clayton and the brotherhood he fostered. Friendships were formed across ranks and many discovered a reality in religion for the first time. The house remained open till the Spring of 1918 when German advances brought it directly into the battle zone. The effect of the house inspired a number of those who had passed through the house to recreate its atmosphere and ethos in peacetime. It is open to visitors and overnight accommodation is available. (See Biography by Rice and Priedeaux-Brune)

VOLUNTARY SECTOR

The need for welfare, social provision, particularly on the Western Front and elsewhere was recognized by several voluntary sector agencies. Deaths and Casualties occurred but they do not appear in this directory.

The Catholic Women's League gave valuable service to the Chaplains and troops in the United Kingdom, France and Flanders, providing hospitality, social care and refreshment.

The Church of Scotland's Guild established twenty five centres, known as "huts". Manned by 350 workers and Ministers, who performed Chaplaincy duties. They were drawn from The Church of Scotland and The United Free Church of Scotland, and served in France and Flanders and in Germany after the hostilities had ended. There was one Chaplain Casualty (The Revd. A. E. Spence) who is not listed in this Directory.

The Church Army opened a hospital at Caen in September 1914. Tents and later huts were provided at many camps and barracks in the United Kingdom and gradually into all theatres of war. By 1918 there were some 800 huts in France and Flanders manned by more than 800 workers. Some were quiet places for reflection and escape while others provided refreshments and writing facilities. There were two casualties.

The Young Men's Christian Association (Y.M.C.A.) served in several of the theatres of war. The aim was to meet in some measure the social and spiritual needs of the troops. This was usually provided in hut canteens behind the front lines. Within ten days of the declaration of war the Y.M.C.A. established no fewer than 250 recreation centres in the United Kingdom providing refreshment and limited social activities. Many were situated at or near railway stations and other places where large numbers of troops would be passing. In November 1914 the first Y.M.C.A. contingent went to France, setting up a similar centre at Le Harvre. Later centres were established at Rouen, Boulogne, Dieppe, Etaples, Calais, Abbeville, Dunkirk, Abeancourt, Paris and Marseilles. Stations were also established along the front and close to the firing line.

The Staff were mainly female or those men who were over military age or below the medical requirements for active service. They also sent volunteer Doctors and Clergy on a four month tour of duty. Later the Y.M.C.A. appointed Chaplains. They were mainly those who felt unable to enlist. Others having done a four month tour of duty felt the need, to resign their pastorates and went full time with the Y.M.C.A. They wore a khaki dress and did valuable work at huts and canteens on the Western Front. There is evidence of them being close to the Front and engaged with the military in Casualty Clearing Stations but the main thrust of their work was behind the lines. A total of 14 Chaplains and 29 volunteers who died are listed by the C.W.G.C. A further 29 volunteers who died are recorded in editions of The Red Triangle.

Those Y.M.C.A. Chaplains who did not return were remembered by their respective congregations and denominations. However this was not always the case and there is evidence that because they resigned their charge and went to serve with the Y.M.C.A, they were not regarded as belonging to their denomination/church. The most notable of these was The Revd. W. A. Wilson of the Presbyterian Church of Ireland who does not appear on their Manse Roll of Honour.

Several Y.M.C.A. Chaplains and volunteers who died were given military funerals, and one Y.M.C.A. lady volunteer driver, Bertha (Betty) Gavin Stevenson was awarded the Croix de Guerre avec Palme (France). She was killed by shrapnel during an enemy air raid at St. Denis, Etaples on the 30th May 1918 aged 21. A graphic account of the incident is to be found in the Red Triangle of the 21st June 1918.

And finally..

COMBATANT CLERGY

Despite a pronouncement from the Archbishop of Canterbury that, "Clergy should not be combatants", Ministers of Religion and many theological Students enlisted as Combatants.

The records of my college, Cuddesdon College Oxford, show a situation that was probably similar with other Institutions. Some 20 former members of the college served as Naval Chaplains, 139 as Army Chaplains and 3 with the Royal Air Force. 8 Priests, 1 Deacon and 13 Ordinands served as combatants. The Army Chaplain casualties are listed. A notable additional entry regarding the Revd. J. C. Fixsen is also included. It is worth mentioning that four members of the domestic staff of the college were also casualties.

In the book, Ambassadors of Christ edited by Mark D. Chapman, mention is made of the demise of Ripon College. "By the end of 1915, there was only one student, and so the Governors decided to close the college for the duration of the war, and the college property was let. The student went to Ridley Hall".

There is no doubt from what I have discovered that many men and women in addition to those who held Army rank of Chaplain exercised a truly Christian ministry throughout the whole of the conflict. Regardless of denomination, intrigues and distrust they served their Lord and Master.

BIBLIOGRAPHY

Books and Article:

Brabant, F. H., 'Neville Stuart Talbot',
London: SCM Press, 1949.

Chapman, Mark D., (ed), 'Ambassadors of Christ',
Aldershot: Ashgate, 2004.

Clifton, A. S., 'Salvation Army's Actions and Attitudes in Wartime 1899 - 1945',
London: Salvation Army Headquarters.

Harrison, Jenny, 'Chaplain Casualties',
Privately Published, 2004.

Howson, P. J., 'Deaths among Army Chaplains 1914 - 1920'
in Journal of the Society for Army Historical Research,
83/333 (2005) pp. 63 - 77.

James, E. A., 'A Record of the Battles and Engagements of
the British Armies in France and Flanders 1914 - 1918',
London: Gale & Polden, 1924

James, E. A., 'British Regiments 1914 - 1918',
London: Samson, 1978.

Jarvis, S. D., and D. B., 'the Cross of Sacrifice Volume 1',
Oakfield: Naval * Military Press, (2000)
[volume 1and volume 2 of the reprint]

Johnstone, T., and Hagerty, J., 'The Cross on the Sword',
London: Geoffrey Chapman, 1996.

Menzies, S., 'Sportsmen Parsons in Peace and War',
London: Hutchinson.

Ussher, R., 'Roll of the sons and daughters of the Anglican Church Clergy
throughout the world and of the Naval and Military Chaplains
of the same who gave their lives in the Great War 1914 - 1918.'
London: English Crafts & Monumental Society, no date

Magazine:

Red Triangle (Quarterly Magazine of the YMCA)

Website:

www.cwgc.org (Website of the Commonwealth War Graves Commission)
www.hellfire-corner.co.uk/coulson.htm (Details of VC winners in RAChD)

Other references are to be found against particular entries and in the Acknowledgements.

BRITISH ARMY CHAPLAIN DEATHS
1914 to 1922

The Revd. William David ABBOTT
Temporary Chaplain 4th Class
Army Chaplains' Department.

He was the son of the late Revd. David Wyley Abbott, some time Vicar of Cardington, Salop. In 1908 he trained for the Priesthood at Lichfield Theological College and was made a Deacon in 1909. Ordained Priest by the Bishop of Worcester, in 1910, he served his Title as Curate of St John Bedwardine, Worcester from 1909 to 1913. He went to St. Paul, Blackheath, in the Diocese of Worcester in 1913. In 1914 he was appointed Organising Secretary for the Society for the Promotion of Christian Knowledge (SPCK) to the Dioceses of Carlisle, Chester, Lichfield, Liverpool, Manchester, Wakefield and all Ireland. He was the husband of R. Abbott, of 75 Mauldeth Road, Withington, Manchester. He enlisted as an Army Chaplain and died in France on the 3rd December 1918 aged 35 and is buried in Janaval Cemetery, Dieppe, Seine - Maritime, Grave Reference II.A.1. He is remembered on the Aldershot Memorial.

The Revd. Armar Edward ACTON
Temporary Chaplain 4th Class
Army Chaplains' Department.
Attached Border Regiment 2nd Battalion.

He was the son of Maud J. and the late Lieut. Col. J. L. C. Acton. (1st Battalion Connaught Rangers) and born at Galway, Ireland. He attended Trinity College Dublin and obtained a B.A. (Jun. Mod.) in 1910. After training for the Priesthood at Wells Theological College, he was made a Deacon in 1912. Ordained Priest in 1913 by the Bishop of Manchester, he served his Title as Curate of St. Mary's, Oldham from 1912 to 1914, and subsequently was Curate of Holy Trinity Bury to 1916. He enlisted as an Army Chaplain and died of wounds in France on the 4th November 1917 aged 28 and is buried in Wimereux Communal Cemetery, Pas de Calais Grave reference IV.L.2. and remembered on the Aldershot Memorial. A memorial from Wells Theological College is now at Sarum College, Salisbury.

The Revd. Frederick William AINLEY
Temporary Chaplain 4th Class
Army Chaplains' Department
Chaplains General Office Boulogne.

He attended the London College of Divinity, and was made a Deacon in 1911. Ordained Priest, by the Bishop of Llandaff in 1914 serving his Title as Curate of St. John's Ebbw Vale, Llandaff, from 1911 to 1912. He was Curate of Magor with Redwick, Llandaff from 1913 to 1915 and then at St. Paul, Leamington from 1915 to 1916. He enlisted as an Army Chaplain and died in France, on the 5th December 1918. He is buried in Terlincthun British Cemetery, Wimille, Pas de Calais, Grave Reference XII.B.23. and remembered on the Aldershot Memorial.

The Revd. William Preston AINLEY
Army Chaplains' Department.

He studied at Jesus College, Cambridge and obtained a B.A. in 1909, and was made a Deacon in 1911. Ordained Priest by the Bishop of Bristol in 1912, he served his Title as Curate of St. Paul, Chippenham and became a Temporary Chaplain to the Forces in 1914. Following a medical he was Medically Boarded on the 1st August 1915 and died on the 12th October 1915. He is remembered on the Aldershot Memorial.

The Revd. John ASH
Temporary Chaplain 4th Class Army Chaplains'
Department. Royal Field Artillery.
Attached 48th Div. Ammunition Col. (Troops).

He was born on the 2nd January 1881 at Bridstow, Northlew, Devon. He was a Local Preacher in his teens and went to college in 1899. In 1901 he became a trainee United Methodist Minister at Kings Brompton. Having failed his exams he was dropped for a while but was re-instated in 1903 at Portland. He was at Swansea from 1905; Southampton and Eastleigh 1908; Newport, Ryde and Cowes from 1913 until he became an Army Chaplain. The husband of the late Mary Ash he was killed in action in Belgium on the 7th September 1917 aged 37. He is buried in Vlamertinghe New Military Cemetery West-Vlaanderen, Grave Reference IX. H. 26. and remembered on the Aldershot Memorial.

The Revd. Frederick William ASHTON
Temporary Chaplain Royal Air Force.

He was born at Sheepwash Shebbear, Devon on 4th May 1885, the son of the late William Henry and Lucy (nee Beeby), Ashton, of Plymouth. After attending Plymouth School, Woodchester, he was apprenticed to the family Poultry business. Ordained a Minister in the United Methodist Church, he served at Stockton on Tees in 1910 and with Middlesbrough from 1912. He was at Tavistock in 1913 and Sheffield, Scotland Street and Leeds Prospect in 1917. He volunteered for active service and became a Temporary Chaplain to the Forces on the 1st November 1918, being attached to The Royal Air Force. He died of acute pneumonia and heart failure at the Base Hospital, Sheffield on 18th November 1918 aged 33. He was the only recorded Chaplain Casualty Serving with The Royal Air Force and is buried in an unmarked grave in Sheffield City Road Cemetery, and remembered on the Screen Wall to the rear of The Sword of Sacrifice.

The Revd. Ernest AVENT
Chaplain 2nd Class Royal Army Chaplains' Department.

(Some Army records show his surname as Aven) The son of The Revd. John Avent and Alice Avent, of Broughton Pogis Rectory, Oxon. He was born on the 17th June 1876. Educated at Hunstanton and Felsted Schools, he studied at Gonville and Caius College, Cambridge where he obtained a B.A. in 1897 and an M.A. in 1906. He trained for the Priesthood at Leeds Clergy School in 1898 and was made a Deacon in

1899 by the Bishop of Royston. Ordained Priest in 1901 by the Bishop of Liverpool, he served his Title as Curate of St. Thomas, Ashton in Makerfield from 1899 to 1903, and was Curate of St. James, Birkdale, from 1903 to 1904. He became an Acting Chaplain to the Forces at Aldershot in 1904 to 1905; Woolwich 1905 to 1906; Gibraltar 1906 to 1911; Garrison Church, Arbour Hill, Dublin 1911 to 1915; B.E.F. 1916 to 1917. He was wounded, and Mentioned in Despatches. He was at Colchester from 1917 to1919. The husband of Jessica May Avent, of "Woodbrae" Curzon Park, Chester, he died at The Military Hospital, York on the 25th August 1920, aged 44 and is buried in Fulford Cemetery, Yorkshire, Grave Reference A.10.

The Revd. George William BAILE
Temporary Chaplain 4th Class
Army Chaplains' Department.
Attached 64th CCS.

He studied at Trinity College Dublin and obtained a B.A. (Resp) and LL.B. in 1886. He was made a Deacon in 1887 by the Bishop of Kilmore and Ordained a Priest in 1888 by the Archbishop of Dublin. He was Curate of St. Peter, Athlone from 1887 to 1888 and at St. Werburgh, Dublin from 1888 to 1892. In the same year he was appointed Deputy Secretary for the Sunday School Society for Ireland and Licensed to the Dioceses of Dublin, Kildare and Glendal. In 1893 he was appointed Acting Chaplain to the Forces at Kilkenny until 1902 when he became Curate of St. Saviour's, Tollington Park. In 1903 he was appointed Consular Chaplain at the British Consulate, at Pernambuco, in the Diocese of Argentina, Brazil. He became a Temporary Chaplain to the Forces in 1916 and died in France on the 27th January 1918. He is buried in Etaples Military Cemetery Pas de Calais Grave Reference XXVIII. E. 10. and remembered on the Aldershot Memorial.

The Revd. Fr. Thomas Leo BAINES
Temporary Chaplain 4th Class
Army Chaplains' Department.
Attached Royal Field Artillery 152nd Brigade.

He was born at Preston Lancs., on the 29th November 1886, the son of Joseph and Elizabeth Baines. After studying at Ushaw Northern Seminary, Durham, for eighteen years as a student, minor and professor he was Ordained by Archbishop Whiteside on the 8th August 1915. He was Professor at Ushaw from Ordination to 1916, when he became Curate at St. Francis of Assisi, Garston, in the Liverpool RC Diocese. He became a Temporary Chaplain to the Forces in 1917, and died of wounds in France on the 31st May 1918 aged 31. An eye witness account recalls, "At 2-30 a.m. he was brought to a Field Hospital having been bombed by a German plane, suffering from, shrapnel wounds in one hand and multiple wounds all over his body. One leg was badly shattered above the knee. He was so shocked that it was impossible to operate. He died at 2 p.m.". A Church of England Chaplain colleague wrote, "He was a perfect Christian with priest written all over him - beloved by all from the General down". He is buried in Aire Communal Cemetery Pas de Calais Grave Reference III. B. 29. and remembered on the Ushaw College and Aldershot Memorials.A letter of Fr. Baines from the Front shortly before his death is in the Ushaw College Notes page 137ff.

The Revd. James BAIRD
Temporary Chaplain 4th Class
Royal Army Chaplains' Department.

He studied Theology and became an Associate of King's College London (A.K.C.) 2nd Class in 1910, then went to St. John's Hall, Durham where he obtained a B.A. (L. Th.) in 1912. He was made a Deacon in 1912 and Ordained Priest by the Bishop of Birmingham in 1913. After serving his Title as Curate of St. George City of Birmingham, he became a Temporary Chaplain to the Forces in 1915. He died in France on the 13th February 1919, and is buried in Longuenesse (St. Omer) Souvenir Cemetery Pas de Calais Grave Reference V. F. 20.

The Revd. Edward Walter BARKER
Temporary Chaplain 4th Class
Army Chaplains' Department.
Attached 176th Trench Mortar Battery.

The only son of Emily Barker, of 12 Cadwell Road, Paignton, Devon, and the late Henry Edward Barker. He was a Late Exhibitioner of Bedford and Queen's College, Cambridge, where he obtained a 2nd cl. Hist. Trip pt. i. and was awarded the Hughes Prize in 1909, and a B.A. in 1910. He studied for the Priesthood at Ridley Hall, Cambridge, and was made a Deacon in 1911. Ordained Priest by the Lord Bishop of London in 1912 serving his Title as Curate of St. John the Evangelist, Notting Hill till 1912, and then moved to St. Michael Chagford. In 1915 he was appointed Curate of St. Luke, Torquay, in the Diocese of Exeter and became a Temporary Chaplain to the Forces in 1916. He was wounded in France on the 9th March 1918 and died on the 18th March 1918 aged 30. He is buried in Achiet-le Grand Communal Cemetery Grave Reference II.C.13. and remembered on the Ridley Hall and Aldershot Memorials.

The Revd. Charles Lees BEDALE
Chaplain 4th Class Royal Army Chaplains' Department.
Attached 176th Trench Mortar Battery.

The son of T. A. and M. Bedale, of Eccles, Manchester, he was a Wesleyan Minister with an M.A. Degree. He commenced his ministry in 1903 as an Assistant Tutor at the Wesleyan Ministerial Training College, Didsbury, Manchester and was Minister at Ulverston in 1906 and Weston-super-Mare in 1909. He returned to Didsbury as Old Testament Tutor in 1910 and became a Chaplain to the Forces in 1916. The husband of Dorothy Rendel Bedale, of "Fieldside" Barton Road, Cambridge, he died on the 8th March 1919 aged 39. He is buried in Cambridge (Histon Road) Cemetery, grave reference 24. B. 26. and remembered on the Aldershot Memorial. (Some researchers show him as a Roman Catholic Priest - The Revd. C. L. Bedale of the Diocese of Westminster. This is incorrect.)

The Venerable Robert Henry BELCHER
Chaplain 4th Class
Army Chaplains' Department.

He studied at the University of London, where he obtained a B.A. (2nd Class Hons.) (Ment. & Mor. Sci.) in 1867, and an M.A. (Ment. & Mor. Sci.) in 1868. He was made a Deacon in 1868 by the Bishop of Jamaica for the Bishop of Exeter. Ordained Priest in 1870 by The Lord Bishop of London, he served as a Curate at St Ives Cornwall until 1869 and then at St. John Baptist Kensington until 1871. He was appointed Assistant Master of King's College School, London in 1871. In 1874 he was Master and Chaplain of King's College School, London until 1876. He went to New Zealand and became Rector of Otago High School, Dunedin, and was Examining Chaplain to the Bishop of Dunedin from 1886 to 1895. He was appointed a Fellow of King's College, London in 1885. Returning to England in 1896, he accepted the Living of Rector of St. Michael, Lewes, in the Diocese of Chichester, and became Archdeacon of Lewes in 1900. In November of 1900 he was commissioned into the Territorial Force CF4 (TF) and was attached to the 25th (County of London) Cyclists Battalion, London Regiment. He died on the 25th October 1916 aged 72 and is buried in Lewes Cemetery Sussex. He was the Author and Editor of *Degrees and "Degrees" - an exposure of traffic in Academical Titles 1873.*

The Revd. Charles Henry BELL, MC
Temporary Chaplain 4th Class
Army Chaplains' Department.
Attached 1st. Battalion Royal Berkshire Regiment.

He was born at North Somercotes, Lincolnshire and was the son of Canon James Bell, of Kettlethorpe. He studied at Christ College, Cambridge where he obtained a B.A. in 1910. He trained for the Priesthood at Wells Theological College, and was made a Deacon in 1912. Ordained Priest in 1913 by the Bishop of Ripon, he served his Title as Curate of St. Bartholomew, Armley, Leeds until 1913 and then at St. Mark's, Woodhouse, Leeds. He became a Temporary Chaplain to the Forces in 1916, and was awarded the Military Cross, London Gazette 26th July 1918, 8775. "During recent operations he did most magnificent work in assisting the wounded. He was in the line during the whole period. He was tireless to assist any stretcher case to the rear, and organized and inspired stretcher bearers to further efforts. He showed utter disregard for his own safety, and set a fine example." Killed in action at Moyenneville, France, on the 23rd August 1918 aged 30, he is buried in Douchy-Les-Ayette British Cemetery, Pas de Calais, Grave Reference II. G. 10. and remembered on the Aldershot Memorial. A memorial from Wells Theological College is now at Sarum College, Salisbury..

The Revd. Arnold John BENNETT, MC
Temporary Chaplain 4th Class
Army Chaplains' Department.
Attached Royal Army Medical Corps 230th Field Ambulance.

He was born at Wincanton, Somerset, the son of Arnold and Annette M. Bennett, of "The Woodlands" Parkstone, Dorset. He trained for the Priesthood at Sarum College in 1905 and was made a Deacon in 1908. Ordained Priest by the Bishop of Salisbury in 1910, he served his Title as Curate of Pewsey until 1911. He was appointed Chaplain to the Railway Mission, at Regina, in the Diocese of Qu' App. until he became a Temporary Chaplain to the Forces in 1914. He was awarded the Military Cross, London Gazette 1st January 1917, Supplement 80. There is no published citation. He died in Egypt on the 26th January 1918 aged 34, and is buried in Kantara War Memorial Cemetery, Grave Reference E. 135. and remembered on the Sarum College and Aldershot Memorials.

Dom Umberto Michael BERTINI
(Some references have his name as Bertina)
Chaplain 4th Class
Army Chaplains' Department.

He was born at Novara, Italy, the son of Ernesto R. Bertini and Palmyra Adele Bertini, of Novara Italy, and Bournemouth. He died of influenza, contracted on active service with the B.E.F. in Italy on the 29th September 1918 aged 33. He was an OSB, Malta, and is buried in Farnborough Abbey, Roman Catholic Churchyard, Hampshire, on the North side of the Church, and remembered on the Aldershot Memorial. In 2001 the Commonwealth War Graves Commission replaced the headstone with a standard CWGC Headstone.

Revd. J. D. Bevins CF4

An entry was found in the War Office Monthly Army List reporting date of death as 7 June 1918. No entries for a clergyman of this name have been traced in any Ecclesial Directories or the Register of Births and Deaths for England and Wales. It appears that the Army List entry should read Rev J D Burns. (See page 13)

The Revd. Fr. Henry Norbert BIRT
Chaplain to the Forces.
Army Chaplain's Department.

He was born in Valparaiso, Chile on May 15 1861. Educated at St. Augustine's, Ramsgate and University College, London, he entered the OSB noviciate at Downside on the 3rd September 1880 and was solemnly professed on the 25th January 1885. He was ordained 13th January 1889. He served at St. Osburg's Coventry from the 20th February 1892 to 29th October 1895. He was a military chaplain in the Boer War from March to November 1901. He was Secretary to the Abbot President Eng. Benedictine Congregation from 1906 to 1914. After volunteering as a chaplain in August 1914, his first post was at Tidworth in August 1915 as chaplain for the 98th Brigade, 33rd Division. He then seems to have been chaplain at the hospital in Netley. He died in London on the 21st August 1919 aged 58. For his publications see the Catholic Who's Who for the period and the Downside Review June 1914.

The Revd. George Bernard Hamilton BISHOP
Temporary Chaplain 4th Class
Army Chaplains' Department.
Attached 6th Battalion Northumberland Fusiliers.

He studied at St. Chad's Hall, Durham, where he won the Capel Cure Prize and obtained a B.A. in 1911. He was made a Deacon in 1911 and Ordained Priest by the Bishop of Peterborough in 1912. He served his Title as Curate of Kettering, until 1913, and then as Curate of St. Mary's, Plaistow, in the Diocese of St Alban's until 1914. He was killed in action, in France, on the 27th May 1918, and is remembered on the Soissons Memorial, Aisne, Reference E. 135 and the Aldershot Memorial. He was the Author of *Religion of Russia* published in 1916.

The Revd. William BLACK
Temporary Chaplain 4th Class
Army Chaplains' Department.

The son of Mrs. and the late Mr. Samuel Black of Aldouran, Newlands, Glasgow. Some records show him as the Assistant Minister at Govan and Kilmalcolm Parish Churches but the Church of Scotland Fasti entry shows that he was Ordained to the Army in 1918 and not to Govan and Kilmalcolm. He died in France, on the 10th July 1918 aged 27, and is buried in Terlincthum British Cemetery, Wimille, Pas de Calais, Grave Reference I. E. 36. and is remembered on the Aldershot Memorial.

The Revd. William Duncan Thomson BLACK
Temporary Chaplain 4th Class
Army Chaplains' Department.
Attached 7th Cameron Highlanders

The son of William B. and Elizabeth Bain Cochrane. He was born on the 10th March 1881 at Glasgow. Educated at John Street School and High School he studied at the University of Glasgow where he obtained an M.A. in 1903. After further study at Glasgow College he became a missionary in Canada in 1904. Licenced by The Presbytery of Glasgow in 1906 he was assistant Minister at Cowcaddens. Ordained and inducted to Fraserburgh South on the 23rd November 1906. Translated and inducted to Rutherglen on the 23rd February 1913. The husband of Janet (Jenny) Liddle Black (nee Cunningham) who he married on 6th November 1907 of 10 Leven Street, Pollokshields, Glasgow, he was killed in action, in Belgium on the 22nd August 1917 aged 36. He is buried in Brandhoek New Military Cemetery No.3, Belgium, Grave Reference II.A.18.

The Revd. Philip John Thomas BLAKEWAY
Chaplain 1st Class Army Chaplains' Department.
Attached Household Cavalry and Cavalry of the Line.
(Including Yeomanry and Imperial Camel Corps)
1st County of London Yeomanry.

The son of Philip and Maria Blakeway, he studied at Magdalene College, Oxford, where he obtained a B.A. in 1891, and an M.A. in 1901. After Theological training at Ely College, he was made a Deacon in 1891 and Ordained Priest by the Bishop of Rochester in 1893. He served his Title as Curate of St. Luke, Camberwell, until 1893 when he became Chaplain and Almoner at Lathom. In 1900 he returned to the parochial ministry as Curate of Lambeth, and St. Andrew's, Battersea

until 1902 when he was appointed a Territorial Chaplain to the Forces at Chichester Barracks. In 1903 he accepted the position of Rector of All Saints, Hastings, and in 1907 he moved to become Vicar of Walberton, in the Diocese of Chichester. He was the husband of Sybil Blakeway, of "The Cottage" Halmaker, Chichester, and died in Egypt on the 16th June 1915, aged 50. He was discovered dead in his bed. Although he had not reported sick, the temperature on the day of his death was 118 degrees Fahrenheit and his death was eventually diagnosed as "climate on a debilitated heart". He is buried in Ismailia War Memorial Cemetery, Grave Reference A.108. and remembered on the Aldershot Memorial. A Memorial for Ely College students is now situated in the King's School Ely.

The Revd. Vincent Coke BODDINGTON
Temporary Chaplain 4th Class
Army Chaplains' Department.
Attached 35th General Hospital.
Some records show him as Victor.

The son of Arthur Onslow Boddington, and Dora Boddington, he was born at Kington in 1886. He was a Choral Student at St. John's College, Cambridge, where he obtained a B.A. in 1908, (Cl. Tr. Sch). In 1909. He was made a Deacon by the Bishop of St. Albans in 1910 and Ordained Priest by the Bishop of Barking for St. Albans in 1911. He served his Title as Curate of East Ham, and became a Temporary Chaplain to the Forces in 1914. He died on the 13th March 1917, aged 30 and is buried in Wokingham (St. Sebastian) Churchyard, Berkshire Special Plot 23. and remembered on the Aldershot Memorial.

The Revd. Edward Keightley BOTWOOD
Temporary Chaplain 4th Class
Army Chaplains' Department.

The son of William Botwood, he was born at Ipswich on the 6th May 1872. Educated at Ayerst High School, he studied at Queen's College, Cambridge, where he obtained a B.A. in 1894. He was made a Deacon in 1895 and Ordained Priest by the Bishop of Manchester in 1896. He served his Title as Curate of Friezland, Yorks, until 1896 when he became Chaplain of Church High School, Harrogate. In 1897 he became Curate of Tintwistle, Cheshire, and in 1898 St. Matthew, Croydon, and St. John Blackheath, from 1899 to 1901. He accepted the living as Vicar of St. Mary, Spital Square from 1901 to 1903, and then St. Mark, Bow, from 1903 until 1910. He moved to the Diocese of Exeter in 1911, to become the Incumbent of Kilmington. The husband of Gwendoline A. Botwood, of Sandford Hall, St. David's, Exeter, he died of illness contracted on active service in Sark, on the 28th July 1916 aged 44. He is buried north of the Church Tower in Kilmington (St Giles) Churchyard, Devon, and remembered on the Aldershot Memorial.

The following entry appeared as addenda to Ussher's Roll of Clergy sons and daughters.

The Revd. James Stanley Bromfield BROUGH

The son of William Bromfield Brough, and Jane Bromfield Brough, of "Westwood", Keston, Kent, he was born in July 1878. Educated at Fettes College, Edinburgh, he studied at Emmanuel College, Cambridge where he obtained a B.A. (3rd cl. Cl. Tripod.) in1900, and an M.A. in 1910. He was Assistant Master at Cargilfields School.

After study at Leeds Clergy School in 1902, he was made a Deacon in 1903 and Ordained Priest by the Bishop of Wakefield in 1904, serving his Title as Curate of Brighouse until 1907. He was then Chaplain of Wells Theological College until 1910 when he became Curate of Penistone until 1912. He was appointed Candidates' Traveling Secretary for the Society for the Propagation of the Gospel (SPG) 1912 to 1917), and was a Temporary Chaplain to the Forces from 1915 to 1917. He was attached to the 39th Division and Mentioned in Despatches. His Index Card shows that he had "a slight rupture which was operated on at Base Hospital". A pencil note states, "alright now". On the 13th February 1917 he sought "permission to resign his commission as from 15th inst.", having been asked to undertake work in England for the Y.M.C.A. This was granted by Field Marshal Sir Douglas Haig on 27th February 1917, and he subsequently returned to England. Following his resignation, a letter was sent to him from the War Office requesting the return of a Field Service Communion Set. Reverend Brough, replied (3rd April 1917) "The Field service set is returned herewith. The Chalice I left with a Chaplain whose own set had been destroyed. (I completed essentials for him from things that were my own property). He died from pneumonia, following influenza on the 11th November 1918 aged 40. His funeral was held at Keston Park Parish Church, Kent. Obituary in The Times November 13th indicated that at the time of his death he was at the Mildmay Park Training Headquarters of the YMCA. The address in Crockford's 1918 is given as, YMCA, Bedford Square, London and he also appears in the deaths of YMCA Volunteers, (The Red Triangle January 1919).

The Revd. William BROWN
Temporary Chaplain 4th Class.
Royal Army Chaplains' Department.

The son of William and Mary Brown, of 1 Mons Avenue, Hebburn on Tyne, Co. Durham born at Bishop Auckland, Co. Durham. In 1911 he entered Lichfield Theological College to train for the Priesthood, he was made a Deacon in 1914 and Ordained Priest in 1915. He served his Title as Curate of Wortley, Leeds, and in 1915 moved to All Saints' with St. James, Hertford in the Diocese of St.Albans. He became a Temporary Chaplain to the Forces in 1916 and died of influenza on 10th March 1919, aged 28. He is Buried in Aldershot Military Cemetery, Grave Reference AG.395., and remembered on the Aldershot Memorial.

The Revd. Cyril Bernard Wilson BUCK
Temporary Chaplain 4th Class
Army Chaplains' Department.
Attached Leicestershire Regiment 1/5th. Battalion.

The son of William Richard and Alice Emmeline Buck, of "Tabards" Ewell, Surrey, he studied at Trinity College, Oxford, where he obtained a B.A. in 1907. He trained for the Priesthood at Cuddesdon Theological College, Oxford, until 1909. He was made a Deacon by the Bishop of Birmingham in 1910, serving his Title as Curate of The Cathedral Church of St. Philip, Birmingham until 1913; Selley Oak 1913 to 1914 and joint Missioner, Birmingham Street Childrens' Union from 1914. He became a Temporary Chaplain to the Forces in 1916. He was killed in action in France, on the 29th September 1918 aged 38, and buried in Busigny Communal Cemetery Extension Nord V. C. 6. and remembered on the Cuddesdon College, Oxford and Aldershot Memorials. (There is no Crockford's record of him being Ordained Priest.)

The Revd. Fr. Matthew Forster BURDESS
Chaplain 4th Class
Army Chaplains' Department.
Attached 1/6th Battalion Gloucestershire Regiment.

The Son of George Burdess, and Rachel Ann Burdess, who was a descendent of the Forsters of Bamburgh, one of whom was General Thomas Forster, who led the Jacobite rising of 1715, he was born at Sunderland in November 1877. His family was noted for its unswerving loyalty to the Stuart cause. He went to St. Cuthbert's Grammar School, Newcastle, and studied at Ushaw College, Durham, in 1894 and the English College, Rome, in 1897 where he obtained D.D. in Philosophy and Theology. Ordained on the 1st November 1903 at St. Cuthbert, Newcastle, he was appointed to the staff of St.Cuthbert's Grammar School, Newcastle and subsequently Professor at Ushaw College, Durham in 1909. After a period of ill health he became a Priest at St. Mary's Stockton on Tees from 1913 to 1915, followed by a short stay at Thornley, Co Durham, until 1916, when he became Priest at St. Thomas, Port Clarence, in the RC Diocese of Hexham and Newcastle. Early in the war he volunteered to go to France, and the Bishop's final permission came at the beginning of Lent 1917. He became a Chaplain to the Forces, and was killed in action five weeks later in France, on the 18th April 1917 aged 39. Records indicate that along with 6 Officers, he was sheltering in a recently captured cellar overnight when a booby trap mine went off killing them all. He is buried in Villers-Faucon Communal Cemetery, Somme, Grave Reference D. 50. and remembered on the Memorial in St. Mary's RC. Church, Stockton on Tees and the Ushaw College and Aldershot Memorials. A full Obituary is to be found in Notes from Ushaw July 1917. (In the book - The Cross on the Sword (Hegarty and Johnstone, he is listed as being from Middlesbrough RC Diocese which is incorrect. Port Clarence is on the Durham side of the river Tees and the postal address was Middlesbrough, hence the error.)

The Revd. Joseph Dobson BURNS
Chaplain 4th Class Army Chaplains' Department.
Attached Royal Garrison Artillery.

The eldest son of Joseph and Helen Burns of Edinburgh, he was born at Portobello, Scotland. Educated at Newington Academy, and George Watson's College, Edinburgh. He studied at the Nottingham Institute in 1906 and was a Student Pastor of Burton Joyce and Minister at the London Road Congregational Church, Newark from 1910 to 1917. In 1914 he became an Officiating Clergyman to the Army and Navy Board, at Newark. He became a Temporary Chaplain to the Forces in August 1917 having resigned his charge. He died of wounds, in France, on the 7th June 1918. The husband of Mary C. Burns, of 2 Denwick Terrace, Tynemouth, Northumberland, he is buried in Ebblinghem Military Cemetery, Nord, Grave Reference II. D. 11. and remembered on the Aldershot Memorial. His Commanding Officer wrote, "Mr. Burns was man first and a Padre afterwards who won the love and esteem of all Officers and men".

The Revd. John CAMPBELL - MacGREGOR
See under MacGREGOR

The Revd. James Leitch CAPPELL
Temporary Chaplain 4th Class
Army Chaplains' Department.
Attached Royal Scots 1st/9th Battalion.

The son of Thomas and Mary Cappell, of Crief, Perthshire, Scotland. He studied at the University of Glasgow, where he obtained an M.A. in 1898. Following training at Edinburgh Theological College, he was made a Deacon in 1900. Ordained Priest by the Bishop of Edinburgh in 1901. He served as Curate of (Old) St. Paul Edinburgh, until 1903 and at Berkswich with Walton until 1910, Blackburn from 1910 to 1912, and at Moseley, in the Diocese of Birmingham until 1915, when he became a Temporary Chaplain to the Forces. The husband of Alice E Cappell, of "Vine House" Revidge Road, Blackburn, Lancs, he died in France, on the 23rd January 1918 aged 41. He is buried in Ste. Marie Cemetery, Le Harve, Seine-Maritime, France, Grave Reference Div.62. I.0.4. and remembered on the Aldershot Memorial.

The Revd. Fr. Timothy CAREY
Chaplain 4th Class Royal Army Chaplains' Department.

The son of Patrick and Mary Carey of Co. Limerick. He was born in Ireland on the 20th February 1878. He went to the Trappist Seminary, Mount Melleray, Ireland, and studied at St. Edmund's College, Ware, entering the Society of Jesus, at Manresa, on the 8th September 1896. (One day in advance of Fr. Denis Doyle). A Teacher at Beaumont (St. John's) from 1903 till 1909, when he studied Theology at Milltown Park. Ordained on the 28th July 1912, he received a Tertianship at Tronchiennes, St. John's in 1913. His last vows were taken on the 2nd February 1914, and at the end of the school year he was transferred to the college staff until he became a Chaplain to the Forces, leaving for France on the 10th October 1916, a week after Fr. McGinity. He died of influenza, in France, on the 27th February 1919, aged 41. He is buried in Audruicq Churchyard and Extension, Pas de Calais, France, near West end of Church and remembered on the Aldershot Memorial. Fr. Rawlinson wrote to the Father Provincial "Since arrival on the 10th October 1916 he has been at Audruicq, where his work has been beyond all praise, his wonderful zeal and energy and his

devotion to duty endeared him to both Officers and men. He founded a Catholic Club which was known throughout the army area and which made a great impression on Cardinal Bourne during his visit to France. He certainly succeeded in stirring up both the soldiers and French civilians to a sense of their religion and organised Christmas Midnight Masses and Corpus Christi processions in a way that few others were able to do. His loss to our Department will be very much felt". Details of his death and funeral can be found in the archives of the British Province of the Society of Jesus, 114 Mount Street, London. W1K 3AH.

The Venerable Walter E. A. CHADWICK
Archdeacon of Kavirando.
Chaplain East African Armies Chaplains' Department.
Listed under East African Chaplains

The Revd. William Gerard CHEESE
Temporary Chaplain 4th Class
Army Chaplains' Department.
Attached Lincolnshire Regiment 8th Battalion.

He studied at St. John's College, Cambridge, where he obtained a B.A. (3rd Class Trip.) in 1905, and an M.A. in 1913. He was made a Deacon in 1906 and Ordained Priest by the Bishop of Peterborough in 1907. He served his title as Curate of Belgrave with Birstall, from 1906 to 1910, and then was Curate of All Saints, City of Peterborough, until 1914. In 1915 he became Vicar of Duddington, in the Diocese of Peterborough, and in the same year Temporary Chaplain to the Forces. He died in France, on the 7th November 1918 and was the brother of Miss B. F. Cheese, of "Roslyn", White Knole Road, Buxton, and is buried in St. Sever Cemetery Extension, Rouen Seine-Maritime, Grave Reference S.V.G.6. and remembered on the Aldershot Memorial.

The Revd. Fr. Stephen CLARKE
Temporary Chaplain 4th Class
Army Chaplains' Department.
Attached Lancashire Fusiliers 7th Battalion.

The son of Patrick Clarke and Rose Clarke of Doonkilmainhamwood, he was born in 1887. In The Diocese of Kilmore Priests and Bishops 1136 - 1988 written by Bishop Francis MacKiernan it is mentioned that he had a B.A. Degree. Ordained on the 23rd June 1912 at Maynooth, Kilmore RC Diocese, he served at Castle Tara and moved to Ballintemple on the 30th October 1913. During Holy Week 1916, he volunteered as a Chaplain to the Forces, and was attached to the Shropshire Light Infantry. Records indicate that he was killed in action on the 4th October 1917 at Passchendaele, Belgium. He is listed on the Tyne Cot Memorial Panel 160. and remembered on the Aldershot Memorial.

The Revd. Frederick Canning CLEAVER
Temporary Chaplain 4th Class
Army Chaplains' Department.

The son of Frederick William and Mary Jane Cleaver, of 348 Fulwood Road, Sheffield he studied at St. Aidan's College, Birkenhead in 1905, and at University College, Durham, where he obtained an L. Th. in 1908. He was made a Deacon in 1908 by the Bishop of Halyn for

London and Ordained Priest in 1909 by the Bishop of Accra, West Equatorial Africa. A Missionary with the Society for the Propagation of the Gospel (S.P.G.) he was at Taizquah from 1908 until 1909, and was seconded from 1909 to 1912 to Accra. In 1916 he became a Temporary Chaplain to the Forces, and died in Iraq on the 17th June 1917, aged 37. He is buried in Basra War Cemetery, Iraq Grave Reference II.B.12.

The Revd. Frederick Walter CLEVELAND, MC
Temporary Chaplain 4th Class
Army Chaplains' Department.
Attached North Staffordshire Regiment
1st/6th Battalion.

The son of the late Samuel George and Eliza Cleveland, of Margate, he was born at Bayswater London, and studied at Mirfield and Lichfield Theological Colleges, until 1909, and at The University of Durham, where he obtained a L. Th. in 1911. He was made a Deacon in 1911 by the Bishop of Stafford for Lichfield. Ordained Priest by the Bishop of Lichfield in 1913, he served his Title as Curate of Christ Church, Tunstall from 1911 until 1913, when he moved to Porthill, Staffordshire, for Mission work in the Potteries, being based at St. Andrew, Porthill. He was Senior Curate at St. Peter's Hornsey from 1913 until 1916 when he became a Temporary Chaplain to the Forces. He was Mentioned in Despatches, and awarded the Military Cross - London Gazette 8th March 1919 page 3238 with no published citation. He died of wounds, in France, on the 11th October 1918 aged 30. He is buried in St. Sever Cemetery Extension, Rouen, Seine-Maritime, Grave Reference S.V.C.2. and remembered on the Aldershot Memorial.

The Revd. Elijah COBHAM, MC
Temporary Chaplain 4th Class
Army Chaplains' Department.
Attached King's African Rifles.

The son of John and Martha Ann Cobham, of Waterloo, Liverpool, and Crowborough, Sussex, he attended Glenalmond School, Perthshire, and studied at Emmanuel College, Cambridge, where he obtained a B.A. in 1903 and an M.A. in 1907. After theological study at Ridley Hall, Cambridge in 1904 he was made a Deacon in 1906. Ordained Priest by the Bishop of Bristol in 1907, he served his Title as Curate of Fishponds, Bristol from 1906 to 1907 and was then Assistant Missioner at All Saints Convent, Fishponds until 1910, when he became Curate of All Saints, Fishponds, Bristol to 1911, and Priest in Charge, of All Saints, Fishponds, Bristol until 1913. In 1913 he was appointed Chaplain of the Colonial and Continental Church, Nakuru, in the Diocese of Mombassa, East Africa. He was awarded the Military Cross - London Gazette 8th March 1918, page 2974 with no published citation. He died of wounds in Tanzania on the 19th September 1917 aged 37. He is buried in Dar-es-Salaam War Cemetery, Grave Reference 5.A.15. and remembered on the Ridley Hall and Aldershot Memorials.

The Revd. Richard Arthur Pell COLBORNE
Temporary Chaplain 4th Class
Army Chaplains' Department.
Attached The London Regiment.
(Royal Fusiliers) 1st/1st Battalion.

The son of Arthur and Margaret Ethel Colborne, of Quy Vicarage, Cambridgeshire, he was born at Sudbury, Suffolk. He studied at Worcester College, Oxford, where he was a Cl. Exhib. in 1905, and obtained a B.A. (2nd Cl. Th.) in 1909, and an M.A. in 1912. He was made a Deacon in 1912 and Ordained Priest by the Bishop of St. Albans in 1913. He served his Title as Curate of St. John Baptist, Great Gaddesden, from 1912 to 1913, and was then Curate of St. Edw. Romford, from 1913 to 1915 before moving to Merton, in the Diocese of Southwark in 1916. He became a Temporary Chaplain to the Forces in 1917, and was killed in action, in France, on the 28th May 1918 aged 31. He is buried in Dainville British Cemetery, Pas de Calais, France, Grave Reference I.D.1. and remembered on the Aldershot Memorial.

The Revd. Fr. Herbert John COLLINS
Chaplain 4th Class
Army Chaplains' Department.
Attached Black Watch (Royal Highlanders)
9th Battalion.

The son of James Thomas and Mary Campbell Collins, of London, he was born on the 27th December 1882, and educated at St. Edmund's, Ware and Oscott. Ordained on the 12th July 1908 by Archbishop Bourne, at St. Edmund's, Ware. A Priest of Westminster RC Diocese, he was at Brentford in 1908 and with The Crusade of Rescue in 1910. He was killed in action, in France, on the 9th April 1917 aged 35. Remembered on the Aldershot Memorial, and the War Memorial at the Church of Our Lady of Willesden, he is buried in Cabaret-Rouge British Cemetery, Souchez, Pas de Calais, France XVII.K.10. Records indicate that he was killed during an advance at Vimy Ridge.

The Revd. George CONDIE
Temporary Chaplain 4th Class
Army Chaplains' Department.

The son of John Morison and Marion McLachlan McDonald Condie, he was born at Glasgow on the 1st April 1873, and educated at Hutchison Grammar School, Glasgow and Glasgow University, where he obtained an M.A. in 1899, and a B.D. in 1902. A Minister of The Church of Scotland, he was licensed by the Presbytery of Glasgow in May 1902, and was Assistant Minister at Bellahouston, Glasgow. Ordained to Stepps on the 3rd August 1904, in the Glasgow Presbytery. He was the first Minister of this parish from 1906. On the 4th December 1912, he was translated to Muthill, in the Presbytery of Auchterarder, and subsequently became a Chaplain to the Forces. He died at Cromarty Military Hospital, on the 30th June 1918 aged 45. He married on the 5th June 1906, Mary Calvert Walker, who died on the 15th November 1912, leaving three young children. The address for next of kin in the CWGC records is shown as 7 Ethel Terrace, Mount Florida, Glasgow. He is buried in Cathcart Cemetery, Renfrewshire, Q.933.61.

The Revd. Arthur COOPER - MARSDIN
(Formerly Arthur Cooper MARSDIN)
Temporary Chaplain 4th Class
Army Chaplains' Department.

The eldest son of Septimus Marsdin, he was born in London. He studied at Jesus College, Cambridge where he obtained a B.A. in 1890 and an M.A. in 1894; Hebrew Prize, University of Edinburgh 1891; ad eund. M.A. (*) Dublin 1894. After further study at the University of Edinburgh, he won the Hebrew Prize in 1891 then went on to receive an M.A. from Dublin in 1894 followed by a B.D. in 1899 and a D.D. in 1913. He was made a Deacon in 1891. Ordained Priest by the Bishop of Wakefield in 1893, he served his Title as Curate of Heckmondwike from 1891 until 1895 and then moved to Bexley, Kent, in 1895 for four years, followed by a move to St. Margaret, Rochester in 1900. In 1902 he accepted the Living of Vicar of St. Matthew, Borstal until 1905, when he became Secretary of the Rochester Diocese, with a Licence to Preach in the Diocese of Rochester. He was made a Honary Canon of Rochester, in 1912 and Proctor in Convocation, for the Dean and Chapter of Rochester from 1913 to 1915. He became a Temporary Chaplain to the Forces on the 11th May 1915 and was posted to Hilsea Garrison, Portsmouth and served there to 1916. Posted to Harwich, he is recorded as having had a breakdown and spent six months in a Sanatorium before being invalided. He died at Thanet, on the 16th August 1918 aged 50. He was married with no children and is remembered on the Aldershot Memorial. Some references show "Ret" which could indicate that he had retired. He was the Author of Caesarius, *Bishop of Arles 1903; The School of Lerins 1905 and The History of the Lerins 1913.*

The Revd. Frederick St. John CORBETT
Chaplain 3rd Class Royal Army Chaplains' Department.
Attached London Regiment (Royal Fusiliers) 3rd Battalion.

He was born at Dublin in 1862, the second son of John Corbett, M.A. Ll.D., and Susanna Jane (nee Manderson). His father was a member of the Senate of Trinity College, Dublin. Frederick studied at Trinity College, Dublin, where he obtained a B.A. in 1884 and an M.A. in 1887, an F.R.S.L. 1901 and an F.R.Hist.S. from 1904 to 1915. He was made a Deacon in 1885 and Ordained Priest by the Bishop of Ripon in 1887. He served his Title as Curate of Hunslet, Leeds, from 1885 until 1890, and was Chaplain to the Leeds Rifles during this period; then Curate of St. Michael, Chester Square, London until 1896. He then accepted the Living as Rector of Long Marton, in the Diocese of Carlisle and was Chaplain to the High Sheriff of Westmorland in 1901, before moving to St. George in the East, with St. Matthew, Pell Street, London in 1903, Chaplain to the Territorial Forces 1911 and Founder of the Church of England Guilds of Sponsors 1911. He was the Commissary in England to the Bishop of the Falkland Islands, from 1913 to 1915. He was Dean of Sion College, and Lord of the Manor of Bradwell, Essex in 1917. He married Elsie Lucy Victoire the eldest daughter of the Revd. Edward A. Askew, Rector of Greystoke, Cumberland. There were two sons and a daughter. He died on the 14th March 1919 aged 57 and is buried in Ruislip, (St. Martin) Churchyard Extension, Middlesex, Grave Reference I.75. He was the Author of; *Sermon Outlines 1891; Echoes of the Sanctuary 1892; The Preacher's Year 1894; The Problem of Life 1896: History of British Poetry 1904; A Thousand thoughts for Practical Preachers 1910.*

The Revd. Fr. Arthur Martin COWD
Chaplain 4th Class Army Chaplains' Department
Attached 81st Field Ambulance.

The son of Mr. Arthur G. and Mrs. Ellen Cowd, of 8 Kirby Road, Earlsdon, Coventry, he was born at Devonport on the 28th November 1890. He studied for the Priesthood at the Scots College, Rome and was Ordained on the 1st November 1915. He was Curate of St. Margaret's RC Church, Canning Town, from the 1st January 1916 residing at 79 Barking Road, Canning Town, East London. He was Commissioned as a Temporary Chaplain to the Forces, 4th Class, on a 2 year contract on the 5th January 1918. He went to Salonika in January 1918 and "remained fit and well until the 9th August". He was attached to the 49th General Hospital B.S.F. and No. 5 Con. Depot; 81st Field Ambulance. In August 1918 he was admitted to the 42nd General Hospital with Dysentery. Following a period of convalescence he returned to duty with the 81st Field Ambulance but was re-admitted to the 42nd General Hospital He was evacuated from Salonika via the Hospital Ship Glengorm Castle on the 13th August 1918 to the Military Hospital, Imtarfa, Malta as an Amoebic Dysentery carrier. A medical report at Malta on the 24th October diagnosed Dysentery and recommended transfer to England. On the 29th November he was invalided to England from Malta. Records show that he died at the 81st General Hospital Marseilles, France, of "influenza and bronicle pneumonia on the 22nd December 1918 aged 28". His body was subsequently re-interred in Mazargues War Cemetery, Marseilles, Bouches du Rhone, France. Grave Reference III.B.57. and he is remembered on the Aldershot Memorial. He had a Brother who was also a RC Priest at East Lulworth Wareham Dorset.

The Revd. George Edward CRAVEN
Temporary Chaplain 4th Class
Army Chaplains' Department.
Attached Rifle Brigade.

The son of the Revd. George Edward Craven, Vicar of Middleton, he studied at Queen's College, Oxford where he obtained a B.A. in 1912 and an M.A. in 1916. He trained for the Priesthood at Ripon College, in 1914 and was made a Deacon. Ordained Priest by the Bishop of

Birmingham in 1915, he served his Title as Curate of Holy Trinity, Smethwick, Birmingham. He died on the 7th December 1918, aged 27, is buried in Mikra British Cemetery, Kalamaria, Greece, Grave Reference 807, and remembered on the Aldershot Memorial. A Memorial fire surround commemorating former students of Ripon College is now situated in Ripon College, Cuddesdon, Oxford.

The Revd. Oswin CREIGHTON
Temporary Chaplain 4th Class
Army Chaplains' Department.

The son of Mandell Creighton (Lord Bishop of London) and Louise Creighton, he studied at Keble College, Oxford, where he obtained a B.A. in 1906, and an M.A. in 1909. He trained for the Priesthood at Bishop's Hostel, Farnham, in 1906 and was made a Deacon in 1907 by the Bishop of Kensington for London. Ordained Priest by the Lord Bishop of London in 1908, he served his Title as Curate of St. James, Norlands, Kensington from 1907 to 1910. He went to Canada as a Missionary of the Edmonton Mission, in the Diocese of Calgary. In 1912 he was appointed Rector of St. Monica Mirror with St. Pancras, Alix, in the Diocese of Calgary and became a Temporary Chaplain to the Forces in 1914. He was prominent at the landings at Y Beach, Gallipoli serving with the Lancashire Fusiliers, 29th Division. He was killed in action, in France, on the 15th April 1918 aged 34, is buried in Choques Military Cemetery, Pas de Calais, France, Grave Reference I.P.34. and remembered on the Aldershot Memorial.

The Revd. William Loraine Seymour DALLAS
Temporary Chaplain 4th Class
Army Chaplains' Department.
Attached The King's Own (Liverpool Regiment)
5th Battalion.

The son of Charles and Emily Dallas of Shanghai China, he studied at St. Edmund's Hall, Oxford where he obtained a B.A. (3rd Class Th. Hon.) in 1907. He trained for the Priesthood at Wells Theological College, in 1908 and was made a Deacon in 1908 and Ordained Priest by The Lord Bishop of London in 1909. After serving his Title as Curate of St. Mary Abbots, Kensington from 1908, he became a Missionary of the Prairie Brotherhood, Edmonton, in the Diocese of Calgary, Canada from1911. Returning to England, he became a Temporary Chaplain to the Forces in 1915. He was killed in action, in Belgium, on the 20th September 1917 aged 33. remembered on the Tyne Cot Memorial Panel 160 and the Aldershot Memorial.
A memorial from Wells Theological College is now at Sarum College, Salisbury.

The Revd. John James DALY
Royal Army Chaplains' Department.

He was a Wesleyan Minister, of the Irish Conference who became a Chaplain to the Forces on the 3rd August 1917, and served in Salonika. A son of the Manse, he returned to Ireland after demobilization, and was a Minister of the Belfast City Mission. He died in Ireland on the 17th November 1921 aged 36. The Obituary notes in Wesleyan Minutes of Conference for 1922, do not link his illness to war service. He is remembered on the Aldershot Memorial.

The Revd. Hatton Bertram St. John de VINE
Chaplain 4th Class
Army Chaplains' Department.
Attached Gordon Highlanders 10th Battalion.

The son of the Revd. Wilson T. de Vine M.A., Rural Dean and Vicar of Tipton, Staffordshire. He was educated at Stone Grammar School, and the High School, Birmingham. After serving his Articles with Messrs Fowler Langley and Wright of Wolverhampton, he qualified as a Solicitor and practiced for a year. He studied at Jesus College, Cambridge where he obtained a B.A. in 1913 and then at Ridley Hall, Cambridge. He was made a Deacon in 1913 and Ordained Priest by the Bishop of Birmingham in 1914. He was Curate of the Cathedral Church of St. Philip, Birmingham. At the outbreak of war he volunteered and became an Army Chaplain serving initially with the West Riding Regiment. He was killed in action in France on the 27th April 1916 aged 36. He is buried in Vermelles British Cemetery, Pas de Calais, France, Grave Reference I.G.29. and remembered on the Ridley Hall and Aldershot Memorials.

An Officer wrote,

"He is one of the bravest men I ever expect to meet. His human kindness and consideration, his unobtrusive familiarity with all ranks, make him beloved of all the men. Perhaps he is the last person they would like to see shot. And he goes anywhere, at any time, where there are men, whether in billets or in saps. Sometimes he is up all night, passing along the lines with a cheery presence and a pack loaded with cigarettes. While on trek he marches with the Brigade, walking every step of the way, though entitled to a horse, carrying a pack like the rest of us, and lending a hand with a rifle or two towards the end of the day. He has been within whispering distance of the Boche, too, gathering identification discs and papers from the dead between the lines. If there is a "strafe" on, depend on it he will be there. What a fine officer he would make. He could have done worlds with a Company". In a letter announcing his death the same officer says, *"He was a brother amongst us. There is no man I would sooner have beside me when hell is loose than De Vine."*

The Revd. Canon Arthur Gordon DEEDES
Temporary Chaplain 4th Class
Army Chaplains' Department.

The son of The Revd. Canon Gordon Frederic Deedes, Vicar of Heydour, Lincolnshire, he studied at Oriel College, Oxford where he obtained a B.A. in 1883 and an M.A. in 1886. After further study at Cuddesdon Theological College, Oxford, he was made a Deacon in 1884, and Ordained Priest by the Bishop of Rochester in 1885. He was Curate of St. John the Divine, Kennington, in the Diocese of Southwark from 1884 until 1911, when he became Vicar of St. John the Divine, Kennington, and was appointed an Honary Canon of Southwark. He was Commissoners Correspondent and Chaplain to St. Gabriel College 1911. Appointed a Temporary Chaplain to the Forces in 1914, he died on the 29th November 1916 aged 55. He is buried in Brookwood Cemetery, Surrey, Grave Reference V.178262 and remembered on the Cuddesdon College, Oxford Memorial.

The Revd. Harry DICKINSON
Temporary Chaplain 4th Class
Army Chaplains' Department.
Attached 28th Battalion London Regiment
(Artists' Rifles).

The son of Richard Henry and the late Cicely Dickinson, 438 Shaftmoor Lane, Hall Green, Birmingham, he was born in Birmingham on the 25th August 1885. His father was the Chief Engineer to Birmingham Corporation Tramways. He studied at Hatfield Hall, Durham, where he won the Long. Prize in 1907 and 1909 and obtained a B.A. in 1907 and an M.A. in 1913. After further study at Queen's College, Birmingham, he was made a Deacon in 1908 and Ordained Priest by the Lord Bishop of Durham in 1909. He served his Title as Curate of Brandon, Durham, and in 1910 he became Curate of St. George, Wolverhampton in the Diocese of Lichfield. He was appointed Chaplain to St. Cuthbert College, Worksop in 1914, was Vicar of St. Mary and St. John, Saltley, from 1915 to 1916 and St. Stephen, Birmingham in 1916. He became a Temporary Chaplain to the Forces retaining his Living. He was killed in action, in Belgium, on the 30th October 1917 aged 32. He is remembered at Passchendaele on the New British Cemetery Special Memorial, Reference 5. and on the Aldershot and Hatfield College, Durham, Memorials.

The Revd. Charles Edmund DOUDNEY
Chaplain 4th Class
Army Chaplains' Department.
Attached 18th Brigade 6th Division.

He was born at Carlisle, in 1868, the son of the late Revd. David and Mrs. Doudney. He studied at Corpus Christi College, Cambridge, where he obtained a B.A. in 1892 and an M.A. in 1896. He trained for the Priesthood at Ridley Hall, Cambridge from 1892 and was made a Deacon in 1894. Ordained Priest by the Bishop of Rochester in 1895 he served his Title as Curate of St. John the Evangelist, Penge from 1894 to 1896. He became Incumbent of Orroroo, South Australia until 1898. He then became Rector of Port Augusta, South Australia until 1902, when he moved once more to become Curate of Christ Church, North Adelaide and in 1904 Rector of Gawler, St. George with Gawler, St. Andrew in the Missionary District of South Australia. Returning to England in 1906, he was Curate of Emmanuel Church, West Hampstead,

and in June 1907 he was appointed Vicar of St. Luke, South Lyncombe, in the Diocese of Bath and Wells. He was the husband of Zoe Doudney of "Domremy" Old Headington, Oxford. He died of wounds, in Belgium, on the 16th October 1915 aged 44. He is buried in Lijssenthoek Military Cemetery, Poperinge, West-Vlaanderen, Belgium, Grave Reference I.A.31. and remembered on the Ridley Hall and Aldershot Memorials.

A Memorial plaque in St. Luke's Church, South Lyncombe, recalls that,
"By his zeal and interest in the parish
This church was rebuilt".
"A Servant of Jesus Christ"
He was succeeded at St. Luke's by his younger brother the Revd. Herbert Doudney.

The Revd. Fr. Denis DOYLE
Temporary Chaplain 4th Class
Army Chaplains' Department.
Attached Leinster Regiment 2nd Battalion.

He was born at Kimberley, South Africa, on the 6th January 1878, and was a pupil at St. Aidan's College, Grahamstown, South Africa. He entered the Society of Jesus at Manresa, in 1886 as a Noviciate, spent two years in Malta and five years at Stoneyhurst College, Lancashire. After studying Theology at St. Beuno's, he was Ordained at St. Beuno's in 1911. He received his Tertianship at Tullamore in 1912, and became Assistant Minister (Accountant) at Manresa in 1913 and Minister in 1914. On the 19th November 1915, he became an Acting Chaplain to the Forces at Richmond Park and went to France in the same month. He was killed in action, in France, on the 17th August 1916. (Jesuit records show that he died of wounds and the date of his death as the 19th of August with a detailed account of his funeral). Other accounts indicate that he died during an advance south towards Longueval, Guillemont, Ginchy and Combles. He was wounded by a shell burst at an advanced dressing station of the 4th Army. His next of kin was his sister who lived in South Africa. He is buried in Dive Copse British Cemetery, Sailly-le-Sec, Somme, France, Grave Reference I.C.6. and is remembered on the Aldershot Memorial.

The Revd. Fr. William Joseph DOYLE, MC
Chaplain 4th Class Army Chaplains' Department.
Attached Royal Dublin Fusiliers 8th Battalion.

He was born at Dalkey, Co. Dublin on the 3rd March 1873, the son of a Magistrate, and was educated at Rosminian College, Ratcliffe, England. He entered the Irish Province of the Society of Jesus at St. Stanislaus College, Tullamore, King's County, (now Co. Offaly) on the 31st March 1891. He studied Philosophy at Enghien, Belgium and at St. Mary's Hall, Stoneyhurst, Lancashire and Theology in Dublin. Ordained in 1907, he was a well known and loved Preacher in Great Britain and Ireland. He became a Temporary Chaplain to the Forces on the 30th November 1915. During his service in France and Flanders, he was at the heavy gas attack on the Loos Salient towards the end of April 1916, when he rescued an Officer. Known as Fr. Willie, he was prominent at Frezenberg Ridge (3rd Battle of Ypres), on the Ypres Salient. Shortly before his death, during the Battle of Langemark, The London Gazette of 1st January 1917 announced the award of the Military Cross. In the book *Fr. William J Doyle SJ* by Alfred O'Rahilly, it states that "Early in January Fr. Doyle was awarded the MC for his bravery at the Somme. For various reasons he disliked this distinction but was glad inasmuch it gave pleasure to his father to whom he wrote on January 4th, 'I am sorry these rewards were given to Chaplains, for surely he would be a poor specimen of the Lord's anointed who would do this work for such a thing. But seeing they are going to, I must say I am really glad because I know it will give pleasure to an old soldier at home, who aught long ago to have had all the medals and distinctions ever conferred. They have given me the MC but his crosses are far more welcome'. He was killed in action, in Belgium, on the 17th August 1917, aged 34, and remembered on the Tyne Cot Memorial, Panel 160 and the Aldershot Memorial. It is said that he was recommended for the VC and it is claimed to have been turned down by his Clerical Superiors. There is no record of an actual offer of a posthumous VC which his Superiors would not have had the right to refuse.

The Revd. Herbert DRANSFEILD

He was made a Deacon in 1892 and Ordained Priest by the Bishop of Rupert Island in 1894. He was Curate of Rounthwaite, Manitoba from 1892 to 1894; Incumbent of Stonewall, Manitoba from 1895 to 1897; Worsborough Dale, in the Diocese of York from 1897 to 1898; St. Andrew's Cathedral, Inverness from 1900 to 1901, then Rector of Arpafeelie with Highfield in the Diocese of Moray from 1901. He was appointed a Temporary Chaplain to the Forces in 1916, and died in 1920. He is commemorated on the war memorial in Inverness Cathedral. (Not serving at time of death).

The Revd. Richard William DUGDALE, MC
Temporary Chaplain 4th Class
Army Chaplains' Department.
Attached Norfolk Regiment 1st Battalion.

The son of the Revd. Sydney Dugdale, Rector of Whitchurch, Salop, he was a Late Exhibitioner of Corpus Christi College, Oxford where he obtained a B.A. (2nd Class Lit. Hum.) in 1912. After training for the Priesthood at Bishop's Hostel, Farnham, he was made a Deacon in 1913. Ordained Priest by the Bishop of Worcester in 1914, he served his Title as Curate of Rugby, in the Diocese of Worcester, and became a Temporary Chaplain to the Forces in 1915. He was awarded the Military Cross, London Gazette 3rd March 1917, page 2193, stating that he was attached to the Middlesex Regiment. "He attended the wounded under very heavy fire without the slightest regard for his own personal safety. He located wounded men in the most advanced positions and guided stretcher parties to bring them in".

He was killed in action, in France, on the 24th October 1918 and buried in Caudry British Cemetery, Nord, France, Grave Reference IV.G.22. and remembered on the Aldershot Memorial. (In Ussher's Roll of Honour he is listed as being in The Royal Air force.)

Editor's note.

In any research there are occasions when a lot of material emerges. The following entry is an example of what lies hidden and is reproduced with grateful thanks to those who supplied it. Although it refers to one particular person I am sure that many such items are known but to a few and held with pride and loving remembrance.

The Revd. Edward Francis DUNCAN, MC
Temporary Chaplain 4th Class
Army Chaplains' Department.
Attached 103rd Infantry Brigade.

The son of John Duncan, a farmer, and Anna Duncan, he was born at Cavan, Co. Tyrone, Ireland, on the 24th November 1884. He studied at Trinity College, Dublin where he obtained a B.A. in 1907 and an M.A. in 1910 having passed the Divinity Testimonium in 1908. He was made a Deacon in 1907 and Ordained Priest by the Archbishop of Dublin in 1909. He served as Curate of St. Mary, Blessington with Kilbride, Co. Wicklow from 1907 to 1911, then moved to Ballycotton, Cloyne, Co. Cork, until 1914. During his ministry at Ballycotton, he was Honary Secretary to the local Lifeboat.

On the 15th November 1911, he went out with the lifeboat crew. The rescue was described in "The Lifeboat" of 1st May 1912. The Revd. Duncan was awarded binoculars by the R.N.L.I, together with a draft of the handwritten thanks of the Institution on Vellum, voted by the Committee of Management on 14th December 1911. It read: "That the best thanks of the Royal National Life-Boat Institution be presented to the Revd. E. F. Duncan, Honorary Secretary of the Ballycotton Branch, in recognition of his very meritorious conduct in going off in the Life-Boat and assisting to save the crew of the S.S. Tadorna, which was wrecked near Ballycotton, in a strong S.S.E. gale, and very heavy sea, on 15th November 1911."

In May 1914 he was appointed Rector of the parish of Kilflyn, in the Diocese of Limerick, where he won the Royal Humane Society medal for saving a life in the River Shannon. He became Temporary Chaplain to the Forces on the 5th May 1915 and served in France from January 1916. By the end of August, the Brigade were back in the Front Line at Armentieres. He was awarded the Military Cross, which was announced in the London Gazette, 25th November 1916 page 11535. "Although himself wounded, he rescued a wounded officer under very heavy fire, displaying great courage and determination." An account of the action records that, "On the night of the 12th October the 27th Battalion Northumberland Fusiliers, sent over a raiding party of 6 officers and 100 men." According to a newspaper of the time, "the Revd. Duncan, at the end of the raid "...discovered that one of the officers was lying wounded in No Man's Land. Regardless of his own safety, he went out and carried the officer back through heavy shell fire from the enemy, who were retaliating vigorously for the British attack. As he was carrying the officer he was struck on the back by shrapnel, but after accomplishing his task he remained on duty."

The London Gazette of the 4th January 1917 also records, that he was Mentioned in Despatches. In March of 1917 the Brigade were in the Front Line at Arras. The War Diary of the 25th Battalion Northumberland Fusiliers has the following entry for 11th March: "About 300 shells fell into Arras during the day, and the Revd. E.F.

Duncan, C.F. was killed, whilst holding a service near the Hdqrs. of the 27th Northd. Fus." He was aged 32 and the husband of Jane Caroline Duncan (nee Church) of Carrick on Shannon, Co. Leitrim. He is buried in Faubourg D'Amiens Cemetery, Arras, Pas de Calais, France Grave Reference II.F.8. alongside the men killed with him. Remembered on the Aldershot Memorial. Those killed with the Revd. Duncan were, Lt. Thomas William Jones, R.A.M.C., 2nd Lt. Ernest James Blight and Lance Serjeant Albert Edward Hopper of the 27th Battalion, Northumberland Fusiliers (Tyneside Irish). An account of his death recalls that, "The day itself had been, "...fine, with a little rain, but good visibility and was the first day in March of which that could be said..." On 12th March 1917 Captain W. H. Davey, 27th Northumberland Fusiliers wrote to Mrs. Duncan;

"As a personal friend and fellow-countryman of your husband's will you allow me to tender to you my heartfelt sympathy in the terrible loss you have just sustained? I know words of consolation are of little avail but I felt you would care to learn anything to be ascertained of Mr. Duncan's last moments before he was killed. He had arranged to hold a church service yesterday (Sunday) afternoon for the men of my battalion and called at Battalion Head Quarters on his way there. We had not seen one another for some time as I had been detached from the Brigade for special duty and he gave me a characteristically hearty reception back and then after we had finished chaffing and joking one another he turned to the Commanding Officer who was in the room and said laughing, "You must excuse us, sir, for this unseemly conduct but you know when two Irishmen meet one another, you have to make allowances." He looked and seemed in splendid form and was in the best of spirits. After a few more words he went off to the service accompanied by several of our Head Quarters officers. Prior to this the Germans had been heavily shelling the town and the bombardment continued after he had gone.

About half an hour later the Sergeant Major of the Company in whose billet the service was being held came round to Head Quarters and informed us that a shell had struck the billet during the service and killed the Padre along with two of the other officers and several men - I at once hastened round and found to my horror that the report was only too true. From the inquiries made I was able to piece together what occurred. The billet was a large building enclosing a courtyard.

In a room on the ground floor on a side of the yard the service was being held. Your husband had just uttered the first sentence of his sermon when a shell crashed through the roof of the adjoining side and killed the sentry who was standing in the gateway. Your husband seeing the man fall rushed out to his assistance followed by the medical officer who was attending the service and another officer.

They had barely reached the man when a second shell hit close beside them and there was no possible chance of escape for any of them. Death must have been instantaneous in each case.

You will thus see that not only did your husband fall when discharging the sacred duties of his office but that he met his death while rushing with his characteristic heroism to give aid and succour to a fallen man. All those whom he left behind in the room where the service was being held escaped unharmed.

The knowledge of this must be a never failing source of legitimate pride to you and all his dear ones, although I realize only too well how unavailing the thought of this to soften the bitterness of your loss. His death has cast a great cloud of sorrow over the Brigade. He was universally beloved by every man, regardless of creed. He had a joke and a hearty word for all, while the men admired him for the bravery he had on so many previous occasions displayed.

I feel his death more than I can say, for as a brother-Irishman we had taken to one another since we first met and were the best of friends. His personal effects will be forwarded to you in due course. The various little things which he was carrying in his pockets at the time were reverently collected and I myself saw them carefully placed in Battalion Headquarters. Once again let me assure you of my deepest sympathy in which I can assure you the whole Tyneside Irish Brigade to a man joins.

Yours very sincerely, W .H. Davey.

On the 24th April 1917 the Tyneside Irish Committee wrote to Mrs. Duncan a letter of condolence part of which read:

"From the first date of his attachment to the Brigade - then stationed at Woolsington Park - he earned the respect and esteem of all who were privileged to make his acquaintance. His genial and constant good nature, his devotion to all ranks in the Brigade, and his solicitude for their general welfare, as well as for their spiritual, endeared him to all. The post of danger held no fears for him, if anyone required his attention. On the contrary, it was his post to help any of the poor fellows should suffer in any way from the want of attention, either spiritually or bodily. And it was a great source of pride to all when his anxiety for the welfare of the men was duly recognised by the authorities, when he was awarded the Military Cross."

Twenty five years after the Tadorna rescue (1. 11. 36), Mrs. Duncan received the following letter from the secretary of the Ballycotton Branch of the R.N.L.I.

Dear Mrs. Duncan

Father O'Shea P. P. Ballyporeen Tipperary who spoke at the presentation of medals to the crew on 27th October, asked me to write to you and tell you how he had spoken of Mr. Duncan. He made very nice references to him and paid him a high tribute. He said "Mr. Duncan was a whole man, and he could not remain inactive." He also said "Several military chaplains who met him at the front told him (Father O'Shea) "That he was a whole man at the front" in conclusion Fr. O'Shea said the Revd. Mr. Duncan was a clergyman of a different church to me "and I say he was the finest man I had the honour to meet. I met him several times in Cork and other places." He also said, "I came to Ballycotton for two reasons, one to shake Patsy Sliney by the hand and secondly, to speak of the bravery of Mr. Duncan." At the lunch at Fawcetts Hotel Fr. O'Shea was talking to Patsy Sliney about the 'Tadorna and Mr. Duncan' and was delighted to hear that Patsy was also at the 'Tadorna' he being 2nd coxswain at the time.

Yours Faithfully, Bob Mahony.

(Some of the information in this entry was supplied by Mr. C. Duncan, the grandson of Revd. E. F. Duncan. MC)

The Revd. Sidney DUNSTAN
Temporary Chaplain 4th Class
Army Chaplains' Department.

He attended Dorchester Missionary College in 1904, and was made a Deacon in 1908. Ordained Priest by the Lord Bishop of London in 1909, he served his Title as Curate of St. Mary, Cable Street, with St. George in the East, from 1909 until 1910. He moved to South Africa and was given a General Licence in the Diocese of Pretoria until 1911; Curate at Boksburg until 1913. Returning to England, he became Curate of St. Mary, Oxford, until 1915. He died on the 16th July 1918, aged 34, and is buried in Mansfield (Nottingham Road) Cemetery, Grave Reference A.3414.

The Revd. John Richard DUVALL
Temporary Chaplain 4th Class
Army Chaplains' Department.
Attached Wiltshire Regiment 7th Battalion.

The son of John William and Anna Duvall, of Walton Road, Ware, Herts, he studied at Selwyn College, Cambridge, where he obtained a B.A. (Th. Trip. pt. i. cl. Ii) in 1911. After further study, at Ely Theological College in 1911, he was made a Deacon in 1912 and Ordained Priest by the Bishop of Liverpool in 1913. He served his Title as Curate of St. Jude, West Derby, Liverpool from 1912 until 1914 and was appointed Vice Principal of St. Boniface College, Warminster until 1915, when he became Temporary Chaplain to the Forces. He died of wounds, in Greece, on the 16th October 1917 aged 28. He is buried in Sarigol Military Cemetery, Kriston, Greece, Grave Reference C.443. and remembered on the Aldershot Memorial. A Memorial for Ely College students is now situated in the King's School Ely.

The Revd. Herbert Hinton EAST
Temporary Chaplain 4th Class
Army Chaplains' Department.
Attached Cheshire Regiment 13th Battalion.

The son of Emma Jane East, of 284 Kew Road, Kew, Surrey, and the late Francis Hyde Hinton East. He studied at St. Chad's Hostel, Regina, Canada, and was made a Deacon in 1912. Ordained Priest by the Bishop of Qu'App. in 1913. He was Curate of Govan, from 1912 until 1913, when he became Org. Missionary in the Diocese of Qu'App. In 1915 he was appointed Incumbent of Lanigan, Qu'App. He became a Temporary Chaplain to the Forces in 1917, and was killed in action, in Belgium, on the 5th August 1917 aged 30. He is remembered on the Ypres Menin Gate Memorial, Panel 56, Belgium, and the Aldershot Memorial.

The Revd. Frank Harrison EDINGER
Temporary Chaplain 4th Class
Army Chaplains' Department.

He was the son of the late Philip and Emily Edinger, and trained for the Priesthood at Kings College, London (A.K.C.) in 1911, when he was made a Deacon. Ordained Priest by the Lord Bishop of London, in 1912 serving his Title as Curate of Camden Town, London until 1914; Ashford, Camden, until he became a Temporary Chaplain to the Forces in 1917. He was drowned at sea, when on board the Hospital Ship Glenart Castle, on the 26th February 1918, aged 33. The Glenart Castle was a Hospital ship, which on the 26th February 1918 was sunk by a torpedo, off the North Coast of Cornwall, near Ilfracombe. She had left Cardiff, bound for Brest to take on patients. Out of a ships compliment of 186, only 31 survived. He was the husband of Maud Mary Edinger, of 4 Church Road, Ashford, Kent. He is remembered on the Hollybrook Memorial, Southampton, Hampshire, and on the Aldershot Memorial.

See also The Revd. John Joseph McILVAINE.

The Revd. Evan EDWARDS
Temporary Chaplain 4th Class
Army Chaplains' Department

Born at Walton, Liverpool, in 1885 the son of Evan and Gwen Edwards of Walton, Liverpool. He attended Bala-Bangor College and in 1912 was a Congregational Minister at Carneddau and Maesbury (Oswestry Town Church). He moved to Shirebrook, Mansfield in 1915 and served in France with the YMCA; becoming a Temporary Chaplain to the Forces in November 1918. Two weeks later he died of influenza at Tidworth Camp on the 27th November 1918 aged 32. He was the husband of Gladys Edwards (nee James) of Fairhaven, Llanrug, Carnarvon, and is buried in Liverpool (Anfield) Cemetery, Grave Reference VI. U. 1375

The Revd. Pierce John EGAN
Temporary Chaplain 4th Class
Army Chaplains' Department.
Attached British West Indies Regiment 1st Battalion.

He studied at Trinity College, Dublin, where he obtained a B.A. and passed the Divinity Test in 1888 and an M.A. in 1899. He was made a Deacon in 1888 and Ordained Priest by the Bishop of Derry in 1889, serving as Curate of Drumragh, Co. Tyrone, until 1893, when he was appointed to the staff of St. Columb Cathedral, Derry, until 1901. He went to St. Mary's Cathedral, Edinburgh, and in 1903, became Cathedral Chaplain until 1912. He was appointed Rector of St. Peter, Galashiels, in the Diocese of Edinburgh. He died in Egypt, on the 6th April 1916, was the husband of Jessie Helen Egan, of 7A Spencer Road, Eastbourne, is buried in Alexandria (Chatby) Military and War Memorial Cemetery, Egypt, Grave reference Q.568. and remembered on the Aldershot Memorial.

The Revd. John Charles ELLIOTT
Temporary Chaplain 4th Class
Royal Army Chaplains' Department.

The son of William Elliott, of Curbar, Derbyshire, studied at Queen's College, Cambridge, where he obtained a B.A. in 1886 and an M.A. in 1890. He trained for the Priesthood at Ridley Hall, Cambridge, and was made a Deacon in 1886. Ordained Priest by the Bishop of Rochester in 1887. After serving his Title as Curate of St. James, Plumpstead, from 1886 until 1890, he was subsequently Curate at Cheltenham until 1891; All Saints, Marylebone until 1894 and Islington until 1896. He then accepted the Living of Holy Trinity, Sheerness, until 1900. He was Vicar of St. Stephen, Clapham Park, from 1900 until 1905; St. Mary, Hornsey Rise, 1905 until 1915; St. John Cheltenham, from 1915 until 1916, when he became a Temporary Chaplain to the Forces until 1919. He died on the 5th October 1920 at Curbar, Sheffield and is buried in the South West part of Baslow (St. Anne) Churchyard, Derbyshire and remembered on the Ridley Hall, Cambridge Memorial. It is probable that he was not serving at the time of death.

The Revd. Edward Williams EVANS
Chaplain 4th Class
Royal Army Chaplains' Department.

Son of the late Archdeacon Evans, of Merioneth, (Canon of Bangor). He studied at University College, Durham, gaining a L. Th. in 1878 when he was made a Deacon. Ordained Priest by the Lord Bishop of Durham in 1879, he served his Title as Curate of Warden, from 1878 until 1881 and then at Matfen until 1882, when he was appointed Cathedral Chaplain of Newcastle on Tyne until 1884. He then accepted the Living of St. Augustine, Tynemouth and in 1887 moved to St. George's, Cullercoats until 1890, when he moved to Maker, Cornwall and was Acting Chaplain to the Forces from 1890 until 1896; Rector of Beverston from 1896 until 1901; Vicar of Dringhouses, from 1901 until 1908; Honary Diocesan Missioner in the Diocese of Gloucester 1902; Rector of Goldsborough, in the Diocese of Ripon from 1908, and Temporary Chaplain to the Forces 1915. The husband of Edith R. Evans, of 71c Harcourt Terrace, London, he died on the 10th February 1919, aged 67. His obituary in Church Times states, "though well over 60 he continued to work until his health collapsed in late 1918. He was buried with full military honours" south of the Church in Maker (SS Macra, Mary and Julian) Churchyard, Cornwall and remembered on the Aldershot Memorial.

The Revd. W. EVANS - JONES
See under JONES.

The Revd. Geoffrey Maynard EVANS, MC
Temporary Chaplain 4th Class
Army Chaplains' Department.
Formerly Lieutenant in the Welsh Regiment.

The son of Samuel and Eleanor Sophia Evans, of "Cartref", Dovercourt, Essex, he studied at Bishop's College, Cheshunt, and was made a Deacon in 1913. Ordained Priest by the Lord Bishop of London. He was Curate of St. Mary Tottenham, from 1913 until he became Temporary Chaplain to the Forces in 1915. The announcement of an award of the Military Cross appeared in the London Gazette on the 4th June 1917 page 5478 with no published citation. He was killed in action, in Belgium, on the 11th August 1917, aged 35, is buried in Divisional Collecting Post Cemetery and Extension, West Vlaanderen, Belgium, Grave Reference II.E.12. and remembered on the Aldershot Memorial.

The Revd. John William Alcock EYRE-POWELL
Chaplain 4th Class Army Chaplains' Department.
Attached Labour Corps 27th Labour Group H.Q.

The son of Richard and Marie Louisa Eyre-Powell, of The Cottage, Colyton, Axminster, Devon and Mont Alto Dalkey, Co. Dublin, he studied at Trinity College, Dublin where he obtained a B.A. in 1907 and an M.A. in 1913. He was made a Deacon in 1910 and Ordained Priest by the Bishop of Bath and Wells in 1912. He was Curate of Abbeyleix, in the Diocese of Leigh, Queen's County, Ireland. Killed in action, in Belgium, on the 16th April 1918, aged 37 he is remembered on the Tyne Cot Memorial, Panel 160, and on the Aldershot Memorial.

The Revd. William James FALSIDE
Temporary Chaplain 4th Class.
Army Chaplains' Department.

The son of the Revd. John Tully Falside, of the United Free Manse, Davington, Eskdalemuir, Dumfries, Scotland and the late Elizabeth Semple Falside, he was a Minister of the United Free Church of Scotland. He studied at the University of Glasgow, where he obtained an M.A. in 1911, and was Ordained and Inducted in the same year to Howgate, by Penicuik. He died of pneumonia, in Italy, on the 7th October 1918 aged 35, is buried in Faenza Communal Cemetery, Italy, Grave Reference I.D.2. and remembered on the Aldershot Memorial.

The Revd. Henry Kingsley FINCH
Temporary Chaplain
Army Chaplains' Department.

A Dowman's Sizar of St. John's College, Cambridge, he obtained a B.A. (3rd Class Trip.) in 1905 and an M.A. in 1910. After study at Wells Theological College, in 1907 he was made a Deacon in 1908. Ordained Priest by the Bishop of Southwell in 1909, he served his Title as Curate of Alfreton, from 1908, until 1912 and was then Curate of St. Mary, Nottingham, until 1914. He became a Temporary Chaplain to the Forces in 1915 and was Medically Boarded as unfit in 1916. The date of death is unknown. He is remembered on the Aldershot Memorial.

The Revd. Fr. William Joseph FINN
Chaplain 4th Class Army Chaplains' Department.

He was born on the 27th December 1875, at Sculercoates, near Hull. His birth details do not record Joseph. After study at Ushaw College, Durham, from 1889 until 1900, he was Ordained on the 5th August 1900 at Middlesbrough. He was Curate at Middlesbrough Cathedral from1900 until 1908; St. Hilda's, Whitby, 1908 until 1909; and Parish Priest at All Saints, Thirsk, from 1909 until 1913. He then became Chaplain to Col. Langdale, at the Holy Family, Houghton Hall, Sancton, near Pocklington in the Middlesbrough RC Diocese until 1915. Previously, he had asked his Bishop for permission to enlist, and this had been refused. In a letter from Bishop Lacey, dated 11th October 1914, it states "I have reconsidered my decision on one condition only namely that when the war is over for one reason or another you cease to be Chaplain to the troops immediately and at once report yourself to the Bishop of the Diocese at that time and that you will not use this leave of absence as a means of seeking release from your own Diocese". He became a Temporary Chaplain to the Forces in 1915. Mentioned in Despatches, he was killed in action at Sedd el Bahr, Turkey, on the 25th April 1915. Lieutenant Patterson DSO wrote,

"He insisted on landing at Gallipoli with the first assault from the vessel *River Clyde* at Helles Bay and was killed. Many anxious eyes were peering about over the protected bulwarks of the *River Clyde*, among them was Fr. Finn, the Roman Catholic Chaplain of the Dublin's. The sight of 500 of his brave boys lying dead or dying on that terrible strip of beach was too much for him, so heedless of the risk, he plunged down the gangway and made for the shore. On the way his wrist was shattered by a bullet, but he went on, and although lead was splattering around him like hailstones, he administered consolation to the wounded and dying, who, alas were so thickly strewn around. For a time he seemed to have some miraculous form of Divine Protection, for he went from one to another through shot and shell without receiving any further injury. At last a bullet struck him near the hip, and on seeing this, some of the Dublins rushed out to him from the protection of the sandbank, and brought him into its shelter. When, however, he had somewhat recovered from his wound, nothing would induce him to remain in safety while his poor boys were being done to death in the open. So out he crawled again to administer comfort to a poor fellow who was moaning piteously a little way off and he was in the act of giving consolation to the stricken man, the heroic Chaplain was struck dead by a merciless bullet".

He is buried in V Beach Cemetery, Turkey, Grave Reference F.4. and remembered on the Memorials in Ushaw College, Beverley Minster and the Aldershot Memorial.

A graphic account of the landing by the Revd. T. A. Harker, who buried Fr. Finn is in the Ushaw College Notes page 183
The story and history of the *River Clyde* is to be found on
http://en.wikipedia.org/wiki/SS_River_Clyde

Photograph with the kind permission of Ushaw College, Durham

The Revd. Oswald Garrow FISHER
Temporary Chaplain 4th Class
Royal Army Chaplains' Department.

He studied at Trinity College, Dublin, where he obtained a B.A. (Mod. In Cl.) in 1913. He went to Bedale School, and won the Kyle Irish Prize in 1914, passing the Divinity Test 2nd Class in 1915. He was made a Deacon in 1916 and Ordained Priest by the Archbishop of Dublin in 1917. He was Curate of St. George, Dublin, from 1916 until 1918, when he became a Temporary Chaplain to the Forces. He died in Iraq, on the 4th November 1920, and is buried in Baghdad (North Gate) War Cemetery, Iraq, Grave Reference VIII.J.9.

The Revd. Fr. John J. FITZGIBBON, MC
Chaplain 3rd Class Royal Army Chaplains' Department.
Attached Army Medical Corps.
17th Field Ambulance.

The second son of Mr. J. Fitzgibbon, a Draper and Nationalist MP for South Mayo, of Castlerea, Co. Roscommon, Ireland, he was born at Castlerea, Co. Roscommon, on the 15th July 1882. He went to Clongowes Wood College, Sallins, County Kildare and completed his apprenticeship as a Draper. He entered the Irish Province of the Society of Jesus, at St. Stanislaus College, Tullamore on the 7th September 1901. He studied Philosophy at St. Mary's Hall, Stoneyhurst, Lancashire, and Theology in Dublin. He was Ordained in 1915. Society of Jesus archives state, "He volunteered in early 1916. His elder brother fell at Gallipoli in 1915. He became Senior Chaplain to the 4th Division. He joined up with Fr. McAuliffe, who died in October 1916. He (Fr. Fitzgibbon) was gassed at the Battle of Polygon Wood, on 5th September 1918 and was killed in the October of that year. He was killed by a shell burst at the advanced dressing station where he was tending the wounded after burying a Catholic soldier".

He was awarded the Military Cross, London Gazette 8th March 1918, page 2974 with no published citation. Military Records show that he was killed in action, in France, on the 18th September 1918. He is buried in Trefcon British Cemetery, Caulaincourt, Aisne, France, Grave Reference B.56. and is remembered on the Aldershot Memorial.

The Revd. Donald FRASER DSO
Chaplain 2nd Class Army Chaplains' Department.

The son of Alexander Fraser of Auchgate, Cannich, Beauly, Inverness-shire, Scotland. Baptist Church Archives state, "He went to the Metropolitan Baptist College, and was a Baptist Minister at Bedworth, from 1902 until 1906, and at Tamworth until his death in 1918". He is listed as a Temporary Chaplain to the Forces from 1915, and was awarded the DSO on the 4th June 1917 London Gazette, page 5470 with no published citation. He was killed in a road traffic accident in France on the 2nd June 1918 aged 42. He is buried in Couin New British Cemetery, Pas de Calais France. Grave Reference A.2. and remembered on the Aldershot Memorial.

The Revd. William Herbert FREESTONE
Temporary Chaplain 4th Class
Army Chaplains' Department.

The son of William and Harriet Maude Freestone, of 4 Clarendon Street, Nottingham, he studied at Keble College, Oxford, where he obtained a B.A. (3rd Class Nat. Sci.) in 1905 and an M.A. in 1909. He was made a Deacon in 1907 and Ordained Priest by the Bishop of Lincoln in 1908, serving his Title as Curate of St. Faith, Lincoln until 1913, when he entered the House of The Resurrection, Mirfield becoming a Temporary Chaplain to the Forces in 1916. He was killed in action, in Greece, on the 14th December 1916 aged 34. He is buried in Mikra British Cemetery, Kalamaria, Greece, Grave Reference 1891 and remembered on the Aldershot Memorial.

The Revd. Reginald Hardwick FULFORD
Temporary Chaplain 4th Class
Army Chaplains' Department.

He studied at Emmanuel College, Cambridge, where he obtained a B.A. in 1908. He was made a Deacon in 1908 and Ordained Priest by the Bishop of Birmingham in 1909. He served his Title as Curate of St. Barnabas, Birmingham, until 1911, and was then Curate of St. George, Edgbaston until 1913, when he moved to St. Andrew, Plymouth, in the Diocese of Exeter. He became a Temporary Chaplain to the Forces in 1914, and was killed in action in Iraq, on the 15th December 1916. He is remembered on the Basra Memorial, Panel 43 and the Aldershot Memorial.

The Revd. Charles Harold GARRETT
Chaplain 4th Class Army Chaplains' Department.
Attached South Staffordshire Regiment.
2nd/6th Battalion.

The eldest son of Mr. and Mrs. C. T. Garrett, Old Town, Clapham, London, he studied at St. Chad's Hall, Durham, where he obtained a B.A. in 1911. He was made a Deacon in 1912 and Ordained Priest by the Bishop of Southwell in 1913. After serving his Title as Curate of The Priory Church, Worksop, he became a Temporary Chaplain to the

Forces, and was killed in action, in Belgium, on the 26th September 1917 aged 28. He is buried in Brandhoek New Military, Cemetery, No. 3, Belgium, Grave Reference I.H.27. and remembered on the Aldershot Memorial.

The Revd. William Duncan GEARE
Temporary Chaplain 4th Class
Army Chaplains' Department.
Attached 165th Infantry Brigade.

The son of Henry Cecil and Caroline Isabella Geare, of 14 Chalcot Gardens, Hampstead, London, he was educated at Westminster School, and studied at Queen's College, Cambridge, where he obtained a B.A. in 1912. After training for the Priesthood at Leeds Clergy School, he was made a Deacon in 1913 and Ordained Priest by the Bishop of Ripon in 1914. He served his Title as Curate of St. Margaret, Ilkley, in the Diocese of Ripon, and became a Temporary Chaplain to the Forces in 1916. He served with the 7th and 9th Battalions, The Kings (Liverpool) Regiment, at Ypres, Belgium and was killed in action, in Belgium, on the 31st July 1917, aged 26. He is buried in Vlamertinghe New Military Cemetery, West Vlaanderen, Belgium, Grave Reference VI.A.1. and remembered on the Aldershot Memorial.

The Revd. Basil Johnson GEDGE
Temporary Chaplain 4th Class
Army Chaplains' Department.
Attached Royal Army Medical Corps.
78th Field Ambulance.

The son of The Revd. Edmund and Mary Elizabeth Gedge, he studied at Selwyn College, Cambridge, where he obtained a B.A. in 1904 and trained for the Priesthood at Cuddesdon College, Oxford, until 1906, when he was made a Deacon by the Bishop of Oxford for Madagascar. Ordained Priest by the Bishop of Madagascar in 1908. he was a Missionary in the Diocese of Madagascar until 1908 and subsequently at Andovoranto until 1913 and then at Mahanoro, Madagascar. He was the husband of M. K. Gedge, "The Priory" Thatcham, Berkshire. He died of wounds, in Greece, on the 25th April 1917, aged 34. and is buried in Doiran Military Cemetery, Greece, Grave Reference I.F.17. and remembered on the Cuddesdon College, Oxford and Aldershot Memorials.

The Revd. Fr. Michael Patrick GORDON
Chaplain 4th Class
Army Chaplains' Department.
Attached XV Corps.

The son of Michael and Mary Gordon, of Chapelton House, Dumbarton, he was a Doctor of Divinity, and a Priest of the Glasgow RC Diocese. He died of wounds, on the 27th August 1917 as a result of counter bombardment fire on 26th August 1917 which hit his billet, at Coxyde, Belgium. Aged 34, he is buried in Coxyde Military Cemetery, Belgium, Grave Reference III.C.13. and remembered on the Aldershot Memorial.

The Revd. Edward Reginald GIBBS
Temporary Chaplain 4th Class
Army Chaplains' Department.
Attached Grenadier Guards 1st Battalion.

The son of The Revd. William Cobham Gibbs, Rector of Clyst St. George and Mrs. Gibbs, of Temple Hill, East Budleigh, Devon, he was a pupil at Haleybury School. He studied at Keble College, Oxford, where he obtained a B.A. in 1910 and an M.A. in 1914. After training for the Priesthood at Cuddesdon College, Oxford, he was made a Deacon in 1911 and Ordained Priest by the Archbishop of York in 1913. He served his Title as Curate of Ardwick le Street, (Woodland Mission Church), from 1911 until 1913 when he became Curate of Armley and was appointed Domestic Chaplain to the Archbishop of York. He was killed in action, in France, on the 29th March 1918 aged 32, is buried in Boisleux-au-mont Communal Cemetery, Pas de Calais, France, Panel 2. and remembered on an Honours Board in All Saints Church, Woodlands, Doncaster, Cuddesdon College, Oxford and the Aldershot Memorial.

The Revd. Ernest Newham GREEN
Temporary Chaplain 4th Class
Army Chaplains' Department.

He studied at King's College, London, (A.K.C.) and was made a Deacon in 1908. Ordained Priest by the Lord Bishop of London in 1909, he served his Title as Curate of St. Mark, Noel Park, until 1910. He moved to St. Martin, Kensall Rise, in the Diocese of London and became a Temporary Chaplain to the Forces on the 8th February 1916. He died after a few days illness on the 26th March 1916, aged 35 and is buried in Willesden New Cemetery, Middlesex, Grave Reference I.340.

The Revd. Herbert GREEN, MC
Chaplain 4th Class Army Chaplains' Department.
Attached 41st Casualty Clearing Station

The son of Henry and Agnes Annie Green, of Catley Park, Linton, Cambridgeshire. He studied at Richmond College, and was a Wesleyan Minister. He enlisted in 1914 as a combatant but was withdrawn in 1916 to become a Chaplain. He was awarded the Military Cross, London Gazette 18th July 1917 page 7230. "he showed the greatest gallantry and coolness in assisting to dress and attend wounded men under heavy fire. Throughout he set a magnificent example to all". The husband of Olive Barough Green, of Little Chesterford, Saffron Walden, he was killed in action, (by shell fired while attending wounded) in Belgium, on the 24th August 1917 aged 28. A Memorial Plaque commemorating students of Richmond College, is now in the Methodist Church House, Marylebone Road, London. He is buried in The Huts Cemetery, Belgium, Grave Reference III.B.13. and remembered on the Aldershot Memorial.

The Revd. Hugh James Bernard GREEN
Temporary Chaplain 4th Class
Army Chaplains' Department.

The son of The Revd. F. J. and Mrs. T. E. Green, of Newstead, Pietermarietzburg, Natal, South Africa, he studied at the University of Oxford, in 1905 and St. Stephen's House, Oxford and Lichfield Theological College in 1907. He was made a Deacon in 1909 by the Bishop of Lichfield, and Ordained Priest in 1913 by the Archbishop of Cape Town. He was Curate of St. George, Walsall from 1909 until 1912, and St. Mary, Woodstock, and Plumpstead, Cape Town until 1915. He died in France, on the 8th December 1918 aged 34. He is buried in Longuenesse (St.. Omer) Souvenir Cemetery, Pas de Calais, France, Grave Reference V.E.75. and remembered on the Aldershot Memorial.

The Revd. Richard Ussher GREER

The son of the then Rector of Kilcoleman and Crossboyle, Co. Mayo, Ireland, he was born near Dungannon, and was a direct descendent of Archbishop Ussher. He studied at Trinity College, Dublin, where he obtained a B.A. in 1890, passing the Divinity Test in 1892 and an M.A. in 1893. He was made a Deacon in 1891 and Ordained Priest by the Bishop of Down in 1892. He was Curate of Holy Trinity Belfast, 1891 to 1892; Carrickfergus, Co. Antrim 1893; St. Michael, Belfast 1893; Vicar of St. Michael, Belfast 1893 to 1902; Incumbent of Christ Church Lisburn, 1902 to 1911; Rector of Seapatrick in the Diocese of Dromore, from 1911 to his death. He was Chaplain to the 36th Ulster Division, 8th Battalion, Royal Irish Rifles, based at Ballykinlar camp. He died of a brain hemorrhage on the 23rd June 1915, and was buried with full Military honours. The clerical information is from Crockford's Clerical Directory of 1914 and is somewhat different to that which appears on a web site.

The Revd. David Howell GRIFFITHS
(Some records show the surname as Griffith)
Temporary Chaplain 4th Class
Army Chaplains' Department.

He was born at Birmingham on the 14th May 1862, and studied at Hatfield Hall, Durham, where he obtained a B.A. in 1885. He was made a Deacon by the Bishop of Manchester in 1887 and Ordained Priest by the Bishop of St. Asaph in 1892. He served his Title as Curate of Waterhead, Lancashire from 1887 until 1889, when he was appointed Assistant Master at St. Drostane's College, Aberlour, Banffshire, Scotland until 1891. Returning to Wales he was Curate of Abergele until 1894, when he was appointed Priest in Charge of Cue, Western Australia. In 1896 he became Rector of Albany, Western

Australia until 1899 and was Archdeacon of Coolgardie from 1900 until 1904. He moved to South Africa and was Priest in charge of Parktown, Transvaal, from 1904 until 1906. Returning once more to Wales, he was Curate of Ruthin with Llanrhydd, from 1906 until 1909. He then became Vicar of Bagillt, until 1912, when he was appointed Rector of Nannerch, in the Diocese of St. Asaph, and subsequently Chaplain at Kinmel Camp, near St Asaph in July 1915.

A certain amount of confusion over his name and date of death has resulted in the following findings. In notes on WO 339/128574 "two years later he wrote to his Bishop saying he was unwell and wished to resign. Nothing further was heard until the Assistant Chaplain, General Western Command at Chester, wrote to the Chaplain General at the War Office on the 6th January 1918 to report that Mr Griffiths had committed suicide. Although there is nothing in the file that directly suggests that his death was the result of his service as an Army Chaplain the ACG would appear to imply so in his letter to the War Office".

In the General Register of deaths for the quarter ending December 1917, a D. H. Griffiths is recorded as having died at Newport, Monmouthshire. Hatfield College Durham shows the date of death as 12th December 1917 at Cross Keys, aged 54. The Commonwealth War Graves Headstone shows the date of death as the 15th December 1915 and his surname as Griffiths. His War Office Record Card is noted 'Suicide' and that he died on the 15th December 1917 aged 53. He was married with five children and came from a clergy family and is buried in a family plot at Usk, (St. Mary the Virgin) Churchyard, Monmouthshire, North East of the Church. The Burial Register held by Gwent Records confirms all the details above but show the date of burial as 15th December 1917 and that the Ceremony was performed by the Revd. H. S. Rees, Vicar of Abertillery.

Fr. Julian Gray, Vicar of the Parish (2006) states that, "the gravestone is of classic war grave design and displays the badge of the Royal Army Chaplains Department. He is buried alongside other members of his family, the graves being protected by a low level wrought iron fence. The Revd. D. H. Griffiths appears to have come from a clerical family- two of his relatives whom he is buried alongside were also Priests. One I think, was his father and the other, possibly a brother. Following the ancient tradition of burying priests so that they face their congregations at the General Resurrection, the graves all face west".

Editor's note August 2007.

The matter of the year of death on the headstone was taken up with the Commonwealth War Graves Commission. Having examined all the evidence they have agreed to replace the headstone with the correct year of death.

The Revd. Fr. Peter GROBEL
Chaplain 4th Class Army Chaplains' Department.

A Priest of the Salford RC Diocese, he served as a Naval Acting Chaplain and was present during the Boxer Rebellion at the capture of Tientsin and at the relief of the Legations at Peking, then was stationed at Malta. He was commissioned as an Army Chaplain from the 25th December 1909, and was with the B.E.F. based at St. Patrick's Soldiers' Club Boulogne. In July 1915 he wrote to Mgr. Bidwell, asking to go to Egypt, as he knew "the East very well, and his friend Fr. Nash was out there, as there was very little doing at Boulogne, and the Dardanelles would have more troops sent out." There is no evidence of any reply. Other correspondence between Fr. Grobel and several other RC Chaplains, and Cardinal Bourne, in May 1916,

questioning the legality of saying more than two Masses per day illustrates the amount of pastoral and spiritual work that they were being called upon to do. Correspondence begun in July 1916, between the War Office and Mgr. Bidwell concerning a promotion to Chaplain 3rd Class resulted in him subsequently being promoted. However RAChD. Records do not support this. It appears the outcome was that his Naval Service did not count and he had to serve at least ten years in the Army before such a promotion. He was Mentioned in Despatches, and died of pneumonia and bronchitis in hospital in France, on the 1st January 1917. He is buried in Boulogne Eastern Cemetery, Pas de Calais, France, Grave Reference VII.A.12. and remembered on the Aldershot Memorial.

Editor's note.

There were Catholic Clubs, some of which were set up by the Catholic Women's League, and it is quite probable that Fr. Grobel was involved with the one at Boulogne.

The Revd. Herbert Edward GUNSON
Temporary Chaplain 4th Class
Army Chaplains' Department.

He studied at St. Edmund Hall, Oxford where he obtained a B.A. (4th cl. Th. Scho.) in 1893 and an M.A. in 1894. He was made a Deacon in 1894 and Ordained Priest by the Bishop of Rochester in 1895. He served his Title as Curate of St. Anne, South Lambeth, until 1898; Acting Chaplain Guy's Hospital 1898 to 1899 and was Curate of St. Olave, Southwark until 1900, when he was appointed Chaplain to the Middlesex Hospital until 1914. He became a Temporary Chaplain to the Forces in 1915. He died on the 23rd August 1918 aged 50, and is buried in Portsdown (Christ Church) Churchyard, Hampshire, 13.

The Revd. Fr. David Michall GUTHRIE
Temporary Chaplain 4th Class
Army Chaplains' Department.
Attached East Lancashire Regiment 8th Battalion.

A Brother of the OSB at Quarr, he died of wounds in France on the 21st November 1916. He is buried in Varennes Military Cemetery, Somme, France, Grave Reference I.C.34. and remembered on the Aldershot Memorial.

The Revd. Fr. John GWYNN
Chaplain 4th Class
Army Chaplains' Department.
Attached Irish Guards 1st Battalion.

He was born at Galway, Ireland, on the 12th June 1866. He entered the Irish Province of the Society of Jesus at Dromore, Co. Down on 18th October 1884, and studied Philosophy at Louvaine, Belgium, and Theology at Milltown Park, Dublin. After he was Ordained in 1899, he taught at Clongowes Wood College, Sallins, Co. Kildare: University College, Dublin, and Mungret College, Co. Limerick. He was a member of the Board of Governors of University College, Dublin. For many years he preached at Annual Retreats of Irish Guards prior to 1914. He died of wounds, in France, on the 12th October 1915, and is buried in Bethune Town Cemetery, Pas de Calais France, Grave Reference II.K.6. and remembered on the Aldershot Memorial. A Memorial Tablet was erected by the Irish Guards, at the Church of the Sacred Heart, Catherham, Surrey.

The Venerable Henry Armstrong HALL CBE
Chaplain 1st Class Royal Army Chaplains' Department.

He was a student at Kings College, London, (A.K.C.), where he won the Trench Gr. Test Prize 1st Cl. and 1st Cl. Preliminary Theological Examination in 1876. After study at University College, Durham, he obtained a B.D. in 1891. He was made a Deacon in 1876 and Ordained Priest by the Bishop of Rochester in 1877, becoming Curate of Holy Trinity, Lee, Kent until 1878, when he was appointed Perpetual Curate of St. George, Douglas, Isle of Man until 1880. He was Vicar of Holy Trinity, Bristol, from 1880 to 1885; Swindon 1885 to 1887; Minister of Brunswick Chapel, St. Marylebone 1887 to 1888; Vicar of St. Mary, Spring Grove, Heston 1888 to 1892; Rector of St. John Baptist, Perth, 1892 to 1898; Vicar of Methley, in the Diocese of Ripon 1898; Rural Dean of Whitekirk, 1908 and Canon Residentiary of Ripon Cathedral 1908 to 1911; Archdeacon of Richmond 1908. In 1912 he was appointed Chaplain to His Majesty King George V. In 1916 he became a Temporary Chaplain to the Forces and Deputy Assistant Chaplain General, W. Command. It is unlikely that he was a war casualty and he died on the 12th May 1921, and is buried in Methley (St. Oswald) Churchyard, Yorkshire, in the South East part near the War Memorial.

The Revd. Frank Robert HARBORD
Chaplain 4th Class Army Chaplains' Department.
Attached 25th Division Chaplain's Depot.

The husband of Edith C Harbord, he was made a Deacon in 1890 and ordained Priest in 1893 by the Bishop of Bloemfontein. He was Curate of Ficksburg from 1890 to1892; Jagarsfontein 1893 to 1895; Bethulie 1895 to 1897; Kroonstad 1897 to 1899, Vicar 1899 to 1903, Rector 1903 to 1905; Rector of Wepener 1905 to 1908 all in the Orange River Colony. He was an Acting Chaplain to the Forces during the Boer War from 1900 to 1902; Curate of Yorktown with Camberley 1909 to 1910; Pershore 1910 to 1912; Vicar of Dunchurch, Rugby, in the Diocese of Worcester from 1912. He died of wounds on the 8th August 1917 in Belgium aged 49. He is buried in Brandhoek New Military Cemetery, Grave reference V.A.1. and remembered on the Aldershot Memorial.

The Revd. Wilfrid John HARDING, MC
Temporary Chaplain 4th Class
Army Chaplains' Department.
Attached Drake Battalion R.N. Division.
(Some records show him as being in the Royal Naval Volunteer Reserve. Chaplains in the Naval Division were a mixture of Army and Navy Chaplains)

He was born at Battersea, London, the son of Richmond Arthur and Alice Emily Harding (nee Tucker) of "Cranmore" Osterley Road, Isleworth on the 2nd December 1885. He attended St. Paul's Preparatory School at Colet Court, Hammersmith; St. John's, Leatherhead and Christ's College, Cambridge where he obtained a B.A. (3rd cl. Th. Trip.) in 1907 and an M.A. in 1912. He trained for the Priesthood at Ripon College, and was made a Deacon in 1912. Ordained Priest by the Bishop of Wakefield in 1913, he served his Title as Curate of Luddenden until October 1914, when he enlisted into the forces, serving in the R.A.M.C. until 29th May 1917. He became a Temporary Chaplain to the Forces, serving on the Western Front, and was awarded the Military Cross. The London Gazette 25th April 1918 5003. "He continually attended to the wounded during four days' operations and repeatedly crossed "No Man's Land "under

heavy fire to bring them in to the front line". He was killed in action while stretcher bearing at Passchendaele, Belgium, on the 31st October 1917 aged 31. He was the husband of Mary Harding (nee Riley), of Cranmore, Isleworth, Middlesex. He is remembered on the Tyne Cot Memorial, Panel 160, and the Aldershot Memorial. The Lieutenant Commander of the Drake Battalion wrote to his widow, "The work for which your husband was awarded the MC was as follows. Stretcher bearers had each case to carry over two miles over the most impossible ground before reaching a road or ambulance. Your husband insisted on going out into No Mans' Land."

A Memorial fire surround commemorating former students of Ripon College is now situated in Ripon College, Cuddesdon. Oxford.

The Revd. James Henry HARDY
Temporary Chaplain 4th Class
Army Chaplains' Department.
Attached Welsh Regiment. 1st/1st Battalion.

The son of Robert Henry and Charlotte Hardy, he was a Congregational Minister, who was killed in action, in Belgium, on the 5th May 1918 aged 45. He was the husband of Mary Stewart Hardy, of 40 Briarbank Terrace, Edinburgh, and is buried in Nine Elms British Cemetery, Poperinge, West-Vlaanderen, Grave Reference XI.B.17 and remembered on the Aldershot Memorial.

The Revd. Theodore Bayley HARDY
VC. DSO. MC.
Temporary Chaplain 4th Class
Army Chaplains' Department.
Attached Lincolnshire Regiment 8th Battalion.

The Revd. Theodore Bayley Hardy was an English recipient of the Victoria Cross, the highest and most prestigious award for gallantry in the face of the enemy that can be awarded to British and Commonwealth forces. In addition to the VC, he had been awarded the Distinguished Service Order, and the Military Cross, making him the most decorated non-combatant of the First World War.

The son of George and Sarah Richards Hardy of Southernhay, Exeter, he was born on the 20th October 1863. He studied at the University of London, where he obtained a B.A. in 1889. From 1891 to 1907 he was Assistant Master at Nottingham High School, and was Headmaster of Bentham Grammar School until 1913. He was made a Deacon in 1898 and Ordained Priest by the Bishop of Southwell in 1899 serving his Title as Curate of Burton Joyce with Bulcote Notts., from 1898 to 1902, when he moved to New Basford until 1907. In 1913 he was appointed Perpetual Curate of Hutton Roof, and Curate in charge of Lupton, in the Diocese of Carlisle, becoming a Temporary Chaplain to the Forces in 1916. There was an initial reluctance to take older clergy straight from civilian life, particularly for service abroad.

He was awarded the DSO on the 18th October 1917.

In the London Gazette dated the 5th March 1918 the following announcement from the War Office was made. "For conspicuous gallantry and devotion to duty in volunteering to go with a rescue party for some men who had been left stuck in the mud the previous night between the enemy's outpost line and our own. He then organised a party for the rescue of this man and remained with it all night, though under rifle-fire at close range, which killed one of the party. With his left arm in splints, owing to a broken wrist, and under the worst weather conditions, he crawled out with patrols to within seventy yards of the enemy and remained with wounded men under heavy fire.

The London Gazette dated the 17th December 1917 announced that he had been awarded the Military Cross.

In a supplement No. 4870 dated the 23rd April 1918 the following announcement was made. "For conspicuous gallantry and devotion to duty in attending the wounded. The ground on which he worked was constantly shelled and the casualties were heavy. He continually assisted in finding and carrying wounded and in guiding stretcher bearers to the aid post".

He was awarded the Victoria Cross. London Gazette, No. 30790, dated 9th July 1918, records the following:

"For most conspicuous bravery and devotion to duty on many occasions. Although over 50 years of age, he has, by his fearlessness, devotion to men of his battalion, and quiet unobtrusive manner, won the respect and admiration of the whole division. His marvellous energy and endurance would be remarkable even in a very much younger man, and his valour and devotion are exemplified in the following incidents: An infantry patrol had gone out to attack a previously located enemy post in the ruins of a village, the Reverend Theodore Bayley Hardy (C.F.) being then at company headquarters. Hearing firing, he followed the patrol, and about four hundred yards beyond our front line of posts found an officer of the patrol dangerously wounded. He remained with the officer until he was able to get assistance to bring him in. During this time there was a great deal of firing, and an enemy patrol actually penetrated between the spot at which the officer was lying and our front line and captured three of our men. On a second occasion when an enemy shell exploded in the middle of one of our posts, the Reverend T. B. Hardy at once made his way to the spot, despite the shell and trench mortar fire which was going on at the time, and set to work to extricate the buried men. He succeeded in getting out one man who had been completely buried. He then set to work to extricate a second man, who was found to be dead. During the whole of the time that he was digging out the men this chaplain was in great danger, not only from shellfire, but also because of the dangerous condition of the wall of

the building, which had been hit by the shell, which buried the men. On a third occasion he displayed the greatest devotion to duty when our infantry, after a successful attack, were gradually forced back to their starting trench. After it was believed that all our men had withdrawn from the wood, Chaplain Hardy came out of it, and on reaching an advanced post asked the men to help him to get in a wounded man. Accompanied by a sergeant he made his way to the spot where the man lay, within ten yards of a pillbox, which had been captured in the morning, but was subsequently re-captured and occupied by the enemy. The wounded man was too weak to stand, but between them the chaplain and the sergeant eventually succeeded in getting him to our lines. Throughout the day the enemy's artillery, machine-gun and trench mortar fire was continuous, and caused many casualties. Notwithstanding, this very gallant chaplain was seen moving quietly amongst the men and tending the wounded regardless of his personal safety".

Another account recalls

"On the 5th, 25th and 27th of April 1918 near Bucquoy and east of Gommecourt, France The Revd. Theodore Hardy showed most conspicuous bravery, tending the wounded under very heavy fire, absolutely regardless of his personal safety. Once he helped to bring in a wounded officer from 400 yards beyond the front line. Then, when an enemy shell exploded in one of our posts and several men were buried, he immediately went, under heavy fire, and managed to dig two of them out. On a third occasion he went out with a sergeant and brought in a wounded man who was lying within 10 yards of a German pillbox".

Another account recalls

"On the 5th, 25th and 27th of April 1918 near Bucquoy and east of Gommecourt, France The Revd. Theodore Hardy showed most conspicuous bravery, tending the wounded under very heavy fire, absolutely regardless of his personal safety. Once he helped to bring in a wounded officer from 400 yards beyond the front line. Then, when an enemy shell exploded in one of our posts and several men were buried, he immediately went, under heavy fire, and managed to dig two of them out. On a third occasion he went out with a sergeant and brought in a wounded man who was lying within 10 yards of a German pillbox".

On the 17th September 1918 he was appointed Chaplain to His Majesty King George V.

He was wounded in action, and died a week later on the 18th October 1918 in Rouen, France, aged 54. He was the oldest chaplain, whose death is known to be recorded as a result of enemy action. He is buried at St. Sever Cemetery Extension, Rouen, France, Grave Reference Block S. Plot V. Row J. Grave1.

He was the husband of the late Florence Elizabeth Hardy (nee Hastings) of Hutton Roof Vicarage, Kirby Lonsdale, Westmorland.

A Memorial Plaque is situated within Carlisle Cathedral.
He is remembered on the War memorial in Hutton Roof Churchyard, and the Aldershot Memorial. The original Medal Group is at the Royal Army Chaplains Centre, Amport House, Andover. SP11 8BE

Extract from Hellfire Corner by Bob Coulson.

The Daughter of The Revd. Hardy, Mary Elizabeth, received a telegram from the King which said "The King is deeply grieved to hear of the death from wounds of your dear Father whose bravery and self sacrifice had won for him the love and respect of all who served with him. His Majesty heartily sympathises with you and yours in your sorrow."

The Revd. Fr. Jeremiah Austin HARTIGAN
Chaplain 4th Class Army Chaplains' Department.
Attached Argyll and Sutherland Highlanders.

The son of Jane Hartigan, of Tar Brook, Croom, Co. Limerick, and the late Dr. J. T. Hartigan, he was born at Foynes, Co. Limerick, on the 18th August 1882. He was educated at the Sacred Heart College, Limerick, and Mungret College, Co. Limerick, he entered the Irish Province of the Society of Jesus, at St. Stanislaus College, Tullamore, Kings County, (now Co. Offaly) on the 7th September 1898. He studied at Beirut, taking a Doctorate in Syriac and Arabic, Philosophy at St. Mary's Hall, Stoneyhurst, Lancashire, and Theology with exiled French Jesuits, at Ore Place, Hastings, England. He was Ordained in 1914, and taught Greek and Latin at Clongowes Wood College. He died of jaundice, at Kut el Amara, Iraq, on the 16th July 1916 aged 33. He is buried in Amara War Cemetery, Iraq, Grave Reference IX.G.19. and remembered on the Aldershot Memorial.

The Revd. Arthur Percival HATFIELD
Temporary Chaplain 4th Class
Army Chaplains' Department.

The son of the Revd. Thomas Spiers Hatfield, and Frances Mary Hatfield, he was born in York in 1891. He studied at Hatfield Hall, Durham, where he obtained a B.A. in 1912. He was made a Deacon in 1913 and Ordained Priest by The Bishop of Southwell in 1914, serving his Title as Curate of St. Peter, Nottingham from 1913. He became a Temporary Chaplain to the Forces in 1916. He served in Mesopotamia, and died in Iraq, on the 9th July 1918. He was the husband of C. Hilda Hatfield (nee Ross), of Sutton Vicarage, Retford, Notts, and is buried in Amara War Cemetery, Iraq, Grave Reference XIV.C.14. and remembered on the Hatfield College and Aldershot Memorials. Hatfield College Durham Clerical Directory, record that two of his brothers, Aubrey and Cyril also were Priests.

The Revd. Noel Elliot HAWDON
Temporary Chaplain 4th Class
Army Chaplains' Department.
Attached 45th Trench Mortar Battery.

The son of Mr. W. and Mrs. M. Hawdon, of Upsall Grange, Yorks, he studied at Jesus College, Cambridge, where he obtained a B.A. in 1908, followed by training for the Priesthood at Wells Theological College. He was made a Deacon in 1909. Ordained Priest by the Archbishop of York in 1910, he served his Title as Curate of St. Lawrence, York until 1910; St. Olav with St. Giles, York, until 1912 when he went to Timaru and was at St. Michael, Christchurch, New Zealand, from 1913 to 1915. Returning to England he was Curate of Helmsley with Sproxton, Yorkshire until 1917. He died of disease (broncho-pneumonia) in France, on the 16th November 1918 aged 32. In his War Office file, it is noted that the telegram informing his parents of his death wrongly went to Milnthorpe. He was one of five children, including one daughter. His father was a well known engineer, who took out a number of patents relating to steelmaking, and retired from Military Service, as Hon. Lieut. Col. of the Durham Light Infantry. Two of his brothers - 2nd Lieut. Cecil Hawdon, of the Yorkshire Regiment, 4th Battalion, and Captain Rupert Ayton Hawdon, of the Royal Garrison Artillery, were killed in action during the First World War. The three brothers are remembered on a Memorial Plaque in St. Cuthbert's Church, Ormesby and St. Barnabas Church Middlesbrough.

A stained glass window to Noel is to be found in the Rievaulx Chapel, which is the original gatehouse to the Abbey. An unusual memorial is in Helmsley Parish Church, and his name also appears on the Cross outside the church. Noel is buried in Terlincthun British Cemetery, Wimille, Pas de Calais, France. Grave Reference XI.B.1. and remembered on the Aldershot Memorial. A memorial from Wells Theological College is now at Sarum College, Salisbury.

The Revd. William Henry HEADING
Temporary Chaplain 4th Class
Army Chaplains' Department.

After studying at the Metropolitan Baptist College, he was a Baptist Minister at Leckhampton; Cheltenham from 1917, and a Temporary Chaplain to the Forces in November 1918. One week later he died of influenza at Tidworth Camp, on the 21st November 1918 aged 29, and is buried in Chatteris General Cemetery, Cambridgeshire. Grave Reference B.640.

The Revd. Alfred HEATH
Chaplain 4th Class Army Chaplains' Department.
Attached Duke of Wellington's (West Riding Regiment).
9th Battalion.

He was the son of Daniel Heath, and Agnes Amelia Heath, of 10 Mount Pleasant, Turner's Hill, Cheshunt, Herts. He was born at Edmonton, Middlesex, and studied at the University of London, in 1907, obtaining an A.K.C. qualification. He was made a Deacon in 1909, and Ordained Priest by the Lord Bishop of London, in 1910, serving his Title as Curate of St. Matthew, Ponders End, London. He was killed in action, in France, on the 30th June 1918 aged 39. He is buried in Toutencourt Communal Cemetery, Somme, France. Grave Reference II.A.1. and remembered on the Aldershot Memorial.

The Revd. David HEGGIE
Temporary Chaplain 4th Class
Army Chaplains' Department.

The son of Andrew and Christina Gorrie Heggie, of Kilwaughter Castle, Larne, Co. Antrim Ireland, he was born on the 3rd June 1874. A Minister of The Church of Scotland, he studied at Edinburgh University, where he obtained an M.A. in 1899. He was Assistant Minister at Inveresk, and Ordained on the 7th May 1903 to Monzievaird and Strowen, in the Auchterarder Presbytery. He married Rosanna Clements on the 7th August 1903 and had a daughter, Rosanna Clements Heggie born on the 10th May 1912. He became a Temporary Chaplain to the Forces, and was attached to the Royal Scots. He died at the Curragh Camp, Ireland, on the 23rd October 1917 aged 33. He is buried in the Curragh Military Cemetery, Co. Kildare, Ireland, Grave Reference 1250. His wife, Rossana Heggie, died at Edinburgh on the 27th September 1922.

The Revd. Robert Morley HENDERSON
Temporary Chaplain 4th Class
Royal Army Chaplains' Department.

He studied at Keble College, Oxford, where he obtained a 3rd cl. Cl. Mod. In 1901 and a B.A. (3rd Class History Hons.) in 1903. He trained for the Priesthood at Cuddesdon Theological College, Oxford, and was made a Deacon in 1904 and Ordained Priest in 1905.

He was Curate of Kettering from 1904 until 1907; Holy Trinity Folkstone 1907 to 1909; St. Mary, Ramsgate 1909 to 1912; St. Paul, Knightsbridge, London 1912. He was appointed Ex. Dioc. Super., for the Diocese of Ross in 1915, and became a Temporary Chaplain to the Forces in 1917. He died on the 3rd February 1919. He is buried in Belgrade Cemetery, Belgium, Grave Reference IV.B.3. and remembered on the Cuddesdon College, Oxford and Aldershot Memorials.

HEWITT. W. CF4 (TCF)

This name is listed, among the deaths in the Army List for January 1918. All the details match with F. W. HEWITT below.

The Revd. Frederick Whitmore HEWITT
Temporary Chaplain 4th Class
Army Chaplains' Department.
Attached 20th Infantry Brigade.

The son of Stanley and Louisa Hughes Hewitt, of Earles Court, London, he was born on the 5th March 1880. Educated at Charter House School, he studied at Corpus Christi College, Cambridge, where he obtained a B.A. in 1901 and an M.A. in 1908. He trained for the Priesthood at Sarum* Theological College. He was made a Deacon in 1903 and Ordained Priest by the Bishop of Chichester in 1904. He served his Title as Curate of St. Peter's Brighton, with Blatchington from 1903 until 1908, and was then Curate of Yorktown with Camberley, until 1910, when he was appointed Vicar of Brixton, Plymouth, in the Diocese of Exeter. He was appointed Temporary Chaplain to the Forces from 1914. The husband of Blanche Hewitt, of Heatherley, Camberley, Surrey, he was killed in action in France, near Vermelles on the 27th September 1915 aged 35. He is buried in Vermelles British Cemetery, Pas de Calais, France. Grave Reference I.G.31. and is remembered on the Ridley Hall, Cambridge and Aldershot Memorials. * Crockford's Clerical Directory shows him as being at Sarum College, but he does not appear on their Memorial. He is listed as being at Ridley Hall Cambridge and appears on their Memorial.

The Revd. Sydney Rangeley HEWITT OBE
Temporary Chaplain 4th Class
Royal Army Chaplains' Department.
Attached Royal Army Medical Corps. 6th Field Ambulance.

The son of Mr. and Mrs. Thomas H. Hewitt of Sydney Cottage, Gawsworth, Macclesfield, he was a Wesleyan Minister, listed as on Supply in 1914 and was at Portsmouth Garrison. He died in Germany on the 16th February 1919 aged 27. He is buried in Cologne Southern Cemetery, Koln, Germany, Grave Reference IX.F.22. and remembered on the Aldershot Memorial.

The Revd. Henry James HOARE
Army Chaplains' Department.

He went to the Church Missionary College, Islington and obtained a 1st cl. Prelim. T.E. in 1889. He obtained a B.A. from the University of Durham in 1898 and was a Fellow of Punjab University from 1903. He was made a Deacon in 1889 by the Lord Bishop of London for Col. Ordained Priest by the Bishop of Lahore in 1890. His Ministry was in India as a C.M.S. Missionary, serving at Peshawar 1889 to 1892; Principle C.M.S. High School Peshawar, 1892 to 1893; Tutor, St. John's Divinity College, Lahore 1893 to 1894; Principal C. M. High School, Dera, Ismail Khan, 1894 to 1897; Principal of Edwardes College, Peshawar, and C.M.S. Missionary at Peshawar 1898 to 1914. He was on furlough from 1897 to 1898, 1903 to 1904 and 1909 to 1911. He became a Temporary Chaplain to the Forces in 1914 and died on the 5th August 1917. (War Office documents record his death as 18th July 1917 and cause as cardiac arrest.) He is remembered on the Aldershot Memorial.

The Revd. Charles William Ackerman HODDER
Temporary Chaplain 4th Class
Army Chaplains' Department.

He studied at Owens College, and was made a Deacon in 1889 by the Bishop of Trinidad for Barbados. Ordained Priest by the Bishop of W. Colorado in 1892, he was Curate of St. George, Grenada, 1889 to 1890; Rector of St. John, Breckenridge 1892 to 1896; Chaplain at Mandalay 1900 to 1906; Curate of Richmond, Surrey 1906 to 1907 and Organising Secretary for the Clergy Pensions Institution from 1907 to 1915. He became a Temporary Chaplain to the Forces. War (Office Records have a letter of resignation dated 29th September 1915 but Army Lists of April 1918 show "retired 29th September 1916"). He died on the 21st October 1918. He is buried in Richmond Cemetery, Surrey, Grave Reference U.4566.

The Revd. Oswald Addenbrooke HOLDEN
Temporary Chaplain 4th Class
Army Chaplains' Department.
Attached 60th Infantry Brigade.

The son of The Revd. Oswald Mangin, and Henrietta Holden of Gailey Vicarage, Staffs, he was a Scholar of Exeter College, Oxford where he obtained a 2nd cl. Mod. in 1895, and a B.A. (2nd cl. Lit. Hum.) in 1897, a 2nd cl. Th. School in 1898 and an M.A. in 1900. He was made a Deacon in 1898 and Ordained Priest by the Bishop of Lichfield in 1899. He served his Title as Curate of Stoke on Trent, to 1902, when he was appointed Rector of Calstone Willington with Blanklands, until 1907 and subsequently Vicar of Penn, in the Diocese of Lichfield. He was Rural Dean of Trysull from 1916, and became a Temporary Chaplain to the Forces in 1917. He was killed in action, in France, on the 1st December 1917 aged 43. His grandson, H.G. Holden, states, 'On the 1st December 1917, my grandfather, Revd. O. A. Holden C.F. was killed whilst going to help the wounded in the vicinity of Villers Plovich (between Cambrai and Peronne). With him was a non-conformist, (Congregational) Chaplain, Revd. Thomas Howell, (see Howell), who I think was attached to the King's Shropshire Light Infantry. Both were apparently killed outright when a shell landed near them in a communications trench both are now buried in Fifteen Ravine British Cemetery' He was the husband of Mary Holden, of "Penn Cot", Cooden Drive, Bexhill on Sea, Sussex, and is buried in Fifteen Ravine British Cemetery, Villers-Plouich, Nord, France, Grave Reference IV.C.15. and remembered on the Aldershot Memorial. His brother in law was also a priest who served as a combatant Lt. Colonel Percy William BERESFORD DSO. Royal Fusiliers 2nd/3rd Battalion.

The Revd. Charles Ivo Sinclair HOOD
Temporary Chaplain 4th Class
Army Chaplains' Department.
Attached Royal Garrison Artillery.

He was the son of the late Sinclair Frankland Hood, J.P. and Grace Hood of Nettleham Hall, Lincoln. A pupil at Haleybury School, he was a Late Demy of Magdalene College, Oxford, where he obtained a B.A. in 1909 and trained for the Priesthood at Cuddesdon College, Oxford. He was made a Deacon in 1911. Ordained Priest by the Lord Bishop of London in 1912, he served his Title as Curate of St. Mary, Somers Town, London, from 1911 and was Head of Magdalene College Mission, Euston, London, from 1912 to 1916, when he became Rector of Sidestrand, Norfolk. He was a Temporary Chaplain to the Forces in 1915 serving at Gallipoli and Egypt, and died of wounds, in Belgium, on the 15th April 1918 aged 31. He was the husband of Christobel M. Hood, (daughter of Sir Samuel Hoare) of Sidestrand, Cromer, Norfolk. He is buried in Lijssenthoek Military Cemetery, Belgium Grave Reference XXVI.FF.9. and remembered on the Cuddesdon College, Oxford and Aldershot Memorials.

The Revd. R. Wilson HOPKINS
Temporary Chaplain 4th Class
Royal Army Chaplains' Department.

He was a Wesleyan Minister at Roath Road, Cardiff in 1901; London Mission 1902; Buxton 1904/5; Scarborough 1908; York 1911; London Bayswater 1914. He became an Army Chaplain on the 27th August 1915 and was at Woolwich Garrison in 1916. Wesleyan Methodist minutes of Conference 1920 state, "On returning to France he developed pneumonia from which he never recovered and passed away peacefully" at the Number 10 Stationary Hospital in Belgium "on the 24th April 1920". He was the husband of Mrs. R. W. Hopkins, of Applegarth Road, West Kensington, London. He is buried in Lissenthoek Military Cemetery, Belgium, Grave Reference XXXI.D.21. and remembered on the Aldershot Memorial.

The Revd. Edgar Charles HOULSTON
Temporary Chaplain 4th Class
Army Chaplains' Department.
Eastern Expeditionary Force.

The son of Sarah Houlston, of 87 Clarence Street, Lower Broughton, Manchester, and the late William Henry Houlston, he was born at Wrexham, Wales. He studied at St. Edmund's Hall, Oxford where he obtained a B.A. and at Bishop's College, Cheshunt. He was made a Deacon on the 4th October 1914 and Ordained Priest on the 19th December 1915. He was Curate of St. Mark, Noel Park in the Diocese of London.

He does not appear in any edition of Crockford's Clerical Directory, but he is in records at the Guildhall Library, London, and his address is given as 85 Albans Crescent, Wood Green, N. He became a Temporary Chaplain to the Forces on the 12th March 1917. At age 25, he must have been one of the youngest chaplains to lose his life. He travelled to France, and embarked on the H. T. Transylvania with troops at Marseilles on 3rd May 1917. His records indicate that he was on his way to his first posting in Egypt (E.E.F). The Transylvania was torpedoed on 4th May 1917, with the loss of 31 Officers, and 382 men. Survivors were landed at Savona, in Italy. War Office records indicate that he was reported as "Missing - believed drowned" on the

4th May 1917. He does not appear on the Savona Memorial, listing those who were lost. Presumably, his body was picked up by a ship attending the sinking, and taken to Marseilles, where he was buried. His body was subsequently re-interred in Mazargues War Cemetery, Marseilles, Bouches du Rhone, France. Grave Reference III.A.18., sometime at the beginning of 1920. He is remembered on the Wood Green and Aldershot Memorials. (See also The Revd. J. T. Ireland, below.) There was also an Anglican Clergyman, William Henry Norman, who was a Sergeant in the Royal Army Medical Corps who drowned.

The Revd. Thomas HOWELL
Temporary Chaplain 4th Class
Army Chaplains' Department.
Attached King's Shropshire Light Infantry. 6th Battalion.

The son of Howell and Mary Ann Howell, of Fishguard, Wales, he was born at Fishguard in July 1884. The family moved to Swansea and was connected with Brecon Memorial College in 1907. He studied at University College, Cardiff, where he obtained a B.A. in 1910. He was a Congregational Minister at Leominster from 1910 to 1914, and then at Bridge Street Church, Walsall, during which time he served with the YMCA in France. He became a Temporary Chaplain to the Forces in 1916 and was killed in action, during the Battle of Cambrai, France, on the 1st December 1917 aged 33. The Principal Chaplain wrote, "he died a hero's death, having stuck to his post in his Division, where he gained the wholehearted love and admiration of Officers and men, ever since his arrival in France seventeen months ago." He is buried in Fifteen Ravine British Cemetery, Villers-Plouich, Nord, France. Grave Reference IV.C.16. and remembered on the Aldershot Memorial. (See also Revd. O. A. Holden)

The Revd. Philip Needham HUNTER
Temporary Chaplain 4th Class
Royal Army Chaplains' Department.

He was made a Deacon in 1890. Ordained Priest in1892 by the Bishop of Sydney, Australia, and was Curate of St. Thomas, Balmain, New South Wales from 1890 to 1892; St. Mary, Balmain, 1892 to 1895; St. Mary, Caulfield, 1895 to 1896; Holy Trinity, Kew, Victoria, 1896 to 1897; St. George, Hobart, 1897 to 1899; Zeeham, Tasmania, 1899 to 1900; He was made an Acting Chaplain to the Forces from 1900 to 1910 serving in South Africa, 1900 to 1905; Singapore, 1905 to 1909, and at Colchester, 1909 to 1910. Leaving the Army he was Chaplain of Java, in the Diocese of Singapore until 1915, when he returned to the Army as a Temporary Chaplain to the Forces. He died on the 14th March 1919. He is buried in Shorncliffe Military Cemetery, Kent. Grave Reference M.744. and remembered on the Aldershot Memorial.

The Revd. Rupert Edward INGLIS
Temporary Chaplain Army Chaplains' Department.

The youngest son of the late Major-General Sir John Inglis KCB, (the defender of Lucknow during the Indian Mutiny) and the late Hon Lady Inglis, he was born on the 17th May 1863. He attended Rugby School, in Warwickshire and went on to University College, Oxford, where he obtained a B.A. (3rd cl. History) in 1885, and an M.A. in 1895. He played rugby as a forward for Blackheath and Middlesex County. He gained his "blue" as a Freshman at Oxford and won 3 caps for England in 1886 playing against Wales, Ireland and Scotland.

He trained for the Priesthood at Ely College in 1889, and was made a Deacon in the same year by the Bishop of Beverley. Ordained Priest by the Bishop of Winchester in 1893, he served his Title as Curate of Helmsley from 1889 to 1890, and was then Curate of Basingstoke from 1892 to 1899. He was appointed Rector of Frittenden, in the Diocese of Canterbury and became a Temporary Chaplain to the Forces in 1915. His diaries and letters are on the Internet and make fascinating reading about Trench life during the First World War. He was involved at the General Hospital at Etaples 10th July 1915; 17th September transferred to 21st Casualty Clearing Station at Corbie; Albert 2nd October; Leave in November; Corbie December. HQ 16th Infantry Brigade 6th Division; 1916 April left Vlanertinghe: Canal Bank near St. Jean; May on home leave; June 17th Bombardment began; September 3rd Parade Service with 2000 men.

His last entry dated 17th September reads,

"I had a good three hours sleep. In a few minutes I will be off to my Dressing Station. I shall probably be back early today". He was killed in action in France, on the 18th September 1916 aged 53, and is remembered on the Thiepval Memorial, Somme, Pier and Face 4C and the Aldershot Memorial. Records would indicate that he was killed, looking for his friend, Captain Thomas Lewis Ingram, DSO MC and RAMC Doctor, who had not returned the previous day. Casualty Records show that he was killed in action on the 16th September 1916. He was the husband of Helen Mary Inglis, of Cuttens, East Grinstead, and the grandson of Bishop Inglis (3rd Bishop of Nova Scotia). The Revd. Neville Talbot recalls, "On Monday afternoon about 3-15 while searching for wounded who had been lying out for several days he was hit by a shell and killed instantly".

A Memorial for Ely College students is now situated in the King's School Ely.

The Revd. John Thomas Craig IRELAND
Temporary Chaplain 4th Class
Army Chaplains' Department.

The son of William Ireland, and Jessie Craig he was born on the 3rd March 1872 at Buckhaven, Scotland. He was educated at Buckhaven, Daniel Stewart's College, Edinburgh and Edinburgh University,

where he obtained an M.A. in 1891. There was further study at New College, Edinburgh. A Minister of the United Free Church of Scotland, he was licenced by the Kirkcaldy Presbytery in 1896, and ordained in Dundee, Natal, South Africa in June 1899. He was minister at Potchefstroom, Transvaal in 1904 and Greyville, Durban, in June 1907. Returning to Scotland he was Inducted at Stow in November 1909. He became a Chaplain to the Forces, serving at Salisbury, in France, and Salonika. He drowned while on board H M Transport Transylvania, torpedoed off Cape Vado, Italy, on the 4th May 1917 with the loss of some 400 lives. He was aged 45, and the husband of Agnes Walker of 18 Braid Crescent, Edinburgh, whom he married on the 28th April 1899. He is remembered on the Memorial at Savona, Italy, and the Aldershot Memorial. The Savona Memorial commemorates some 275 casualties who died when the Transylvania went down and have no known grave.

The Revd. Charles Thomas Claude JEFFERYS
Chaplain 4th Class Army Chaplains' Department.

He studied at St. Chad's Hall, Durham, where he obtained a L. Th. in 1906, and was made a Deacon in 1906. Ordained Priest by the Bishop of Llandaff in 1907. He was Curate of St. Mary, Monmouth until 1910 and Micheldver with East Stratton, in the Diocese of Winchester, until 1913 when he moved to All Saints, Mile End, in the Diocese of London, becoming a Temporary Chaplain to the Forces in 1916. He died on the 20th November 1918. He is buried in Bath (St. James's) Cemetery, Somerset, Grave Reference Y.F.43. and remembered on the Aldershot Memorial.

The Revd. David JENKINS
Temporary Chaplain 4th Class
Royal Army Chaplains' Department.

The son of William and Margaret Jenkins, of Cefn Cribbwr Bridgend, Glamorgan, he was educated at St. Paul's Missionary College, Burgh in 1905. He studied at University College, Durham, where he obtained a L.Th. in 1909. He was made a Deacon in 1910, by the Bishop of Llandaff and Ordained Priest by the Bishop of St. Asaph for Llandaff in 1911. He was Curate of Newcastle with Laeston Tythegston until 1912; St. Augustine, Penarth with Lavernock, 1912 to 1915 and St. John, Derby, in the Diocese of Southwell, until he was appointed a Temporary Chaplain to the Forces, on the 12th February 1918. The brother of Mrs. Watkins, 23 Copr Road, Cefn, Cribbwr, Bridgend, Glamorganshire, he died of pneumonia on the 6th March 1919 aged 32. He is buried in the South East part of Pyle, (St. James) Churchyard, Glamorganshire.

The Revd. Ernest Edward JOHNSON
Chaplain 4th Class Army Chaplains' Department.
Attached Lancashire Fusiliers 15th Battalion.

The son of Edward Thomas and Ann Jane Johnson, of 52 Mowbray Street, Byker, Newcastle upon Tyne, he was born in 1885. His father was a Joiner. He studied at Hatfield Hall, Durham, where he obtained a B.A. in 1909, and an M.A. in 1916. He was made a Deacon in 1909 and Ordained Priest by the Archbishop of York in 1910, serving his Title as Curate of St. Anne's, Sheffield until 1912 and at St. James, Wath on Dearne, to 1916, when he became the first Priest in Charge of New Rossington, Sheffield. Some time later he became a Temporary Chaplain to the Forces. After being wounded, he died of pneumonia, in France, on the 1st December 1918 aged 33.

He was the husband of Elsie M. B. Johnson, of "The World's End", Cobham, Surrey. He is buried in Le Cateau Communal Cemetery, Nord, France, Grave Reference I.32. and remembered on the Wath on Dearne War Memorial, and on a Memorial Tablet in Wath on Dearne Parish Church, Hatfield College, and Aldershot Memorials. Notes from Hatfield College, Durham, Clerical Directory, indicate that he was a prominent cricket player for South Yorkshire teams, and known as the "Miners Parson" because at times he worked on the coalface at New Rossington Pit.

The Revd. Edward JOHNSON - SMYTH
Chaplain 4th Class Army Chaplains' Department.

The son of Thomas Johnson-Smyth, J. P. and Maud, his wife, of Glenavy, Co. Antrim, Ireland, he studied at Trinity College, Dublin, where he obtained a B.A. in 1893, passed the Divinity Test 2nd Class in 1894, and an M.A. in 1898. He was made a Deacon in 1895 and Ordained Priest by the Bishop of Rochester in 1896. He served his Title as Curate of St. Crispin, Bermondsey, until 1897, and at St. Thomas, Birmingham, until 1898 when he became C.M.S. Missionary at Multan until 1906; Furlough 1906 to 1907; Chaplain at Davos Platz, 1907 to 1908; C.M.S. Missionary at Srinagar, 1908 to 1911. Returning to England, in 1911 he was Curate of Brampford Speke, (in charge of Ballykeel Cowley) in the Diocese of Exeter. The husband of M. S. Johnson-Smyth, of "Pawa Domus" Cherry Garden Road, Canterbury, he died in France, on the 10th February 1917 aged 44. He is buried in St. Sever Cemetery, Rouen, Seine-Maritime, France, Grave Reference B.4.11.

The Revd. Basil JONES
Chaplain 4th Class Army Chaplains' Department.
Attached Royal Garrison Artillery.

The son of George and Emma Jones, he trained for the Priesthood, at St. Deiniol College, Lampeter, where he obtained a B.A. in 1911, followed by a Course at Wycliffe Hall, Oxford. He was made a Deacon in 1911 and Ordained Priest by the Bishop of Oxford in 1912. He served his Title as Curate of Thame, Oxford until 1914, when he moved to St. James, Gloucester. The husband of Dora M. Jones, of 48 Conduit Street, Gloucester, he died in France, on the 25th October 1918 aged 32. He is buried in Ste Marie Cemetery Le Havre, Seine-Maritime, France, Grave Reference Div. 62.V.N.2. and remembered on the Aldershot Memorial.

The Revd. Peter JONES - ROBERTS
Chaplain 4th Class Royal Army Chaplains' Department.

He was a Wesleyan Minister who began his ministry in 1886 and was at Tregarth (Welsh) in 1887; Coedpoeth 1889; Llanrwst 1891; Bangor 1892; Dolgelly 1895; Bagillt 1898; Canarvon 1899; Llarwst 1891; Towyn 1904; Tregarth 1906; Blaenau Ffestiniog 1908 and at St. Paul's Methodist Church, Bangor, Caernarvon, Wales from 1911. Like his sons, he joined the Army, and was a Chaplain in 1916. He went to France, with the 38th Welsh Division, and was present at the attack on Mametz Wood, Somme, in July 1916. One of his sons, Lieutenant Cadwaladr Glyn Roberts, Royal Welch Fusiliers, 9th Battalion, died during this attack. Records indicate that he never recovered from his experiences in France, and he died as a result of drowning while on a fishing trip in the Menai Straits, on the 23rd June 1921 at the age of 58.

He was the husband of S. E. Jones-Roberts, of "Glynawel" College Road, Bangor. He is buried in Bangor (Glanadda) Cemetery, Caernarvonshire, Wales. W.C.P.13. (See Up to Mametz - Llewelyn Wyn Griffith; Witness these Letters - G D Roberts)

The Revd. Thomas Glasfryn JONES
Temporary Chaplain 4th Class
Army Chaplains' Department.

The son of Mr. and Mrs. John Jones of 3 Meidoym Road, Llangeitho, he was a Late Welsh Exhib. of St. Deiniol College, Lampeter where he obtained a B.A. in 1905 and was at St. Michael's College, Aberdare in 1906. He was made a Deacon in 1907 by the Bishop of St. Asaph, and Ordained Priest by the Bishop of Bangor for St. Asaph, in 1908. He was Curate of Mostyn, St. Asaph until 1916 when he became a Temporary Chaplain to the Forces. He died of wounds on the 12th April 1917 aged 33. He is buried in new ground to the north of Llangeitho (St. Ceitho) Churchyard, Cardingtonshire, Wales, and remembered on the Aldershot Memorial.

The Revd. William Edgar JONES
Chaplain 4th Class Army Chaplains' Department.
Attached Yorkshire Regiment 9th Battalion.

The son of Mrs. A. Jones of "The Garth", Aberayron, Cardiganshire, and the late Mr. J. B. Jones. He was a Late Exhib. St. Deiniol College, Lampeter, where he obtained a B.A. in 1904. After training for the Priesthood at Ely Theological College, he was made a Deacon in 1905 and Ordained Priest by the Bishop of Lincoln in 1906. He served his Title as Curate of St. John the Divine, Gainsborough, until 1908, when he moved to St. James, Croydon, until 1910, and then at St. Augustine, Tonge Moor, Bolton, in the Diocese of Manchester, from 1911. He died of wounds, in France, on the 24th October 1918, aged 30. He is buried in Roisel Communal Cemetery Extension, Somme, France, Grave Reference II.D.25. and remembered on the Aldershot Memorial. A Memorial for Ely College students is now situated in the King's School Ely.

The Revd. William EVANS - JONES
(Some records list him as W E JONES)
Temporary Chaplain 4th Class
Army Chaplains' Department.
Attached Royal Welsh Fusiliers 2nd Battalion.

The son of Eliza Evans Jones, of Rowen, Portdinorwic, Carnarvonshire, Wales, and the late David Jones, he studied at the Baptist College, Bangor, Wales. He was a Baptist Minister at Caersalem, Carnarvon, and enlisted into the 16th Battalion Royal Welsh Fusiliers and was discharged as wounded. He became a Temporary Chaplain to the Forces in 1917 and was killed in action, in France, on the 8th October 1918, aged 24. He is buried in Prospect Hill Cemetery, Gouy, Aisne, France, Grave Reference IV.E.2. and remembered on the Aldershot Memorial. A Newspaper cutting of an Obituary notice in the archives at Regent's Park College, Oxford, states, "he went over the top as was his custom. Our young friend went over with the men and was killed while bending over a soldier who had been mortally wounded and rendering him what help and consolation he could". In a letter to his mother Lieutenant Colonel C.C. Norman wrote, "you will be proud to know that he died nobly; and in the act of mercy which he was performing at the time, he upheld the noblest traditions of his calling. We happen to know that he was held in the highest esteem by the men of his Battalion because he gave himself unreservedly to serve them. He identified himself with the rank and file in everything and shared their life and hardships and dangers. This was perhaps due to the fact that he had been in the ranks himself".

The Revd. Alan Cecil JUDD, MC
Temporary Chaplain 4th Class
Army Chaplains' Department.
Attached Sherwood Foresters.
(Notts and Derby Regiment) 2/5th Battalion.

The son of Bertram George Scott Judd, and Emma Donna Judd, he was educated at St. Paul's School, and studied at Exeter College, Oxford, where he obtained a B.A. in 1909, and an M.A. in 1912. He was made a Deacon in 1913 and Ordained Priest by the Bishop of Shantung in 1913. He served with the Society for the Propagation of the Gospel (S.P.G.), as a Missionary at Tai An Fu, in the Diocese of Shantung from 1913, becoming a Temporary Chaplain to the Forces in 1916. He was awarded the Military Cross - London Gazette 23rd April 1918, page 4873. "in attending to wounded under shell fire. He searched shell holes for wounded, assisted them to the dressing station, and in one case carried a man on his back. His cheerfulness had a splendid effect in the front line trenches, which he continually visited." He was killed in action, in France, on the 21st March 1918, aged 31. He is remembered on the Arras Memorial, Pas de Calais, France, Panel 10, and the Aldershot Memorial.

The Revd. Fr. Bernard KAVANAGH
Chaplain 4th Class Army Chaplains' Department.

He was born at Limerick, on the 7th November 1864 but lived mainly in London.

Extract from the CSSR Archives

"He took vows at Bishop Eaton on the 8th December 1883, and after studies at Teignmouth, he was Ordained Priest on the 20th December 1889 at Clapham. He began his Apostolate for souls, in various houses to which he was assigned, whether on missionary or parochial work. He excelled in defending Catholic doctrine in public streets and parks. When at Edmonton, he frequently went to the Green where often heretics or Nationalists attacked the Church. Fr. Kavanagh, with his quick mind and ready flow of speech, was more than a match for his opponents, and won approval of bystanders even if they were not converted. When the war began, he was permitted to go as a Chaplain to the land Forces, Egypt, being his first assignment. He ministered to their spiritual needs with zeal, as many Officers testified after his death, for it was in the exercise of his ministry that he met his death. He was a man of keen intelligence and well versed in letters and a lover of the Scriptures. To keep himself fervent he often said to himself the words of his saintly Patron Bernard - "For what hast thou come". He was not strong in physique and had frequent headaches; to a man of his temperament and mental ability the daily routine of our life was something of a hardship - a sacrifice which he had begun when he first made his vows of which was consummated at Jerusalem. In the battlefield, where Fr. Kavanagh was with his troops, the soldiers had been warned that they must go forward almost bent double or crawl as best they could, but on no account to raise their head. Forgetful of this warning, Fr. Kavanagh raised his head and a bullet struck him dead. He was in the act of anointing a man". He died of wounds sustained at the advance on Jerusalem, on the 21st December 1917 aged 53. He is buried on the Mount of Olives, in Jerusalem War Cemetery, Israel, Grave Reference Q.82. and remembered on the Aldershot Memorial.

Extract from the CSSR Archives.

"On the 21st December 1917 the dreadful war which for four years raged through almost all the countries of the world brought to death two Priests of this Province. "(See also Revd. Fr. Charles Watson)." A stained glass window was erected behind the Sanctuary at Edmonton, the cost being met by money left by Fr. Kavanagh. His brother became a Jesuit and his sister a Notre Dame Nun".

The Revd. William Henry KAY, MC
Temporary Chaplain 4th Class
Army Chaplains' Department.
Attached Dorsetshire Regiment 5th Battalion.

The son of Henry Kay F.C.S. and Emily Kay, of 6 South Road, Handsworth, Birmingham. He studied at the University of London, where he obtained a B.A. in 1911. He was made a Deacon in 1913 and Ordained Priest by the Bishop of Birmingham in 1914, serving his Title as Curate of All Saints, Birmingham, becoming a Temporary Chaplain to the Forces in 1915. He was awarded the Military Cross - London Gazette 14th November 1916 page 11057. "For conspicuous gallantry and devotion to duty in action. He took command of a company which had lost all its officers, and pulled it together. On another occasion he reinforced the firing line with his company, and assisted to hold a captured enemy position until relieved. He had shown a total disregard of danger and has set a splendid example." He was killed in action, in France, on the 5th April 1918 aged 29. He is buried in Mazingarbe Communal Cemetery Extension, Pas de Calais, France, Grave Reference III.C.3. and remembered on the Aldershot Memorial.

The Revd. John KELLIE
Army Chaplains' Department.
Attached Cameron Highlanders 6th Battalion.

The son of Robert Muir Kellie and Janet Frew Kellie (nee Smith), he was born on the 4th February 1883. Educated at Kilmarnock Academy, and the Universities of Glasgow, where he obtained an M.A. in 1904; B.D. 1907 and Edinburgh and Erlangen where he became a Ph. D. in 1909. He was licensed by the Presbytery of Irvine in May 1907; Assistant at Cathcart, and ordained on the 23rd March 1910. He married Margaret Orr Ramsay, the daughter of James Ramsay, Provost of Maybole, on the 12th August 1913 and had a daughter - Jean Ramsay born on the 26th November 1914. He was a Temporary Chaplain 4th Class from 1915, and was killed in action, in Belgium, on the 1st August 1917 aged 34. (Church of Scotland Records show his death as 31st July 1917). He was Mentioned in Despatches, and his widow resided at 30 Park Circus, Ayr, Scotland. Remembered on the Ypres Menin Gate Memorial, Panel 56, and the Aldershot Memorial. He was the Author of "Philosophical Position of Alexander Fraser (Thesis) published Edinburgh 1909.

The Revd. James KIRK, MC
Temporary Chaplain 4th Class
Army Chaplains' Department.
Attached Seaforth Highlanders 2nd Battalion.

The son of James and Janet Kirk (nee Reekie), of Kirkford, near Cowdenbeath, Fife, Scotland, he was born at Beath, Fife, on the 4th May 1873. Educated at Cowdenbeath School, and Dunfermline High School, and the Universities of St. Andrews, where he obtained an M.A. in 1896 and Edinburgh. He was a Minister of the Church of Scotland and Licensed by the Presbytery of Dunfermline on the 1st May 1901 and was Assistant Minister at New Greyfriars, Edinburgh. Ordained on the 14th May 1903, at Forteviot, Perthshire, and then at Old Machur, Aberdeen from the 2nd March 1910 and at Dunbar from the 23rd April 1913. He married Elizabeth Mary Mackay, of Edinburgh, on the 2nd April 1904, with a daughter, Betty Mackay, born on the 17th March 1905. He was awarded the Military Cross in June 1917 with no published citation. He died of wounds, in France, on the 1st April 1918 aged 44, and his widow resided at 8 Woodhall Terrace, Juniper Green, Midlothian, Scotland. He is buried in Wimereux Communal Cemetery, Pas de Calais, France. Grave Reference IV.E.2. and remembered on the Aldershot Memorial.

The Revd. Robert Mansel KIRWAN
Temporary Chaplain 4th Class
Army Chaplains' Department.

The son of Richard Kirwan of Gittisham, Devon, he studied at Keble College, Oxford, where he obtained a B.A. in 1885, and an M.A. in 1894. He was made a Deacon in 1888 and Ordained Priest by the Bishop of Sarum (Salisbury) in 1889 serving his Title as Curate of Westbury until 1891. He was appointed Assistant Chaplain (Ecclesiastical Establishment) at Allahabad from 1891 to 1893 followed by ministry at Cawnpore 1893 to 1895; Lucknow Canton 1895 to 1898; Meerut 1898 to 1902; Chakrata 1902 to 1905; 1905 - 1906; he was on furlough from 1906 returning to Lucknow Canton in 1908. He was Chaplain at Bareilly in the Diocese of Lucknow from 1912 to 1914. Returning to England on furlough, he became a Temporary Chaplain to the Forces in 1915. He died on the 23rd May 1916, and is buried in Kensington (Hanwell) Cemetery Middlesex, Grave Reference 166.7&8.

The Revd. Fr. Simon Stock KNAPP. DSO. MC
Chaplain 3rd Class Army Chaplains' Department.
Attached Irish Guards 2nd Battalion.

The son of Thomas and Teresa Knapp (nee Davis), he was born at Burgess Hill, Sussex, on 13th April 1858. Educated at St. Edmund's, Ware, which was a Roman Catholic Primary and Secondary School, he excelled at cricket. Aged 18, he applied to the Order of Carmalite Friars, at Kensington. He took the French Novitiate at Lyons, in 1880. In that year, the French Government threatened expulsion of religious orders from the realm, and he returned to England to continue his studies at St. Edmund's Theological College, Ware, and was Ordained in 1883 at Ware. He volunteered at the beginning of the Boer War in 1889, serving with the 6th Inniskilling Dragoons, and Allenby's Flying Corps. At the outbreak of the First World War, he once more volunteered. On the 13th October 1914 he was attached to the 1st Royal Irish Rifles, and subsequently, the Irish Guards. Throughout the whole of the War, he served in the front line, and was twice Mentioned in Despatches. He was awarded the Military Cross on the 14th January 1916 - London Gazette page 579, and the DSO on the 4th June 1917 - London Gazette page 5471, with no published citation for either award. He died of wounds, sustained at the Battle of Pilkem Ridge, (Boesinghe); Belgium on the 1st August 1917 aged 59. A Memorial window commissioned by the Irish Guards, in the Carmelite Church, Kensington, was destroyed by a German flying bomb in 1944. He is buried in Dozinghem Military Cemetery, Belgium, Grave Reference II.C.1. and remembered on the Aldershot Memorial.

The Revd. Cecil LANGDON
Temporary Chaplain 4th Class
Army Chaplains' Department.
Attached Border Regiment 11th Battalion.

The son of the late Augustin William Langdon M.A. Barrister at Law, Lincoln's Inn, he studied at Selwyn College, Cambridge, where he obtained a B.A. (Jun. Opt.) in 1904, and an M.A. in 1909. He trained for the Priesthood at Ely Theological College, and was made a Deacon in 1905. Ordained Priest, by the Bishop of Chichester, in 1906, serving his Title as Curate of All Saints, Hove, from 1905 until 1911, and Curate of Preston, St. John, Brighton, until 1914, when he became Incumbent of Horsham Road, Sussex. He was a Temporary Chaplain to the Forces in 1916, and was killed in action, in Belgium, on the 31st October 1917 aged 35. He was the husband of E. M. Langdon, "Orchard Cottage" Aspley Heath, Woburn Sands, Bedfordshire. He is buried in Gwalia Cemetery, Ypres, Belgium, Grave Reference II.E.11. and remembered on the Aldershot Memorial. A Memorial for Ely College students is now situated in the King's School Ely.

The Revd. Henry Heaton LAWSON
Chaplain 4th Class Army Chaplains' Department.
Attached Northumberland Fusiliers 2nd Battalion.

The son of Mr. and Mrs. W. H. Lawson of "West House", The Greave, Rochdale, he studied at the University of Manchester where he obtained a B.A. in 1910 and an M.A. in 1911. After training for the Priesthood at Ripon College, he was made a Deacon in 1914 by the Bishop of Richmond for Ripon and Ordained Priest in 1915 by the Bishop of Knaresborough for Ripon, serving his Title as Curate of St. Andrew, Stourton, in the Diocese of Ripon from 1914. He was killed in action, in France, on the 24th March 1918 aged 29. He was the husband of Helen (Hettie) Lawson, of Sandfield, Bacup, Lancashire. He is buried in Fouquescourt British Cemetery, Somme, France, Grave Reference III.A.1. and remembered on the Aldershot Memorial. A Memorial fire Surround commemorating former students of Ripon College is now situated in Ripon College, Cuddesdon, Oxford.

The Revd. Herbert Nettleton LEAKEY
Temporary Chaplain 4th Class
Army Chaplains' Department.

The son of Charles Montague and Agnes Leakey of Goldsworthy House, Gunnislake, Cornwall, he studied at St. John's College, Cambridge, where he obtained a B.A. in 1912. Following a short spell at Ripon College, he was made a Deacon in 1913. Ordained Priest, by the Bishop of Exeter in 1914, he served his Title as Curate of St. Paul, Devonport, from 1913 until 1914, and then at Charles Church, Plymouth, becoming a Temporary Chaplain to the Forces in 1917. He died of meningitis, in Madagascar, on the 24th July 1917 aged 27. He is buried in Dar es Salam War Cemetery, Grave Reference 4.C.5. and remembered on the Aldershot Memorial. A Memorial fire surround commemorating former students of Ripon College is now situated in Ripon College, Cuddesdon, Oxford.

The Revd. Herbert Peter LEDBITTER
Temporary Chaplain 4th Class
Army Chaplains' Department. AMTD Base.

The son of Annie Ledbitter, he trained for the Priesthood at Kelham Theological College, Newark, and was made a Deacon in 1913. Ordained Priest by The Lord Bishop of London in 1914. He served his Title as Curate of St. Augustine, Haggerston in the Diocese of London from 1913 until he became a Temporary Chaplain to the Forces in 1915. He died of disease, in France, on the 28th February 1917 aged 27. He is buried in Le Treport Military Cemetery, Seine-Maritime, France, Plot 2 Row O Grave 3. and remembered on the Aldershot Memorial.

The Revd. Fr. James Thomas LEESON
Chaplain 4th Class Army
Chaplains' Department.
Attached Royal Fusiliers 13th Battalion.

The son of James and Mary Ellen Leeson (nee Smith), he was born at Litherland, Lancashire, on the 6th June 1877. After study at St. Edward's College, Liverpool, and St. Joseph's Seminary, Upholland Lancashire. He was Ordained by Bishop Whiteside on the 6th June 1903. He was Professor at St. Edward's College until 1905. He served in the Liverpool RC Diocese as Curate at St. Mary's, Douglas, Isle of Man 1905 to 1906; St. Mary's, Barrow in Furness, 1906 to 1907; St. Mary's, Widnes, 1907 to 1911; St. Philip Neri, Liverpool 1911 to 1915. He became a Chaplain to the Forces in 1915, and was much respected by the Officers and men of the Royal Fusiliers. He was killed in action, in France, on the 23rd April 1917. He is buried in Point - du - Jour Military Cemetery, Athies, Pas de Calais, France, Grave Reference II.G.14. and remembered on the Aldershot Memorial.

The Revd. James Herbert Reginald LENDRUM
Chaplain 4th Class
Army Chaplains' Department.
Attached King's Own (Royal Lancaster) Regiment.
8th Battalion.

The son of Robert and Clara Lendrum, of London, he studied at University College, London, where he obtained a B.A. in 1909 and an A.K.C. in 1913. Crockford's Clerical Directory 1914 list him as being made a Deacon in 1913, by the Bishop of St. Albans, serving as Curate of St. Mary, Apsley End, from 1913 but there are no further entries. He was killed in action, in France, on the 22nd August 1918 aged 31. The husband of Eleanor Mary Lendrum, of The Square, St. Neots, Hunts, he is buried in Bienvillers Military Cemetery, Pas de Calais, France, Grave Reference XIX.E.14. and remembered on the Aldershot Memorial.

The Revd. Gerald James LESTER
Chaplain 4th Class
Army Chaplains' Department.
Attached CME Loco Works.

He was the son of the Revd. Edward Augustus and Mrs. Mary Frideswide Lester, of Bishop's Nymphton, Devon, where he was born in 1885. Educated in Surrey, he studied at Hatfield Hall, Durham, where he obtained a B.A. in 1910. He was made a Deacon in 1911 and

Ordained Priest by the Lord Bishop of Durham in 1912, serving his Title as Curate of St. Thomas, Bishop Wearmouth, Sunderland until 1914, and at Cambois, near Blyth, Northumberland, till 1916. Appointed Rector of Rackenford, Devon in 1916. Hatfield College, Durham, Clerical Directory, indicates that "he enlisted into the Army Chaplains' Department on moving to Devon, being attached to the CME Loco Works. He was fatally wounded, and died in France, on the 16th December 1918 aged 33. The husband of Eleanor Lester, of 13 Rivers Street, Bath, he is buried in St. Sever Cemetery Extension, Rouen, Seine-Maritime, France, Grave Reference S.V.L.9. and remembered on the Hatfield College and Aldershot Memorials.

The Revd. Archibald Owen Carwithen LONGRIDGE
Temporary Chaplain 4th Class
Army Chaplains' Department.
Attached 11th General Hospital Boulogne.

The son of Michael Longridge, he studied at Trinity College, Cambridge, where he obtained a B.A. in 1905 and an M.A. in 1909. Following study at Ely Theological College, he was made a Deacon by the Lord Bishop of London, in 1906 and Ordained Priest by the Bishop of Wakefield, in 1907. He was Curate of St. John, Bethnal Green, from 1906 to 1907; Elland, Yorks 1907 to 1908; St. Peter, Coventry, 1908 to 1909; St. James, Exeter, 1909 to1911; Clyst, St. George, and Assistant Missioner in the Diocese of Exeter, 1911 to 1914; Sawton, 1914 to 1916. He became a Temporary Chaplain to the Forces in 1915, and died of pneumonia, on the 12th October 1918 aged 38. The Church Times of 18th October 1918 states that "he had suffered gas poisoning in France". He served with the RAF at Grantham and died at Topsham. He was the husband of Constance Longridge, of 2 Clystlands, Topsham. He is buried in Topsham Cemetery, Devon, Grave Reference 1.1684. and remembered on the Aldershot Memorial. A Memorial for Ely College students is now situated in the King's School, Ely.

The Revd. Fr. Patrick LOOBY
(Also known as Patrick LUBY).
Chaplain 4th Class
Army Chaplains' Department.

The son of Denis and Alice Looby, he was born at Cahir, Co. Tipperary, Ireland on the 23rd February 1889. He studied at St. John's, Waterford, and the Irish College, in Paris. He was Ordained by Bishop Sheehan, on the 21st June 1914. He was Curate of St. Alphonsus, in the Liverpool RC Diocese, becoming a Chaplain to the Forces in 1915. He was killed in action, at the Battle of Passchendaele, Belgium, on the 26th October 1917. Buried in Poelcapelle British Cemetery, Grave Reference VI.E.13., he is remembered on the Aldershot Memorial.

The Revd. John CAMPBELL - MacGREGOR
Chaplain 4th Class Army Chaplains' Department.
Attached 4th Battalion Cameron Highlanders.

He was born at Ardenny, Taynuilt, Argyll, Scotland, the son of John MacGregor, (Surgeon) and Catherine Campbell, on the 2nd November 1869. He studied at the University of Glasgow, F.R.G.S. 1908; B.D. 1912. A Minister of The Church of Scotland, he was Licenced by the Presbytery of Lorn, in May 1898, and was Assistant Minister at Kilfinichen, and then at Stevenston, Maxwell, Glasgow. He was Ordained to Strachur, and Strathlachlan, in the Dunoon Presbytery, on the 17th July 1901, and translated and admitted to St. Oran's (Gaelic) Parish Church, Edinburgh, on the 29th June 1911, and was Edinburgh Presbytery Dean. He married on the 3rd September 1902, Robina Ralston McIntyre, the daughter of Alexander Campbell McIntyre, Minister of Kilbrandon. She died at Connel, on the 25th October 1939. He became a Chaplain to the Forces, and died of wounds, at Dieppe, France, on the 4th November 1916 aged 47. He is buried in Janval Cemetery, Dieppe, Seine-Maritime, France, Grave Reference I.D.5. and remembered on the Aldershot Memorial.

Author of Appreciation of Wordsworth's 'Ode on the Intimations of Immortality' published at Ardrossan 1898. Comparative Geography for the use of teachers Published at Ardrossan 1898.

The Revd. Alban Bodley MACE
Chaplain 4th Class Army Chaplains' Department.
Attached Duke of Cornwall's Light Infantry 2nd Battalion.

The son of The Revd. J. C. and Mrs. Mace, late of Hawley, Hampshire, he studied at Queen's College, Oxford, where he obtained a B.A. (3rd cl. Th. Hons.) in 1907, and an M.A. in 1911. He trained for the Priesthood at Wells Theological College, in 1909, and was made a Deacon in 1910. Ordained Priest by the Bishop of Wakefield in 1911, he served his Title as Curate of Lightcliffe, from 1910 until 1911, and was then Curate of Alverstoke, until 1913 and thereafter at Brighouse, in the Diocese of Wakefield. He was killed in action, in Greece, on the 3rd October 1916 aged 31, by a high explosive shell near Yenikeui.

The husband of Evelyn Mace, of 3 St. Mark's Road, Alverstoke, Gosport, Hampshire, he is buried in Struma Military Cemetery, Greece, Grave reference II.H.1. and remembered on the Aldershot Memorial. A memorial from Wells Theological College is now at Sarum College, Salisbury.

The Revd. Charles William Wykeham MAJOR
Chaplain 4th Class
Royal Army Chaplains' Department.

The son of Charles and Ellen Major, of Bridgewater, Somerset, he became in 1905 an A.K.C. at London University and was made a Deacon. Ordained Priest by The Lord Bishop of London in 1906, he served his Title as Curate of All Hallows, East India Docks, London, from 1905 until 1907. He then went as Curate of Camborne, until 1908; Furnham Chard, 1908 to 1911; Salcombe, in the Diocese of Exeter, 1911 to 1914; St. Mary Church, Exeter, 1914 to 1917; He was appointed Rector of Combe Raleigh, Exeter in 1917. The husband of Ida Anne Major, of 23 Westbourne Gardens, Folkestone, he died in Germany, on the 19th March 1919 aged 41. He is buried in Cologne Southern Cemetery, Koln Nordrhein - Westfal, Grave Reference IX.B.9. and remembered on the Aldershot Memorial.

The Revd. Charles Antonio MARONA
Chaplain 3rd Class
Army Chaplains' Department.

He became an A.K.C. at London University in 1876 and trained for the Priesthood at Chichester College, in 1878. He was made a Deacon in 1879. Ordained Priest by the Bishop of Chichester, in 1880, he served his Title as Curate of Rye, until 1889. He was Vicar of St. Andrew, Portslade - by - Sea, from 1889 to 1902; St. Saviour, Preston, Sussex, 1902 to 1910; Rector of Hurstpierpoint, Chichester, from 1910. He died on the 28th February 1915, and is buried in Hurstpierpont (Holy Trinity) Churchyard, Sussex.

The Revd. Cecil Radcliffe MARTYN
Temporary Chaplain 4th Class
Royal Army Chaplains' Department.

The son of Henry Matthews Martyn, and Helena Sara Martyn, he was born at Countess Wear, near Topsham, Devon, in 1875. His father was the owner of a Paper Mill, at Countess Wear. He studied at Hatfield Hall, Durham, where he obtained a B.A in 1899. He was made a Deacon in 1900 and Ordained Priest by the Bishop of Worcester in 1901, serving his Title as Curate of St. John Baptist, Bedwardine, Worcester from 1900 to 1906. He was then Curate of Polesworth with Dordon, until1910. He became Rector of The Quinton, with Warley Woods, until 1912, and was Vicar of Tamerton Foliott, in the Diocese of Exeter, from 1912. He became a Temporary Chaplain to the Forces, in 1915 and was twice Mentioned in Despatches. Having been wounded, he died of pneumonia, in France on the 3rd March 1919 aged 44. He was the husband of Christine F. M. Martyn (nee Stewart), who he married in April 1903, of "Crescent House", Effingham Road, Surbiton, Surrey. He is buried in St. Sever Cemetery Extension, Rouen, Seine-Maritime, France, Grave Reference S.V.M.8. and remembered on the Hatfield College, and Aldershot Memorials. Notes from Hatfield College, Durham, Clerical Directory, record that his name was omitted from the First World War Memorial Board in the college chapel for over 85 years, and was inscribed thereon in 2005.

The Revd. Fr. Lewis Joseph MATTHEWS
Chaplain 1st Class
Army Chaplains' Department.

A Priest of Westminster RC Diocese, he was born in 1856 and Ordained in 1879. (An 'Aloysium Matthews' of the Institute of St. Andrew, was Ordained at St. Thomas' Seminary, Hammersmith on the 20th December.) He served in the Nile Expedition of 1898, and in the South African Campaign, when he was Mentioned in Despatches. The senior serving RC Chaplain at the outbreak of The First World War, approaching 60, he was considered too old for service overseas. He died in the Military Hospital, Millbank, on the 26th May 1916, and is buried in Kensall Green (St. Mary's) Roman Catholic Cemetery, Grave Reference Cardinals 2650.

The Revd. Fr. Cornelius (Raphael) McAULIFFE
Chaplain Army Chaplains' Department.

The son of Michael McAuliffe and Margaret Begley, who was the sister of three Franciscans, he was born at Meenoline North, near Templeglantine, Co. Limerick, Ireland, on the 13th March 1866. He entered the OFM Irish Province, at Killarney, on the 16th October 1903; Professed on the 12th November 1904; Ordained in Rome, on the 24th September 1910. On the 2nd December 1915, he became Chaplain to the 4th Division and served in Egypt, and was at the landing of the ANZAC, at Ari Burnu, with Fr. Patrick Dore (see under New Zealand in Commonwealth Section) and in France. He was attached to the 17th Ambulance Unit. Returning home, on the 6th October 1916, to visit his sick mother, he died of severe seasickness, on board HMT Viper before it reached Southampton, aged 29. Despite the anti-chaplain bias of Bishop Edward Thomas O'Dwyer, he was buried with full military honours, in the Franciscan Plot, of Mount St. Lawrence Cemetery, Limerick, Ireland, Plot 30861 and is remembered on the Aldershot Memorial. The senior Catholic Chaplain said of Fr. McAuliffe that, 'as a chaplain he ranked as one of the best. He never spared himself for his men; he went wherever they went and consequently he was loved by them'. He was singled out by Protestant chaplains as most kindhearted to all with whom he came in contact. - Father B. Bradley - Irish Franciscan chaplains in World Wars I and II.

It has been suggested, in The cross on the sword - Johnstone and Hegarty, that Father McAuliffe, despite his Official death record, 'probably died of a heart attack following the strain of the trenches'. It is worth noting that he was 'one of the two full military funerals for a chaplain during the war'. The other was for the Bishop of Nottingham, Robert Brindle, DSO." He was with Kitchener at Khartoum and died in June 1916. He was Mentioned in Despatches five times. Interesting biographical notes in *Sportsmen Parson in Peace and War* Mrs. Stuart Menzies.

The Revd. Fr. John Joseph McDONNELL
Chaplain 4th Class Army Chaplains' Department.

The son of the late Edmund and Johanna McDonnell, of Cork, Ireland, he was of the CM Irish Province. He was with the 55th Machine Gun Corps, at Givency, France, which came under heavy attack, and was killed attending wounded under fire, on the 9th April 1918 aged 41. He is buried in Beuvry Communal Cemetery Extension, Pas de Calais, France, Grave Reference II.B.8. and remembered on the Aldershot Memorial.

The Revd. Fr. Henry Cuthbert McGINITY
(Some records show name as McGinty)
Chaplain Royal Army Chaplains' Department.
Royal Army Medical Corps 23rd Field Ambulance.

The son of Francis Patrick and Edith Rachel McGinity, of Waterloo, Liverpool, Lancashire, he was born at Waterloo, on the 28th March 1882. Educated at Stoneyhurst College, Lancashire, he entered the Society of Jesus at Manresa, as a Noviciate in 1900, and took his vows in 1902. He went to Stamford Hill, until 1910, and then to Louvaine, to study Philosophy. He taught at Preston, in 1909 and at the Seminary in 1911, studying Theology at Milltown Park in 1913. Ordained on the 31st July 1916 at Milltown Park, he became a Chaplain to the Forces from the 3rd October of that year. He went to France, where he was Mentioned in Despatches in December 1917. A letter of his dated 28th November 1917, announced his arrival in Italy. He died at the 39th Casualty Clearing Station, on the 8th November 1918 after exposure on the Piave, Italy. He is buried at Giavera British Cemetery, Italy, Arcade Plot 5, Row C, Grave 11. and remembered on the Aldershot Memorial.

The Revd. Fr. John Joseph McILVAINE
Chaplain 4th Class
Army Chaplains' Department.
Attached Sherwood Foresters
(Notts and Derby Regiment) 2nd/7th Battalion.

The son of Eleanor Hatton (formerly McIlvaine), and the late William McIlvaine. He was a Roman Catholic Priest, who was drowned at sea, while on board the Hospital Ship Glenart Castle on 26th February 1918 aged 39. He had been previously wounded, and gassed, on the 2nd October 1917 at the battle of Polygon Wood, Belgium. The Glenart Castle was a Hospital ship which, on the 26th February 1918, was sunk by a torpedo off the North Coast of Cornwall, near Ilfracombe. She had left Cardiff, bound for Brest, in France, to take on patients. Out of a ships compliment of 186 only 31 survived. Remembered on the Hollybrook Memorial Southampton, Hampshire and the Aldershot Memorial. He is not listed as a casualty in The Cross on the Sword. See also The Revd. Frank Harrison EDINGER.

The Revd. Stanley Gibson McMURTRIE
Temporary Chaplain 4th Class
Royal Army Chaplains' Department.

The son of Hugh McMurtrie, he was born on the 8th November 1887 at Frome. Educated at Bath College, he was a Late Scholar of St. Catherine's College, Cambridge where he obtained a B.A. (June Opt) in 1899. He was made a Deacon in 1903 by the Bishop of Ossary, and Ordained Priest by the Bishop of Down in 1905. He served as Curate of Grange Sylvae with Shankill, County Kilkenny, from 1903 to 1905; Sea Patrick, (Banbridge) county Down, 1905 to 1907; Minor Canon of Kilkenny Cathedral, 1907 to 1909; p b Cho. 1908 to 1909; St. Saviour, Woolcott Park, Bristol, 1910 to 1912; St. James with All Saints, New Brighton, in the Diocese of Chester 1912 to 1916, when he became a Temporary Chaplain to the Forces in 1914. He was Vicar of St. John's Egremont, in the Diocese of Chester in 1917 where he died on the 14th June 1919, and is buried in Egremont (St. John) Churchyard, Cheshire, Grave Reference South 284.

The Revd. Charles Gustave Clark MEISTER, MC
Chaplain 4th Class Army Chaplains' Department.
Attached 7th Seaforth Highlanders and
10th Argyll and Sutherland Highlanders.

The son of Frederic Meister and Charlotte Clark Meister, he was born in Edinburgh, in 1883 and educated at George Watson's College, Edinburgh. He was a student of Arts at Edinburgh University, from 1907 and obtained an M.A. in 1910. After further study at Edinburgh Theological College in 1910, he was made a Deacon in 1912 and Ordained Priest by the Bishop of Edinburgh in 1913. He served in the Episcopal Church of Scotland, as Curate of Old St. Paul's Edinburgh, from 1912 and became a Temporary Chaplain to the Forces in November 1915. He was Mentioned in Despatches in 1916, and awarded the Military Cross - London Gazette 1st January 1918 page 42, with no published citation. He was killed in action, in Belgium, on the 18th April 1918. He is buried in La Clytte Military Cemetery, Belgium Grave Reference IV.E.1. and remembered on the Aldershot Memorial.

The Revd. George MILLAR
Temporary Chaplain 4th Class
Army Chaplains' Department. 13th General Hospital.

The son of George and Jessie Rennie Millar, he was born in Dundee, on the 19th May 1872. He was educated at John Russell School, Dundee, and Edinburgh University, where he obtained a Lit. A. in 1894. Further study followed at the United Presbyterian College, Edinburgh. He was a student assistant at Abbeyhill, Edinburgh followed by a period as student missionary at Uphall, from 1897 to 1898. Licensed by the United Presbyterian Presbytery of Dundee, in March 1898, he was Ordained and Inducted at Uphall on the 2nd August 1898 and translated and admitted on the 18th May 1904 as Minister of Paterson United Free Church, Kirkwall, Orkney. He served as a Chaplain to the Forces in Orkney, from 1914 to 1917, when he went to France. The husband of Agnes Hendrie Millar (nee Downie), of Lenzie, Scotland, he died in France, on the 26th August 1917 aged 45. He is buried in Boulogne Eastern Cemetery, Pas de Calais, France, Grave Reference VII.A.27. and remembered on the Aldershot Memorial. His widow resided at 70 Colinton Road, Edinburgh.

The Revd. Charles Wand MITCHELL
Temporary Chaplain 4th Class
Army Chaplains' Department.
Attached East Yorkshire Regiment 8th Battalion.

He studied at Bishops College, Lennox, where he obtained a B.A. in 1897 (Mackie Prize for English and Latin Essay and Prince of Wales Gold Medal for Classics 1897); 1st cl. Th. Hons. 1898; M.A. 1900. He was resident Tutor at Bishops College, Lennox 1900 to 1902, and Late Thorpe Scholar of Emmanuel College, Cambridge, taking advanced Study Th. Trip. Pt. ii, and Jeremie Prize, 1903; Tyrwhitt Scholar 1904, Oriental Trip. and B.A. 1904, M.A. 1911. He was Assistant Master at Merchant Tailors' School, from 1905, and was made a Deacon, in 1907. Ordained Priest by The Lord Bishop of London in 1908, serving as Curate of St. Thomas, Streatham Hill in the Diocese of Southwark. He became an M.R. Asiatic S. in 1913. He was the Author of; St. Ephraim's Prose Discourses against Mani Marcion and Bardaisan Vol, 1 1912; Work in Syriac Pentateuch 1913. He became a Temporary Chaplain to the Forces in 1915, and died of wounds in France, on the 8th May 1917. He is buried in Faubourg D'Amiens Cemetery, Arras, Pas de Calais, France. Grave Reference IV.E.28. and remembered on the Aldershot Memorial.

The Revd. Fr .Walter Philip MONTAGU
Chaplain 4th Class Army Chaplains' Department.
Attached Royal Garrison Artillery 22nd Brigade.

The fifth of seven sons of Lt. Cmdr. Robert Acheson Cromie Montagu RN Retired, and Annie Margaret Montagu (nee McMicking), of Cromore, Portstewart, Co. Londonderry, Ireland, he was born on the 7th May 1886. Educated at Stoneyhurst College, Lancashire, he entered the Society of Jesus at Manresa, on the 8th September 1903, taking his Noviceship and Juniorate. He was at St. John's, Beaumont, from 1909 to 1915, and went to St. Beuno's to study Theology, being Ordained by dispensation on the 25th April 1917. He became a Chaplain to the Forces in May 1917 and died of wounds, in France, on the 31st October 1918 aged 32. The Tablet reported: "He was admitted to the 45th Casualty Clearing Station on the evening of the 28th October suffering from very severe wounds of his thighs and received the last sacraments at his own request." He is buried in Awoingt British Cemetery, Nord, France, Grave Reference III.A.1. and remembered on the Aldershot Memorial. Stoneyhurst Magazine page 395 records that four of his brothers served in the Army or Navy, the youngest Lieut. Alec C. Montagu being lost on H.M.S. Bulwark on the 26th November 1914. H.M.S. Bulwark was a Formidible-Class Battleship. There was a powerful explosion on 26th November 1914 at 07.50 a.m., while moored to a bouy in Kethole Reach, four miles west of Sheerness, in the medway Estuary. (Foul play was suspected). Out of a ships compliment of 750 only 14 survived. Two died subsequently and the remainders were seriously injured.

The Revd. Fr. Robert John MONTEITH
Chaplain 4th Class Army Chaplains' Department.
Royal Field Artillery 70th Army Field Artillery Brigade.

The son of Joseph Monteith, of Carstairs, Lanarkshire, Scotland, he was a Priest of the Society of Jesus. He died of wounds in Belgium, sustained at the Battle of Passchendaele, on the 27th November 1917 aged 40. He is buried in Ribecourt British Cemetery, Nord, Belgium, Grave Reference I.D.11. and remembered on the Aldershot Memorial.

The Revd. Edgar Noel MOORE, MC
Temporary Chaplain 4th Class
Army Chaplains' Department.
The King's (Liverpool Regiment) 20th Battalion.

The son of Arthur Louis and Augusta Cicilia Moore, of St. John's Wood, London, he studied at Exeter College, Oxford, where he obtained a B.A. (2nd cl. Med. Hist.) in 1911. He was made a Deacon in 1913 and Ordained Priest by the Lord Bishop of London in 1914. He served his Title as Curate of St. Simon Zelotes, Bethnal Green, in the Diocese of London from 1913, and became a Temporary Chaplain to the Forces in 1916. He was awarded the Military Cross - London Gazette 9th January 1918, page 631 "While the Battalion to which he was attached was forming up in the assembly position, they were heavily shelled, but with splendid disregard of danger he walked along the top tending the wounded and consoling the dying. Throughout four days of heavy fighting, he displayed a magnificent example of courage to all ranks whilst burying the dead and assisting to carry stretchers, under heavy shell fire." He was killed, in Belgium, on the 5th January 1918 aged 29. He is buried at Railway Dugouts Burial Ground, Grave Reference VII.V.5. and remembered on the Aldershot Memorial.

The Revd. Samuel MORRISON
Chaplain 4th Class Royal Army Chaplains' Department.

The son of Captain William Morrison, he was born at Carrickfergus, Co. Antrim, Ireland. A Presbyterian Minister, he relinquished his Commission on the 20th May 1920 and died on the 24th July 1920, aged 60. He was the husband of Janet Isabella Morrison, of 50 College Road, Whalley Range, Manchester. He is buried in Manchester Southern Cemetery, Grave Reference S.CE.4. and remembered on the Aldershot Memorial.

The Revd. James White NAIRN

A Congregational Minister, who was Chaplain to two local military hospitals at Haslingden, Lancashire. He died in December 1917. He appears in the Congregational Obituaries but was not commissioned.

The Revd. William Owen O'CONOR
Chaplain 3rd Class.
Royal Army Chaplains' Department.

The name above is that listed by The CWGC. His entry accompanied by a signature in the Register at Cuddesdon College, Oxford, shows him as William "Richard O'Connor." He studied at Trinity College, Dublin, Ireland where he obtained a B.A, in 1899 and an M.A. in 1903. He trained for the Priesthood at Cuddesdon College, Oxford, in 1901 and was made a Deacon in 1902. Ordained Priest by the Bishop of Worcester in 1903, he served his Title as Curate of Balsall Heath until 1907; Chaplain at Ecclesiastical Establishment at Lahore, Canton 1907 to 1909: West Ridge (Rawalpindi) 1909 to 1910; Sialkot 1910; Simla 1911 to 1912; Karachi 1912 to 1913; Lahore 1913 to 1916; Karachi 1916. Some records show him as T/Major, Indian Army, Indian Ecclesiastical Establishment. He died at Hamadan. in Iran, on the 24th January 1919. He is buried in Tehran War Cemetery, Iran, Grave Reference V.A.7. and remembered on the Cuddesdon College, Oxford and Aldershot Memorials. Indian Ecclesiastical Establishment Chaplains were not commissioned Army Chaplains. Those who served outside India were transferred and Commissioned into the Army

Chaplains' Department. O'Conor is listed in the Cuddesdon Register as being, "On active service 1918". But he does not appear in the Army Lists or London Gazette for that year.

The Very Revd. Fr. Laurence O'DEA
Chaplain 4th Class Army Chaplains' Department.

The Son of Kyran and Mary O'Dea, of William Street, Kilkenny, Ireland, he was an OSF Priest at Crawley. He died on the 4th November 1917 aged 66, and is buried in Crawley Monastery Burial Ground Sussex.

The Revd. Wilfred Rathmel Ogle

The son of Dr. John William Ogle of St. Georges, Hanover Square, London, he was born in 1859. Educated at Eton, he studied at Trinity College Oxford, where he obtained a B.A. in 1881, and an M.A. in 1884. He was made a Deacon in 1882 and Ordained Priest by the Archbishop of Dublin in 1883. Curate of St. Stephen, and Minor Canon of St. Patrick's Cathedral, Dublin from, 1882 to 1884; Curate of St. Mark, Audley Street, London, from 1884 to 1888; Resident Chaplain to the Lord Bishop of London from 1888 to 1891, and Chaplain to the Bishop from 1888 to 1896. During this period, he was Curate of Tamworth, 1892 to 1893, and St. Stephen the Martyr, Marylebone, from 1893 to 1896 when he became Vicar of Highgate, London. He appears among the deaths, as a Chaplain on the Army List for April 1917, (TF Chaplain attached 7th Duke of Cambridge (Middlesex) Hornsey. He died at Edmonton in 1916 aged 57. He may not have been deployed as there are no further details known.

The Revd. Fr. James (Isidore) O'MEEHAN
Chaplain 4th Class
Royal Army Chaplains' Department.
Attached to a Casualty Clearing Station.

The son of Thomas and Catherine O'Meehan (Nee O'Dwyer), he was born at Ennis, Co. Clare, Ireland, on the 5TH July 1867. He entered the OFM Irish Province, on the 14th October 1885. Ordained in Rome on the 11th June 1892. He served at Franciscan Colleges at Capranica, and Munltyfarnham, and volunteered in June 1915. He served in France, and at a Casualty Clearing Station in Mesopotamia. He died on the 19th December 1919, aged 52, as a result of an accidental gun shot, while landing from a boat at Kut el Amara on the River Tigris,

Iraq. Some records suggest that his death was the result of a shooting incident while hunting on the River Tigris. The Principal Chaplain GHQ Mesopotamian Expeditionary Force - The Revd. R Williams wrote, "He was universally respected and liked. A worthy Chaplain". He is buried in Amara War Cemetery, Iraq, Grave Reference XII.E.3.

The Revd. William McNiell ONSLOW CARLETON
(Some records show CARLTON).
Army Chaplains' Department.

He was a Congregational Minister/United Board from South Africa, who became a Temporary Chaplain to the Forces on a one year contract from the 14th July 1917. He completed his service and relinquished his commission on the 29th July 1918. He died on the 4th/5th October 1918 aged 44, when the Japanese liner Hirano Maru, in which he was returning to South Africa, was torpedoed off the Irish coast. He is remembered on the Aldershot Memorial.

The Revd. Benjamin Garniss O'RORKE DSO
Chaplain 2nd Class
Royal Army Chaplains' Department.

The son of J. W. and Annie O'Rorke, he studied at Exeter College, Oxford, where he obtained a B.A. (3rd cl. Th. Hons.) in 1897, and an M.A. in 1901. He trained for the Priesthood at Wycliffe Hall, Oxford in 1897. He was made a Deacon in 1898, and Ordained Priest by the Bishop of Exeter in 1899, serving his Title as Curate of St. Peter, Tiverton, until 1901. He was an acting Chaplain to the South African Field Force from 1901 to 1902 (Medal and 4 clasps); Chaplain to the Forces 1902; Aldershot 1902 to 1904; Bloemfontein 1904 to 1905; Roberts' Heights, Pretoria, 1905 to 1909; Bordon, 1909 to 1914. In 1910, he was appointed Honorary Organising Secretary for S.P.G. / C.M.S. to British Army and was Commiss. to the Bishop of Accra from 1913 to 1914. In 1914 he was a Chaplain to the British Expeditionary Forces. The husband of Myra Roberta O'Rorke, of 17 Evelyn Court, Cheltenham, he died on the 25th December 1918 aged 43. He is buried in Falmouth Cemetery, Cornwall, Grave Reference L.B.9. and remembered on the Aldershot Memorial. He was the Author of 'African Missions 1912', and 'In the hands of the enemy 1915'.

The Revd. Fr. Donal Vincent O'SULLIVAN
Army Chaplains' Department
Attached 1st Irish Rifles.

The son of Hannah O'Sullivan, of 6 High Street, Killarney, Ireland, and the late D. F. O'Sullivan, he was a Priest in the Kerry RC Diocese. He was killed in action, in France, on the 5th July 1916 aged 26, and is buried to the right of the entrance to the extension, of Bouzincourt Communal Cemetery, Somme, France. He is remembered on the Aldershot Memorial

The Revd. The Hon. Maurice Berkeley PEEL
MC and Bar
Chaplain 4th Class Army Chaplains' Department.

The youngest son of Arthur Wellesley Peel, First Viscount Peel, former Speaker of the House of Commons, and Adelaide Peel (nee Dugdale). He was born on the 23rd April 1873. A Late History Exhib. of New College, Oxford, he obtained a B.A. (2nd cl. Modern History) in 1895. After training for the Priesthood at Wells Theological College, in 1897, he was made a Deacon in 1899 and Ordained Priest by the Lord Bishop of London in 1901. After serving his Title as Curate of St. Simon, Bethnal Green, from 1899 to 1906, he was appointed Rector of Wrestingworth and Vicar of Eyeworth from 1906 to 1909. He became Vicar of St. Paul, Beckenham, in the Diocese of Rochester, until 1915. He was made a Temporary Chaplain to the Forces in 1914, being attached to the 7th Division, and was awarded the Military Cross in 1915. Having been wounded at the Battle of Festubert, he returned home and was appointed Vicar of Tamworth where his grandfather, Sir Robert Peel, had been the Member of Parliament and Home Secretary who reorganised the London Police. He rejoined the 7th Division in early 1917 and received a Bar to his Military Cross.

He was killed in action, while tending the wounded on the 14th May 1917, aged 44. during the second Battle at Bullencourt, France. It is believed he was with the Welsh Fusiliers. He was the husband of the late Emily Peel, and is buried in Quant Road Cemetery, Buissy, Pas de Calais, France, Grave Reference V.A.31. and remembered in St. Denys Church, Little Barford, the Sandy War Memorial, Bedfordshire and the Aldershot Memorial. See A Hero Saint Revd. G.V. Sampson. Successor to him at New Beckingham. A memorial from Wells Theological College is now at Sarum College, Salisbury.

The Revd. George Southey PARDOE
Temporary Chaplain 4th Class
Army Chaplains' Department.

The son of George Owen Pardoe, and Letitia Pardoe, of Shropshire, he studied at University College, Oxford, where he obtained a B.A. (3rd cl. Hons) in 1904. He was made a Deacon in 1904 and Ordained Priest by the Lord Bishop of London in 1905, serving his Title as Curate of All Saints, South Acton, until 1907. He was appointed Vicar of Muncaster in the Diocese of Carlisle, and Chaplain to Lord Muncaster. He became a Temporary Chaplain to the Forces in April 1917. He was the husband of Gertrude Pardoe, of Southcote, Baldock, Herts. He died of a cerebral haemorrhage, in Israel on the 15th October 1918, aged 41. He is buried in Jerusalem War Cemetery, Israel, Grave Reference R.106. and remembered on the Aldershot Memorial.

The Revd. Prebendary Somerset Edward PENNEFATHER
Chaplain 2nd Class Army Chaplains' Department.

The son of John Pennefather K.C., of Merrion Square, Dublin, he studied at Trinity College, Dublin, Ireland, where he obtained a B.A. in 1871 and an M.A. in 1876; ad eund. M.A. Durham 1876; Hon.D.D. Aberdeen 1895; Fellow of King's College, London 1898. He was made a Deacon in 1871 and Ordained Priest by the Bishop of Oxford in 1872, serving his Title as Curate of East Claydon, until 1874. He was Vicar of Christ Church, Wakefield, 1874 to 1875; Kenilworth 1875 to 1882; Jesmond 1882 to 1888; St. George, Jesmond, 1888 to 1897; Vicar of St. Mary Abbot, Kensington, in the Diocese of London 1897. Honary Canon (St. Edwin the King) Newcastle upon Tyne Cathedral, from 1888 to 1907; Acting Chaplain to the Forces, Kensington Barracks 1898 to 1906; Rural Dean of Kensington, 1901 to 1913; Prebendary of Brondesbury, in St. Paul's Cathedral, London 1907; Acting Chaplain to the Forces, Kensington Barracks 1908; Proctor In Convocation 1908. The husband of the late Catherine Emily Pennefather, he died on the 29th August 1917 aged 69, and is buried in Kensington (Hanwell) Cemetery, Middlesex, Grave Reference 22.56.21 and 22.

There is a certain amount of confusion about his status. He had been a Territorial Chaplain in London for many years before the outbreak of war. He was mobilized on the 5th August 1914 to serve as a Chaplain to the 1/2nd London territorial Division. Some time later his files shows, "surplus to war establishment". Returning to his parish, he became Chaplain to 13th Battalion London Regiment. Under Army Order 12 of 1916, he was appointed as officiating Chaplain to Kensington Barracks and apparently drew pay for what was a civilian duty. His War Office death record indicated that he had never been demobilized.

The Revd. Charles Benjamin PLUMMER
Temporary Chaplain 4th Class
Army Chaplains' Department.
Attached 61st Infantry Brigade.

The son of the Revd. Canon Francis Bowes Plummer, and Edith Mary Plummer, of Halewood Rectory, Halewood, Liverpool, he studied at Trinity College, Oxford, where he obtained a B.A. (2nd cl. Th. Hons.) in 1912. He trained for the Priesthood at Wycliffe Hall, Oxford, and was made a Deacon in 1913 and Ordained Priest by the Bishop of

Liverpool in 1914. After serving his Title as Curate of St. Clement, Toxteth Park, he became a Temporary Chaplain to the Forces in 1914. He was killed in action, in France, on the 12th March 1917 aged 27. He is buried in Carnoy Military Cemetery, Somme, France, Grave Reference A.5. and remembered on the Aldershot Memorial.

The Revd. Basil Pemberton PLUMPTRE, MC.
Chaplain 4th Class
Army Chaplains' Department.
Attached London Regiment
(1st Surrey Rifles) 1/21st Battalion.

The son of The Revd. Charles P. and Clara Plumptre, of 11 South Park, Sevenoaks, Kent, he studied at Emmanuel College, Cambridge, where he obtained a B.A. (2nd cl. Cl. Trip.) in 1905, and an M.A. in 1910. Following training for the Priesthood at Ridley Hall, Cambridge, he was made a Deacon in 1906 and Ordained Priest by the Bishop of Southwark in 1907. He served his Title as Curate of St. Mary Magdalene, Bermondsey, in the Diocese of Southwark until he became a Temporary Chaplain to the Forces in 1915. He was awarded the Military Cross - London Gazette 27th July 1916 page 7430 "when attached to a Dressing Station he rendered great assistance in dressing the wounded under heavy shell fire." He was killed in action, in Belgium, on the 16th July 1917 aged 34, and buried in La Clytte Military Cemetery, Grave Reference II.F.36. and remembered on the Ridley Hall and Aldershot Memorials.

Walter Harry POWLEY
Chaplain 4th Class
Royal Army Chaplains' Department.

The son of James and Elizabeth Ann Powley, he appears in the Army List 1918 as Salvation Army and was the only Salvation Army Officer / Army Chaplain to lose his life. He was commissioned on the 8th April 1918. He died of influenza, in the General Military Hospital, Edmonton on the 23rd February 1919 aged 41. He was the husband of Margaret Elizabeth Powley, of "Rosebank" 192 Brownhill Road, Catford, London. He is buried in Abney Park Cemetery, London. Grave Reference E4.2.RN.17242. and remembered on the Aldershot Memorial.

The Revd. Arthur Morrell PRATT
Chaplain 4th Class
Army Chaplains' Department.
Attached South Staffordshire Regiment
6th Battalion.

A Late Exhib. of Queen's College, Cambridge, he obtained a B.A. (4th cl. Hon. Th.) and an M.A. in 1905. He was made a Deacon by the Bishop of Islington for London in 1902 and Ordained Priest by the Lord Bishop of London in 1903. He served his Title as Curate of St. Peter, Bayswater, until 1908; Curate of Willenhall 1908 to 1909. He was appointed Vicar of St. Giles, Willenhall, Staffordshire, in the Diocese of Lichfield in 1909. He was the husband of Violet Pratt of "Redcroft" Branksome Park, Bournemouth. According to Army Records (WO 374/55025) he died in France, following an accidental fall from his horse on the 29th June 1917 aged 42. He is buried in St. Sever Cemetery, Rouen, Seine-Maritime, France, Grave Reference Officers B.8.5. and remembered on the Aldershot Memorial.

The Revd. Fr. Matthew Vincent PRENDERGAST
Chaplain 4th Class
Army Chaplains' Department.

The son of Patrick Prendergast of Ballysaggart, Lismore, Co. Waterford, Ireland, he was a Priest of the Waterford RC Diocese on loan to Middlesbrough RC Diocese. Some records show him as having been a Priest at St. Nicholas Church, Bristol. He died, in Egypt, on the 16th September 1918 aged 37. He is buried in Cairo War Cemetery, Grave Reference M.179. and remembered on the Aldershot Memorial.

The Revd. Foster RAINE
Chaplain 4th Class
Army Chaplains' Department.

He was born at Prudhoe, Northumberland on the 18th March 1889, the son of the last Circuit Minister at Sunderland, Thornhill. He studied at Victoria Park College in 1908 and was a United Methodist Minister in the Scilly Islands in 1911. He was at Helston Porthleven in 1913 and enlisted for Army Service in 1916, becoming an Army Chaplain in 1917. He died on the 6/7th December 1918, aged 29. A newspaper cutting dated 8th December 1918, in the archives of the Museum of Army Chaplaincy, states

"CHAPLAIN'S STRANGE END

At an inquest on the Revd. Foster Raine, Army Chaplain, who was found hanging in a train from Penzance at Plymouth Station yesterday, it was stated that the deceased was wearing a pair of lady's high heeled brown boots. The Inquiry was adjourned". He is buried in St. Martin's Churchyard, Isles of Scilly, and remembered on the Aldershot Memorial.

The Revd. William Henry RANKINE
Chaplain 2nd Class
Royal Army Chaplains' Department.
Attached Transport.

The son of Adam R. Rankine, Master of the General Assembly School, Carronshore and Joanne Currie, he was educated at the University of Edinburgh, where he obtained an M.A. in 1883, and a B.D. in 1886. A Minister of The Church of Scotland, he was Licensed by the Presbytery of Kirkcaldy on the 4th May 1886, and Ordained to Slamannan, Scotland on the 9th November 1887; St. Boswell's 1891; Titwood 1897. He was appointed a Chaplain to the Forces in 1914, and served in the Mediterranean from 1915 to 1916; Transport Administrator January 1918. He was then Minister at Kirkmichael in 1918. He married Helen Anderson, on the 12th December 1888, and died on the 11th July 1921 probably after demobilsation. He is buried in the South West corner of Kirkmichael Parish Churchyard, Ayrshire, Scotland. He was a regular contributor to the Scottish Outposts - Edinburgh 1914 and Hastings Dictionary of Christ and the Gospels and the Author of *A Hero of the Dark Continent - a biography of the Revd. William Affleck Scott Edinburgh 1896. The Call to Discipleship, Kelso 1897. The Secret of Christian Giving Glasgow 1899.*

The Revd. George Harvey RANKING
Temporary Chaplain 4th Class
Army Chaplains' Department.
Attached IV Corps Heavy Artillery.

The son of Harvey Ranking, a Foreign Merchant and Banker, and Margaret Ranking (nee Humfrey), he was born in 1872 at London. He was educated at Orwell House, Clifton on Dunsmore, Warwick, 1881 and Husby School. Following a career in the family business (John Ranking and Co London) and involvement with Missions in Notting Hill and Lambeth, he studied at New College Oxford in 1903. After further study at Bishops Hostel, Farnham, in 1904, he was made a Deacon. Ordained Priest by the Bishop of Winchester in 1905, he served his Title as Curate of St. Andrew, Farnham, from 1904 to 1907; Curate at Lambeth until to 1911. In 1906 he married Violet Evelyn Paget, the daughter of Col. Paget, Scots Guards. He moved to Ardwick le Street (Curate in charge of Woodlands from 1911 to 1914); Perpetual Curate of Woodlands, in the Diocese of Sheffield, from 1914 until 1915, when he was appointed Vicar of Fornhurst, Chichester, becoming a Temporary Chaplain to the Forces in 1917. Killed in action, in France, on the 20th November 1917 aged 46, he is buried in Hermies British Cemetery, Pas de Calais, France, Grave Reference F.3. and remembered on the Honours Board at All Saints Church, Woodlands, Doncaster, and the Aldershot Memorial. His widow, Violet Ranking resided at Open Combe, Arley Heights, Haslemere, Surrey, and died in 1946 aged 81 in West Sussex.
See also Doncaster Chronicle December 1917.

The Revd. Hardwicke Drummond RAWNSLEY

He appears among the deaths in the Army List for July 1920 with no further details. The Royal Army Chaplains Department has no record of him. He was Vicar of Crosthwaite, Keswick, and he was appointed Chaplain to the King in 1912. Information about him is worth looking up on the Internet, as he was connected with the Lakeland Poets, Beatrix Potter, and a Founder of the National Trust. (See www.nationalarchives.gov.uk)

The Revd. Eric Oswald READ
Chaplain 4th Class
Army Chaplains' Department.
Attached Dorsetshire Regiment 5th Battalion.

The son of George O. and Dora Read, he was born at Thetford, Norfolk, and studied at Corpus Christi College, Cambridge, where he obtained a B.A. in 1912 and was Scho. Canc. Linc. in 1912. He was made a Deacon in 1913 and Ordained Priest by the Bishop of Southwell, serving his Title as Curate of East Retford, in the Diocese of Southwell, until 1916 and then at Alfreton. The husband of Alice Read, of "Gorsefield" Giles Lane, Canterbury, he was killed in action, in France on the 3rd October 1918 aged 30. He is buried in Chapel Corner Cemetery, Sauchy-Lestree, Pas de Calais, France, Grave Reference C.3. and remembered on the Aldershot Memorial.

The Revd. Clifford Hugh REED, MC
Temporary Chaplain 4th Class
Army Chaplains' Department.

The son of William Henry and Caroline Reed, of "Thornlea" Cowley Road, Exeter, he was an M.A. and a Wesleyan Minister. From 1912 he was at The Lays School and became a Chaplain to the Forces in 1915. He was awarded the Military Cross - London Gazette 14th November 1916 Page 11064, "For conspicuous courage and devotion to duty on many occasions in the firing line, in helping with the evacuation of wounded. On one occasion he led a party of stretcher bearers under heavy shell fire to the advanced aid posts, rendering conspicuous service at great personal risk. He had previously rendered valuable service under fire." He was killed in action, in Belgium, on the 7th June 1917 aged 28. He is buried in Oosttaverne Wood Cemetery, Grave Reference I.A.12. and remembered on the Aldershot Memorial.

Editor's note

The Lays School in Cambridge was a Wesleyan foundation and still functions as a Public School, maintaining a particular ethos. There was traditionally a Wesleyan then Methodist Minister appointed as Chaplain.

The Revd. Walter H. RICHARDS
Chaplain 3rd Class
Royal Army Chaplains' Department.
Attached Transport.

A Wesleyan Minister, he was at Ramsey, Isle of Man in 1903; British Guyana in 1906 and at Pembroke in 1912. He served as an Army Chaplain from 1914 to 1920, and is listed as being at Stafford in 1915. He died on the 19th February 1920. He is buried in Clynnog Fawr (St. Beuno) Churchyard, Caernarvonshire, Wales, West of St. Beuno's Chapel. Although listed in The Cross of Sacrifice there is no evidence to support that he was serving at the time of his death.

The Revd. Peter JONES - ROBERTS
See under JONES.

The Revd. Charles ROBERTSON, MC
Temporary Chaplain 4th Class
Army Chaplains' Department.

The son of Hope and Catherine McLeish Robertson, of Kinclaven, Perthshire, Scotland, he was born in 1880. A Church of Scotland Minister, he studied at the University of Edinburgh, where he obtained an M.A. in 1900. He was licenced by the Presbytery of Dunkeld, in 1905 and was assistant minister at Govan, and St. John's, Edinburgh. He was Ordained on the 12th November 1908 to the Middle Parish, St. Andrews. He enlisted into the R.A.M.C. and served with Forces at Salonika, and was appointed Chaplain to the Forces serving with the Argyll and Sutherland Highlanders. He was awarded the Military Cross with no published citation. He died of wounds, in Greece, on the 3rd October 1918 aged 39. He is buried in Mikra British Cemetery, Greece, Grave Reference 421. and remembered on the Aldershot Memorial.

The Revd. Francis Cavendish ROCHE
Chaplain 4th Class Army Chaplains' Department.

The son of the late George Major Roche, of Dublin, and Jane Roche, of Rosemary Lodge, Felixstowe, he was born at Dublin. He served in the South African Campaign as a Trooper in the Irish Horse. He studied at Trinity College, Dublin, where he obtained a B.A., Divinity Test (1st cl.); Downe's Prize, and Warren Prize in 1908, and an M.A. in 1913. He was made a Deacon in 1908, and Ordained Priest by the Bishop of Down in 1909, serving as Curate of Ballymena until 1911; Mortlake with East Sheen, in the Diocese of Southwark, from 1911. He was at Sulva Bay, Gallipoli, and died of enteric fever at Alexandria, Egypt on the 14th November 1915 aged 33. He is buried in Alexandria Memorial Cemetery, Egypt, Grave Reference J.2. and remembered on the Aldershot Memorial.

The Revd. Benjamin Corrie RUCK - KEENE
Temporary Chaplain 4th Class
Army Chaplains' Department.
Attached East Yorkshire Regiment 8th Battalion.

The son of The Revd. Edmund Ralph and Mrs Emma Ruck-Keene, nee (Corrie) Rector of Copford, Colchester, he was born on 25th May 1889. He studied at Keble College, Oxford where he obtained a B.A. and at Bishop's College, Cheshunt in 1912. He was made a Deacon in 1913, and Ordained Priest by the Lord Bishop of London in 1914, serving his title as Curate of St. James the Great, Bethnal Green, in the Diocese of London, becoming a Temporary Chaplain to the Forces in 1917. He was killed in action, in Belgium, on the 26th September 1917, aged 28. He is buried in the Ypres Reservoir Cemetery, Belgium, Grave Reference I.F.37, and remembered on the Aldershot Memorial. His brother Lt. Edgar Ralph Ruck-Keene served in the Royal Welsh Fusiliers and was killed in action on the 16th January 1916 aged 27 at Richebourg St. Vaast.

The Revd. Fr. Michael RYAN
Chaplain 4th Class Army Chaplains' Department.

The son of Patrick and Sabina Ryan, of Loughrea, Co. Galway, Ireland, he was a Priest in the OCD, and Commissioned in July 1915. He served in France, before being transferred to India, where he contracted the plague, and died, at Kirkee, on the 1st November 1916 age 59. Remembered on the Kirkee 1914-1918 Memorial, India, Face 11. and the Aldershot Memorial.

The Revd. Samuel John Woodhouse SANDERS

The son of The Revd. Samuel and Phoebe Sanders, he was born at Hadnall, Salop., and baptised on the 15th February 1846. Educated at Ludlow Grammar School, he studied at St. John's College, Cambridge, where he obtained a B.A. in 1864, and an M.A. in 1868, L.L.M. 1873, L.L.D. 1885. He was made a Deacon in 1870 and Ordained Priest by the Bishop of Ely in 1871. Curate of Kempstoon, Berkshire, and Vice Master of Bedford Co. School from 1869 to 1872. Headmaster of Northampton Grammar School, from 1872 to 1893, and Curate of St. Peters, Northampton, from 1874 to 1893. Vicar of St. Nicholas, Leicester, from 1893; St. Martin, Leicester, 1893 to 1909. Honary Canon of Peterborough 1890 to 1915. Surrogate for Archdeacon of Leicester 1893, and Bishop of Peterborough 1894. Vicar of Rothley with Keyham, Chadwell, and Wykeham in the Diocese of Peterborough 1909 to 1915. He married on 16th July 1872, Roberta Henrietta Douet, a Widow of Leicester and daughter of The Revd. C.P. Douet, Rector of Metcalfe, Jamaica. There was a second marriage on the 24th April 1894 to Annie Elizabeth Pegg. The Army List for February 1916 showed him among the deaths, as a CF2 (TF) with no further details. He was the Author of, *Facts and Figures 1870.* Brief Notes on structural Botany 1870.

The Revd. Cecil Herbert SCHOOLING
Temporary Chaplain 4th Class
Army Chaplains' Department.
Attached 122nd Infantry Brigade.

The son of Frederick and Lily Schooling, of "Hilly Dene" Bromley, Kent, he was born at Wandsworth Common, London. After study at Pembroke College, Cambridge, where he obtained a B.A. in 1906, and an M.A. in 1910. He trained for the Priesthood at Wells Theological College. He was made a Deacon in 1907. Ordained Priest by the Bishop of Wakefield in 1908, he served his Title as Curate of All Saints, Wakefield, until 1910, and subsequently as Curate of St. John Baptist, Croydon, in the Diocese of Canterbury until 1916, when he became a Temporary Chaplain to the Forces. He died of wounds, in Belgium, on the 21st June 1917 aged 32. He is buried in Lijssenthoek Military Cemetery, Belgium, Grave Reference XIII.A.21. and remembered on the Aldershot Memorial. A memorial from Wells Theological College is now at Sarum College, Salisbury.

The Revd. James SHAW

A Presbyterian Minister in Quetta, he was called up for Chaplaincy service early in 1918 at the advanced age of 73. He was demoblised on the 15th February 1919. Although not a casualty he was the oldest serving chaplain of the First World War.

The Revd. Fr. James SHINE
Chaplain 4th Class Army Chaplains' Department.
Attached Middlesex Regiment 21st Battalion.

The son of Thomas and Mary Shine, of Ballylaffin, Ardfinnan, Cahir, Co. Tipperary, Ireland, he was a Priest from the Waterford RC Diocese, on loan to Dunkeld RC Diocese, Scotland. He died of wounds, in France, on the 21st April 1918 aged 37. He is buried in Boulogne Eastern Cemetery, Pas de Calais France, Grave Reference VII.B.40. and remembered on the Aldershot Memorial.

The Revd. Thomas Jasper SHOVEL
Chaplain 4th Class Army Chaplains' Department.
2nd/2nd Wessex Field Ambulance.

The son of Thomas and Ellen Shovel, of Upton Cross, Linkinhorne, Cornwall, he was born on the 2nd August 1884. He trained at Richmond College, and was a Wesleyan Minister. He was at Tredegar in 1905; Hitchin 1909; Hunts Mission 1912; Hollyhead 1913 and at Preston in 1916. An obituary Notice recalls that "He was Ordained as a Methodist Minister in July 1912 after which he worked in the Hitchin & Stevenage area under the Reverend John Pellow. He lived in Green Street, Stevenage and joined the Royal Army Chaplains Department on the 16th January 1918 as a Chaplain 4th Class. After a short introduction to Army life he embarked from Folkestone on the 29th January 1918 for France where he was attached to the 2/2 Wessex Field Ambulance on the Western Front. He died from shrapnel wounds received in the field on 5th October 1918 aged 34. His name is amongst those that are not recorded on the Stevenage War Memorial". A Memorial Plaque commemorating students of Richmond College is now in the Methodist Church House, Marylebone Road, London. He is buried in Louverval Military Cemetery, Doignies, Nord, France, Grave Reference A.6. and remembered on the Aldershot Memorial.

The Revd. Frederick Seaton SMITH
(Shown as Fred in Crockford's Clerical Directory 1917).
Chaplain 4th Class Army Chaplains' Department.
York and Lancaster Regiment 13th Battalion.

He was born at Pocklington, Yorkshire, and studied at St. Denial's College, Lampeter, where he obtained a B.A. in 1913, in which year he was made a Deacon. Ordained Priest by the Bishop of Ripon in 1914, he served his Title as Curate of St. John, Bradford, until 1915, and was Curate at All Souls, Leeds, until 1916. He died, in France, on the 15th November 1918, aged 31. He is buried in Terlincthun British Cemetery, Wimille, Pas de Calais France, Grave Reference XI.A.29. and remembered on the Aldershot Memorial.

The Revd. Peter George SMITH
Chaplain 4th Class
Royal Army Chaplains' Department.
Attached 9th Scottish Rifles in Germany.

The son of Peter S. and Jessie Smith (nee Downie), he was born on the 23rd March 1878 at Glasgow. His father was Congregational minister at Govan. He was educated at Hutchesons Grammar School, and the University of Glasgow, where he obtained an M.A. in 1900, and a B.D. in 1904. He was Licenced by the Presbytery of Glasgow, on the 6th May 1903, and was Assistant Minister at St. Stephen's, Glasgow. Ordained by the Dunblane Presbytery to Kemnay on the 11th November 1904, and translated on the 20th November 1908 to Kippen, and was an assistant Minister at Ollaberry, Killeen and Whiting Bay. He married Jessie Boland, of Stonehouse, on the 23rd March 1905, becoming a Chaplain to the Forces on the 8th April 1918, serving in Germany, with the Black Watch, and 9th Scottish Rifles. After a short illness he was Medically Boarded on the 15th October 1919 at No 2 Scottish General Hospital and Gazetted on the 20th November 1919. The diagnosis was Gastric Carcinoma. It was argued that he enlisted with this condition but that it was aggravated by military service. He relinquished his Commission on the 20th November 1919, and died on the 3rd December 1919. He is remembered on the Aldershot Memorial.

The Revd. Alexander SPENCE, MC
Chaplain 4th Class Army Chaplains' Department.
Attached Royal Inniskilling Fusiliers.

He studied at Trinity College, Dublin, Ireland, where he obtained a B.A. (Mods) in 1913. He was made a Deacon in 1914, and Commissioned on the 5th June 1916. (As there was no 1916 edition of Crockford's, no further record of his Priesting and ministry can be found). He was awarded the Military Cross, London Gazette 18th October 1917, page 10711, "for conspicuous gallantry and devotion to duty. He worked for twenty hours attending to the wounded in an aid post during an attack. On the following day, hearing that some wounded were lying out in shell holes he went out in daylight under machine-gun fire and brought back several wounded men to the aid post. He rendered splendid, service and showed great gallantry and contempt of danger." He was a Prisoner of War and died of wounds, in enemy hands, on the 31st March 1918. His grave is in Roye New British Cemetery, Somme, France, Reference IV.C.17. and he is remembered on the Aldershot Memorial.

The Revd. Hubert Octavius SPINK
Chaplain 4th Class Army Chaplains' Department
Attached 55th (West Lancs) Division.

The son of Joseph Simeon Spink, and Lucy Dorothea Spink, he was born at Dulwich, London. After studying at St. Aidan's College, Birkenhead, in 1902 he was made a Deacon in 1904, and Ordained Priest by the Bishop of Liverpool in 1905 serving as Curate of St. Philip, Orrell Hey, (Litherland) until 1905; St. Cypr. Edge Hill, Liverpool, until 1909; It is recorded that he obtained a B.A. in 1907, and an M.A. in 1911, from the University of Durham. He was Incumbent of St. Andrew, Kowloon, Hong Kong, from 1909 to 1912, and was then Vicar of St. Clement, Toxteth Park, Liverpool. He had been wounded on several occasions and was killed, in action, in France, on the 9th August 1916 aged 38. In Khaki Vignette The Revd. Philip J. Fisher, a Primitive Methodist Minister, and Chaplain to the Forces, writes movingly about Spink. They were serving together at West Peronne, on the Somme, France, in 1916. "He appears to have gone to the aid of some wounded soldiers during the night and to have been killed by shell fire". He is buried in Dive Copse British Cemetery, Sailly-le-Sek, Somme, France, Grave Reference II.D.46. and remembered on the Aldershot Memorial.

The Revd. Harvey STAUNTON
Chaplain 4th Class
Army Chaplains' Department.

The son of the late Revd. Francis Staunton, of Staunton Hall, Nottingham Rise, and of Mrs. L. A. Staunton Lees, of 5 The Mount, St. Leonards on Sea. He was born on 21st November 1870. He was educated at Bromsgrove School and studied at Selwyn College, Cambridge, where he obtained a B.A. in 1895, and an M.A. in 1916. He was a Rugby 'blue' in 1891, and was made a Deacon in 1896. Ordained Priest by the Bishop of Oxford, in 1897, he served his Title as Curate of Boxford, Berkshire, until 1898 and subsequently Curate of Pleasley, Mansfield, until 1900; Plumtree, Nottingham, until 1902. He was Chaplain to Notts County Asylum, from 1902 to 1907, when he was appointed Rector of Broughton Sulney, until 1911. He became Chaplain (A.C.I.S.) in the Diocese of Nagpur, India, from 1911 to 1916. He married Mabel Healing, of Plymard, Cheshire. He died, in Iraq, on the 14th January 1918 aged 45. He is buried in Baghdad (North Gate) War Cemetery, Iraq, Grave Reference XX.J.7. and remembered on the Aldershot Memorial.

The Revd. Silas William STEVENS

The son of James and Mary Ann Stevens, he was born on the 11th October 1854, at Beaulieu, Hants. Educated at St. Austin's School, and St. John's Hurstpierpoint. He was a Late Exhib. of St. John's College, Cambridge, where he obtained a B.A. and an Ll.B. (2nd Class Law Trip.) in 1884, and an M.A. in 1892, LL.M. in 1901. He was made a Deacon in 1885 and Ordained Priest by the Bishop of Winchester in 1886. Curate of All Saints, Ryde, Isle of Wight from 1885 to 1887; Chaplain to the Royal South Hants Infirmary, 1887; Vicar of Burley, Hants, 1889 to 1890; Rector of St. Laurence, Southampton, 1890 to 1915. He appears as a CF1 (TF) in Army List for January 1916 with no further details. He died on the 23rd October 1915 at Southampton aged 61.

The Revd. James Robert STEWART
Chaplain 4th Class
Army Chaplains' Department.
Attached Worcestershire Regiment 2nd Battalion.

The son of a Missionary family whose father, mother and younger brother were amongst other missionaries massacred at Hwasang, Korea, during the ant-foreign riots in 1895. He studied at the University of Sydney, where he obtained a B.A. in 1903, and went to Moore Theological College, in 1903. He was made a Deacon in 1904 and Ordained Priest by the Bishop of Winchester in 1905, serving his Title as Curate of St. James, Shirley, Hants, from 1904 to 1907. He joined the Church Missionary Society and was a Missionary at Teh-Yang from 1907 to 1910, when he became Principal of the Anglican Hostel, Chen-tu, in the Diocese of Western China. He was killed, in action, in France, on the 2nd January 1916, aged 35. He is buried in Bethune Town Cemetery, Pas de Calais, France, Grave Reference II.L.11. and remembered on the Aldershot Memorial.

Editor's note.

A newspaper cutting indicates that he died while "conducting a military funeral service, an enemy shell exploded in the midst of the mourners". He was killed instantly and others in attendance were seriously wounded.

The Revd. Robert Arthur STEWART
Temporary Chaplain 4th Class
Army Chaplains' Department.
Attached 57th CCS.

Formerly of Aldershot, he was a Presbyterian Minister, who had a ministry at Aldershot and died in France, on the 3rd November 1917. He is buried in St. Pol Communal Cemetery Extension, Pas de Calais, France, Grave Reference H.3. and remembered on the Aldershot Memorial.

The Revd. Basil Robert STREETEN
Chaplain 4th Class Army Chaplains' Department.
Attached Lancashire Fusiliers 2nd/5th Battalion.

The son of Mrs. Streeten, of Swinford, Sidcup, Kent, he was a Late Somerset Exhib. of St. John's College, Cambridge, where he obtained a B.A. (3rd cl. Th. Trip.) in 1911. After training for the Priesthood at Wells Theological College, he was made a Deacon in 1912 and Ordained Priest by the Bishop of Southwell in 1913. He served his Title as Curate of Gedling, in the Diocese of Southwell, from 1912. He died, in France, on the 1st November 1918, and is buried in Don Communal Cemetery, Annoeullin, Nord, France, Grave Reference I.A.27. He is remembered on a Memorial in Holy Trinity Church, Lamorbey, Kent, and the Aldershot Memorial. A memorial from Wells Theological College is now at Sarum College, Salisbury.

The Revd. Fr. Joseph STRICKLAND
Chaplain 4th Class Army Chaplains' Department.
Attached 12th Brigade 4th Division.

The son of Captain Walter Charles Strickland RN, and his wife Nobile Luisa Bonici Mompalao, he was a Priest of the Society of Jesus Roman Province. Part of his Noviciate was spent at Manresa, and he studied Theology at St. Beuno's. He was appointed Chaplain, at Sleaford Camp, in 1914, and served in France, with the 12th Infantry Brigade, from 1914 to 1916. He was one of the first batch of three RC Chaplains to go to France, with Fr. M. King, and Fr. Raymond-Barker. He died in Malta, of pleurisy, on the 15th July 1917 aged 53, and is buried in the Addolorata Cemetery, Ossuary of the Jesuit Fathers, and remembered on the Aldershot Memorial.

The Revd. Alexander STUART
Temporary Chaplain 4th Class
Army Chaplains' Department.
Royal Irish Rifles 12th Battalion.

The son of the Revd. J. C. Stuart, of Clare, near Tandragee, Ireland, he was one of five brothers who entered the ministry. He was educated at Tanioky National School, near Poyntzpass, and Agnes National School, Belfast. He studied for the ministry at Magee College, Derry, Ireland, and the Assembly's College, Belfast, and New College, Edinburgh and at Princeton, USA. A minister of the Presbyterian Church of Ireland, he was licenced by the General Assembly, on the 3rd June 1912. He was assistant minister at Agnes Street Church, Belfast and was Ordained on the 21st May 1915 to Bessbrook. He was with the YMCA, in Egypt, during the early part of 1916. He became a Temporary Chaplain to the Forces, and was killed in action, two weeks after he had arrived in France, on the 24th October 1917.

He was the first Irish Presbyterian Chaplain casualty of the First World War. He is buried in Ruyaulcourt Military Cemetery, Pas de Calais, France, Grave Reference F.5. and remembered on the Aldershot Memorial.

The Revd. Stephen John SULLINGS
Chaplain 4th Class
Army Chaplains' Department.
Royal Army Medical Corps
54th East Anglian Division.

The son of the late Mr. and Mrs. Thomas Sullings, of Stanford-le-Hope, Essex, he was a Wesleyan Minister being Ordained at the Victoria Australia Conference of 1892. He was with the Sussex Mission in 1901; London Mission 1904; Hull 1907 and at Burnley, Fulledge, in 1910. He was one of the first to be commissioned in August 1914, and was invalided home from Gallipoli. He died at Birmingham of enteric Fever, contracted at Gallipoli on the 21st November 1915 aged 47. The husband of the late Edith Sullings, he is remembered in Birmingham (Lodge Hill) Cemetery, Warwickshire, Screen Wall, Reference B10.1.143. and on the Aldershot Memorial.

The Revd. Andrew Neil SUTHERLAND
Temporary Chaplain 2nd Class
Army Chaplains' Department.

He was born on the 9th May 1855 at St. Andrews Free Church Manse, Dunfermline, Scotland, the son of the Revd. Andrew Sutherland, and Amelia Sutherland (nee MacDiarmid). He was educated at Glasgow Academy, and Glasgow University, where he obtained an M.A. in 1878. Further study took place at the University of Tubingen in 1879, and the Glasgow Free Church College. A Minister of the Free Church of Scotland, he was Licenced by the Free Church Presbytery of Glasgow, on the 11th May 1880, and was assistant minister at, Maxwelltown Free Church, Dumfies, from1880. He was Ordained and Inducted to Muthill Free Church, Perthshire, on the 14th April 1881, and translated to Rothsay Free Parish, on the 11th May 1886; McCheyne Memorial Church, Dundee, on the 26th March 1902. He married Christina Purves, the daughter of the Revd. David Purves, of Maxwelltown Free Church, Dumfries, on the 22nd March 1883. He was a Chaplain to the Forces based at the 1st General Hospital, Aberdeen, from 1915 to 1916, and died on the 16th January 1918. He is buried in the Glasgow Western Necropolis Grave Reference K.402.

The Revd. George Charles Walrond SWEET
Chaplain 4th Class
Royal Army Chaplains' Department.

The son of The Revd. C. F. Sweet, and Mrs. Maud Sweet, of Symondsbury Rectory, Bridport, he studied at Bishop's Hostel Farnham in 1914, and at Keble College, Oxford, where he obtained a B.A. in 1915. He was made a Deacon in 1915 and Ordained Priest by the Bishop of Winchester in 1916, serving his Title as Curate of St. Paul, Southsea, in the Diocese of Winchester. He became a Temporary Chaplain to the Forces in 1918, and was accidentally drowned at Oxford on the 7th August 1919 aged 29. He was the husband of Phyllis Walrond Sweet, of Outreau, West Bay, Bridport, Dorset, and is buried in Sampford Arundel (Holy Cross) Churchyard, Somerset.

The Revd. William TAYLOR
Chaplain 3rd Class Army Chaplains' Department.

The son of Peter T. and Margaret Taylor (nee Hughes), he was born on the 3rd November 1863, at Muthill, Perthshire, Scotland. Educated at Muthill School, he studied at the University of Glasgow, where he obtained an M.A. in 1884. A minister of the Church of Scotland, he was Licenced by the Presbytery of Auchterarder, on the 4th May 1887, and was assistant minister at the North Parish, Stirling. He was Ordained on the 11th December 1891 to Dallater and Dunbarton, and was subsequently at Melville, Queen Street, Montrose. He married Jane Gow Latta, of Dunbarton on the 5th February 1895. He was appointed Chaplain to the Forces in 1902 and attached to the 1st Forfar Royal Garrison Artillery, and the North Scottish Royal Garrison Artillery M (A) in 1910. He died on the 19th October 1916. His widow resided at 40 Stratheam Road, Edinburgh, and he is buried in Montrose (Sleepyhillock) Cemetery, Angus, Grave Reference D.2.51. He was the Author of; *Sabbath Keeping* - A sermon preached before the Synod of Angus and The Mearns 1902. *Twelve favourite Hymns, their message and their writers* Paisley 1907.

Editor's note.

This entry has puzzled me for some time, but my memory recalls certain events of my boyhood. I was brought up by my grandparents who resided in the County of Angus (Forfarshire). At the beginning of the twentieth century, my grandfather was a ploughman. He had many memories of The First World War, one of which was the hauling of heavy artillery to the cliff tops between Arbroath and Montrose. At times the task was too great for farm horses, and Steam Traction Engines used for threshing wheat were requisitioned for this purpose.

The Revd. Thomas J. Thorpe
Army Chaplains Department.

A Wesleyan Minister who was commissioned at the outbreak of war, he died from illness on the 20th February 1915 at Woolwich. His ministry indicates an involvement with the Army on behalf of his church. (See Preface) In 1879 he was Minister on supply and was part of the First London District Mission in 1880. He was at Aldershot in 1883, London Hind Street 1886; Woolwich Garrison 1889; Aldershot 1896; London Clapham 1899; Kent Mission 1902; Wiltshire Mission 1906 and Woolwich Garrison in 1910.

The Revd. William Henry TOMKINS
Temporary Chaplain 4th Class
Army Chaplains' Department.
Attached South Staffordshire Regiment 7th Battalion.

A son of the Manse, he was born at Rushden, Northamptonshire. In early manhood he went to London and was connected with a large publishing house. He studied at the Metropolitan Baptist College. He was Minister at Yalding, Kent from 1901 to 1904; Batley, Yorkshire 1904 to 1907; Morley, Yorkshire 1907 to 1914. President of Leeds District Yorkshire Association in 1912, and Doncaster from 1914 to 1917. He became a Temporary Chaplain to the Forces in January 1917, serving at Salonika, and in Palestine. He was killed in action, in France, on the 28th September 1918 aged 40. He is buried in Cagnicourt British Cemetery, Pas de Calais, France, Grave Reference I.C.7. and remembered on the Aldershot Memorial.

The Revd. Ernest Wilberforce TREVOR
Chaplain 4th Class Army Chaplains' Department.
Attached Rifle Brigade 13th Battalion.

The son of The Revd. G. W. Trevor, and Mrs. A.F. Trevor, of 3 Bloomfield Place, Bath, he was born at Marton in Cleveland, Yorkshire. He studied at University College, Oxford, where he obtained a B.A. (3rd cl. Mod Hist.) in 1908, and an M.A. in 1912. He trained for the Priesthood at Wells Theological College, in 1908, and was made a Deacon in 1909. Ordained Priest by the Bishop of Peterborough in 1910, he served his Title as Curate of Kettering, until 1911, and at Lenham, Maidstone, from 1912 to 1914; St. Peter in Thanet, in the Diocese of Canterbury 1914. He died in France, on the 14th November 1916 aged 30. He is buried in Hamel Military Cemetery, Beaumont-Hamel, Somme, France, Grave Reference II.D.21. and remembered on the Memorial in Beverley Minster and the Aldershot Memorial. A memorial from Wells Theological College is now at Sarum College, Salisbury.

The Revd. Francis Henry TUKE
Chaplain 4th Class Army Chaplains' Department
Attached 53rd Brigade.

He studied at Trinity College, Cambridge, where he obtained a B.A. in 1889. He was made a Deacon by the Bishop of Rochester in 1890, and Ordained Priest by the Bishop of Gibraltar for Rochester in 1891. After serving his Title as Curate of St. George, Camberwell (Trinity College Cambridge Mission), in 1890, he was Curate of Hatchford, Surrey from 1893 to 1894; Addlestone 1894 to 1896; Vicar of Ripley, Surrey, 1896 to 1901; Hope under Dinmore, and Chaplain of Dinmore Chapel 1902 to 1908 in the Diocese of Hereford; Halmer with Huntington, Diocese of Hereford from 1908. The husband of Jane Ellen Tuke of "Moss Croft" Halmer, Hereford, he was killed in action in France, on the 20th July 1916 aged 49. He is remembered on the Thiepval Memorial, Somme, France, Pier and Face 4C, and on the Aldershot Memorial.

The Revd. Albert Thomas VERYARD
Chaplain 4th Class Army Chaplains' Department.
Attached 15th Trench Mortar Battery.

He studied at the Metropolitan Baptist College, and was the Baptist Minister at Longley Road, Tooting, from 1912 to 1917, becoming a Temporary Chaplain to the Forces in 1916. He was killed in action, in France, on the 28th June 1917 aged 33. He is buried in Roclincourt Military Cemetery, Pas de Calais, France, Grave Reference II.C.9. and remembered on the Aldershot Memorial.

The Revd. John James WALLACE
Temporary Chaplain 4th Class
Army Chaplains' Department.
Attached North Staffordshire Regiment 8th Battalion.

The son of the late John Lishman Wallace, and of Mary A. Wallace, of 6 Dunvegan Gardens, Eltham Park, London, he was an A.K.C. (1st cl.) in 1907, and was made a Deacon in 1907. Ordained Priest, by the Bishop of Wakefield in 1908, he served his Title as Curate of Marsden, until 1909, and at Outwood, in the Diocese of Wakefield, until he became a Temporary Chaplain to the Forces in 1917. He died of wounds, in France, on the 8th November 1918 aged 39. He is buried in Awoingt British Cemetery, Nord, France, Grave Reference III.E.13. and remembered on the Aldershot Memorial.

The Revd. Fr. Charles WATSON
Chaplain 4th Class
Army Chaplains' Department.

He was the son of Thomas and V. Watson, of Grange of Barrie, Gedinne, Belgium, and a Priest of the CSSR. He studied at Ushaw College from 1881 to 1885. Extract from the CSSR Archives. "On the 21st December 1917, the dreadful war which for four years raged through almost all the countries of the world brought to death two Priests of this Province". (See also Revd. Fr. Bernard Kavanagh). "He was born on the 26th August 1867, in Belgium, the son of a Scotsman and a Belgian lady. He was a fluent speaker of French and was, for a time, a student at Ushaw College, Durham. He made his Noviciate at Bishop Eaton, and was professed there on the 8th September 1891. After studies at Teignmouth, he was Ordained Priest on the 21st September 1897. Until the war he was assigned to various houses and gave many missions. He was an expert at planting and pruning fruit trees, an art which he practiced at many Presbyteries. He engaged in this hobby till he met his death". He died from sunstroke, on the 22nd July 1918 aged 51, and is buried in Basra War Cemetery, Iraq, Grave Reference IV.Q.8. and remembered on the Ushaw College and Aldershot Memorials. Extract from the CSSR Archives 22nd July 1918 "Fr. Charles Watson was the second of our Fathers who acted as Military Chaplains to the Forces in the 1914 - 1918 war to meet his death. His first sphere of activity was with the troops in Egypt then he passed to Mesopotamia and it was near Baghdad that he died of sunstroke. Fr. Watson was near Baghdad in Mesopotamia and all were warned not to go out in blazing sunlight with head uncovered".

The Revd. John Edmund Malone WATSON, MC
Temporary Chaplain 4th Class
Army Chaplains' Department.
Attached Middlesex Regiment 21st Battalion.

The son of the Revd. John Watson, of Charlemont Rectory, Co. Tyrone, Ireland, he studied at Trinity College, Dublin, Ireland in 1908, passed the Divinity Test in 1909, and was made a Deacon in 1910. Ordained Priest by the Bishop of Down in 1911. He was Curate of St. James, Belfast, in the Diocese of Connor, until 1916, when he became a Temporary Chaplain to the Forces. Awarded the Military Cross, London Gazette 16th September 1918 page 11031 "for conspicuous gallantry and devotion to duty. During six days fighting this Chaplain was in line with the Battalion and in close touch with the men, being indefatigable in his attention to the wounded. His fine example and cheerfulness under very trying circumstances greatly encouraged the wounded." He was the husband of Mary K. Watson, of "Ard-Stratha", Antrim Road, Belfast, and died of wounds, in France, on the 10th April 1918 aged 31. He is buried in Haverskerque British Cemetery, Nord, France, Grave Reference E.11. and remembered on the Aldershot Memorial.

The Revd. Fr. John A. WATTERS
Chaplain 4th Class
Army Chaplains' Department.
Attached 115th Infantry Brigade HQ.

The son of Mary Watters, of Frenchgrove, Hollymount, Co. Mayo, Ireland, and the late James Watters, he was a Priest in the Plymouth RC Diocese. He died, in France, on the 7th November 1918 aged 26. He is buried in Awoingt British Cemetery, Nord, France, Grave Reference III.G.9. and remembered on the Aldershot Memorial.

The Revd. Cyril Narramore WERE
Chaplain 4th Class
Army Chaplains' Department.

The son of Edward Ash Were, (Bishop of Stafford), and Julia Leite Were, he studied at Christ Church, Oxford, where he obtained a B.A. in 1903, and an M.A. in 1907. He trained for the Priesthood at Bishop's Hostel Farnham, in 1903, and was made a Deacon in 1904. Ordained Priest in 1905, by the Bishop of Winchester, he served his Title as Curate of Bramshott, until 1907. He was Rector of Samford Brett, 1907 to 1908; Curate of Addlestone, 1909 to 1911, and Domestic Chaplain to the Bishop of Lichfield, 1911 to 1913; Domestic Chaplain to the Bishop of Southwark 1914. The husband of Mildred Gladys Were, of 14 Christchurch Road, Reading, he died, in France, on the 9th January 1918 aged 36. He is buried in Outtersteene Communal Cemetery Extension, Bailleul, Nord, France, Grave Reference II.D.53. and remembered on the Aldershot Memorial.

The Revd. Fr. Charles B. WHITEFOORD
Chaplain 4th Class
Army Chaplains' Department.
Attached London Regiment (City of London Rifles).
6th Battalion.

Educated at Rugby School, he studied at Merton College, Oxford, and was a Priest in the Shrewsbury RC Diocese. The brother of Mr. C.A. B. Whitefoord, of 36 Broad Street, Ludlow, Salop, he died of wounds, in France, on the 30th May 1918. He is buried in Bagneux British Cemetery, Gezaincourt, Somme, France, Grave Reference II.E.23. and remembered on the Aldershot Memorial.

The Revd. Walter Charles WILKS, MC
Chaplain 3rd Class
Army Chaplains' Department.
Attached South Staffordshire Regiment 7th Battalion.

The son of Samuel Hawes Wilks, and Maria Nice Wilks, he was a Wesleyan Minister in Transvaal South Africa in 1905 and became a Chaplain to the Forces in 1915. He was awarded the Military Cross, London Gazette 14th November 1916 page 11044. "for conspicuous gallantry and devotion to duty. He tended the wounded for 48 hours under very heavy fire, displaying great courage and determination." He is listed as being killed in action. Records indicate that he was killed by a shell, while rescuing the wounded near Poelcapelle, Belgium, on the 4th October 1917 aged 35. He is buried in Bard Cottage Cemetery, Belgium, Grave Reference V.A.1. and remembered on the Memorial in Beverley Minster and the Aldershot Memorial.

The Revd. Harold William WOOD
Chaplain 4th Class
Army Chaplains' Department.
Attached Royal Garrison Artillery 282 Siege Battery.

The son of the Revd. Arthur William, and Sarah Ann Wood, he studied at Bristol Baptist College, where he obtained a B.A. He was a Baptist Minister at Sheppard's Barton, Frome, from 1913 to 1918. He served with the YMCA at Salonika, and became a Temporary Chaplain to the Forces in 1918. The husband of Mrs. H. F. Wood, of Woodside, Alum Chine Road, Bournemouth, he died in France on the 1st November 1918 aged 31. He is buried in Terlincthun British Cemetery, Wimille, Pas de Calais, France, Grave Reference VI.F.45. and remembered on the Aldershot Memorial.

The Revd. Disney Charles WOODHOUSE
Chaplain 4th Class
Army Chaplains' Department.
Attached Royal Sussex Regiment 12th Battalion.

The son of The Revd. Arthur Chorley and Mrs. Woodhouse, of Pampisford Vicarage, Cambridge, he studied at Clare College, Cambridge, where he obtained a B.A. (2nd cl. Th. Trip) in 1905: Carus Gr. Test Prize in 1906, and an M.A. in 1909. He trained for the Priesthood at Ridley Hall, Cambridge, in 1905, obtaining a 1st cl. Prelim T.E. in 1906 at the University of Durham, and a B.D. in 1911. He was made a Deacon in 1906 and Ordained Priest by the Bishop of Birmingham in 1907. He was Curate of Aston-juxta, Birmingham, from 1906 until 1909; Lecturer at Bishop Wilson Theological School, Isle of Man, 1909 to 1911; Vice Principal. Bishop Wilson Theological School, Isle of Man, 1911 to 1912; Diocesan Chaplain to the Bishop of Sodor and Man, 1909 to 1913; Principal Bishop Wilson Theological School, Isle of Man 1913; Vicar of St. Ninian's, Douglas, Isle of Man, 1913; Examining Chaplain to the Bishop of Sodor and Man, 1913. He died, in France, on the 6th October 1916 aged 32. He is buried in Boulogne Eastern Cemetery, Pas de Calais, France, Grave Reference VII.A.5. and remembered on the Ridley Hall and Aldershot Memorials.

THE COMMONWEALTH

In Christ there is no East or West,
In him no South or North,
But one great fellowship of love
Throughout the whole wide earth.

John Oxenham 1852 - 1941.

The contribution made by Armed Forces of what is now the Commonwealth played an important part and should not be underestimated. They were involved in every theatre of war and some had their own Chaplaincy Departments.

Chaplain casualties from the Indian Army and East African units listed do not include attached Chaplains from the Army Chaplains' Department.

AUSTRALIAN ARMY'S CHAPLAINS' DEPARTMENT
WORLD WAR I

The Revd. Albert Edward BATES
Chaplain 4th Class
Australian Army Chaplains' Department.
Attached 3rd Australian Auxiliary Hospital.

The son of William Henry and Christina Bates, he was a native of Burwood, Sydney, and a Presbyterian Minister. He enlisted on the 30th September 1918 from Ashford Manse, Inverell, New South Wales. He was the husband of C. M. E. Bates, of Woodland Avenue, Pymble, nr. Sydney, and died on the 9th February 1919 aged 34. He is buried in Brookwood Military Cemetery, United Kingdom, Grave Reference IV.K.8.

The Revd. Michael BERGIN, MC
Chaplain 3rd Class
Australian Army Chaplains' Department.

The son of Mrs. Bergin, of "Fancroft" Roscrea, Ireland, he was a Church of England Priest, and a school teacher at the Holy Family College, Fagala, Cairo, Egypt. He enlisted on the 13th May 1915, and died, in Belgium on the 12th October 1917. He is buried in Renninghelst Churchyard Extension, Belgium, Grave Reference 1.

The Revd. John Kemp BRUCE
Chaplain 4th Class
Australian Army Chaplains' Department.
Attached 3rd Australian Hospital.

He was a Presbyterian Minister who enlisted on the 1st November 1917 at Wahroonga, New South Wales. The husband of Mrs. B. Lecate, Dragon Street, Warwick, Queensland, he died of influenza at sea, on the 9th February 1918 aged 38, and is remembered on the Hollybrook Memorial, Southampton, United Kingdom.

The Revd. John DEMPSEY
Chaplain, Australian Army Chaplains' Department.

The son of Patrick and Martha Dempsey, he was born in Belfast, Ireland, and was a Congregational Minister. He enlisted at Burwood, New South Wales on the 20th November 1916. He was the husband of Lily E. Dempsey, of Ethel Street, Burwood, New South Wales, and died of pneumonia on the 13th June 1917 aged 36. He is buried in the Cairo War Memorial Cemetery, Egypt, Grave Reference F. 262.

The Revd. William James DUNBAR. 1889.
Chaplain 4th Class
Australian Army Chaplains' Department.
Attached 11th, Australian Light Horse.

The son of William and Victoria Matilda Dunbar, of 88 Lord Street, Orange, New South Wales, he was a Methodist Minister, and enlisted on the 14th September 1915. He died on the 7th November 1917 aged 37. He is buried in Gaza War Cemetery, Israel, Grave Reference XII. E. 3.

The Revd. Andrew GILLISON
Chaplain 4th Class
Australian Army Chaplains' Department.

The son of John Gillison and his wife, Jane Brootch, he was a native of Scotland and a Presbyterian Minister. He enlisted from St. George's Manse, St. Kilda, Victoria on the 23rd October 1914. He was the husband of Isobel Gillison, of "St. Andrew's" Burke Road, Upper Hawthorn, Victoria, Australia. Mentioned in Despatches, he died of wounds on the 22nd August 1915 aged 47. He is remembered on the Special Memorial Reference B. 62. at Embarkation Pier Cemetery, Turkey.

The Revd. Alfred Ernest GOLLER
Chaplain 4th Class
Australian Army Chaplains' Department.

The son of John George Martin Goller and Matilda Goller, he was a Church of England Priest. He enlisted on the 16th January 1917 at Lancefield, Victoria. He was the husband of Hilda Goller, of 81 South Road, Brighton Beach, Victoria, Australia, and died on the 29th September 1918 aged 35. He is buried in Templeux-le-Guerard British Cemetery, France, Grave Reference II. F. 29.

The Revd. David de Venny HUNTER
Chaplain 4th Class
Australian Army Chaplains' Department.
Attached 55th Battalion, Australian Infantry, A.I.F.

The son of George and Jane Hunter (nee De Venny), he was born in Ireland. A Methodist Minister, he enlisted from the Parsonage, Ballina, New South Wales on the 24th August 1916. He was the husband of Marion Hunter, of "Girrawheen", Pyrmont Street, Ashfield, New South Wales. He was killed in action, on the 28th September 1917 aged 41. He is buried in Hooge Crater Cemetery, Belgium, Grave Reference II.F.16

The Revd. Spencer Edward MAXTED
Chaplain 4th Class
Australian Army Chaplains' Department.
Attached 54th Battalion Australian Infantry A.I.F.

The son of the late Henry Edward and Alice Rachael May Maxted, he was born at Sydney. He studied at the Australian College of Theology in 1903 (L. Th. 1st Cl.) and at Trinity College, Melbourne, where he obtained a B.A. and won the Bromby Prize in 1909, and an M.A. in 1911. He obtained a B.D. from the University of London in 1911. He was made a Deacon in 1907 and Ordained Priest by the Archbishop of Melbourne in 1908. He was Curate of St. Andrew's, Clifton Hill from 1907 to 1909, and Ferntree, Guly, to 1910, and Christ Church, St. Kilda in 1910, in the Diocese of Victoria. He was appointed Curate of St. Celement's, Marrickville, New South Wales until 1913 and was Minister of St. Oswald, Haberfield, New South Wales and Rector of the Church from 1913 to 1914. Some records indicate that he was 613 Private 1st Field Ambulance reinforcements - 22nd December 1914. Appointed Temporary Chaplain to the Forces in 1915, and is recorded as having enlisted at Marrickville, Sydney on the 9th November 1915. He was killed between the 19th and 20th of July 1916. The husband of Gertrude 0. Maxted, of Corner Merrivale Road, and Nithsdale Street, Pymble, New South Wales, he is buried in Rue-Petillon Military Cemetery, Fleurbaix, France, Grave Reference I. K. 2.

The Revd. Alfred METTERS
Chaplain 1st Class
Australian Army Chaplains' Department.

The husband of Mrs. O. G. Metters, of Melbourne. He died on the 1st March 1918 and is buried in Adelaide (West terrace) Cemetery, Grave Reference Gen.LN.6. 14E/5E. (GRM/5*).

The Revd. William Johnstone STEVENS
Chaplain 3rd Class
Australian Army Chaplains' Department.
Attached. 5th, Australian Infantry Brigade.

The son of William John and Susannah Marian Stevens, he was a native of Wycombe, England. A widower, and a minister of the Presbyterian Church, he enlisted at Bathurst, New South Wales, on the 19th April 1915. He died on the 15th November 1917 aged 49. He is buried in Brookwood Military Cemetery, England, Grave Reference. XI. B. 18.

The Revd. Fr. Edward John SYDES
Chaplain Australian
Army Chaplains' Department.
Attached Field Ambulance Brigade.

The son of Samuel George and Rosanna Sydes, he died of sickness on the 15th November 1918 aged 55. He is buried in Kensal Green (St. Mary's), Roman Catholic Cemetery, United Kingdom, Grave Ref. 2. 3991.

CANADIAN ARMY'S CHAPLAINS' DEPARTMENT
WORLD WAR I

The Revd. Fr. G. E. R. CROCHETIERE
Chaplain 4th Class
Canadian Army Chaplains' Department.
Attached 22nd Battalion Canadian Infantry
(Quebec Regiment).

The son of Alphonse Crochetiere and his wife Josephine Cornier Crochetiere, of Arthabaskaville, P.Q. Canada, he was Ordained a Priest on the 9th July 1905 at Nicolet Seminary. He died on the 2nd April 1918 aged 39, and is buried left of centre path, between two french tombs, in Bailleulmont Communal Cemetery, France.

The Revd. William Henry DAVIS, MC
Chaplain 4th Class
Canadian Army Chaplains' Department.
Attached 4th Canadian Mounted Rifles.
(Central Ontario Regiment).

The son of James and Anne Davis, of Davistown, King's County, Ireland, he died on the 9th August 1918 aged 34, and is buried in Le Quesnel Communal Cemetery, France, Grave Reference 1.

The Revd. Joseph ELLIOTT
Honorary Captain
Canadian Army Chaplains' Department.

The son of the late Thomas Elliott, of Bayfield, Ontario, he died on the 12th December 1919 aged 50. The husband of Eleanor Rose Elliott, of Golerich, Ontario, he is buried in London (Woodland) Cemetery, Canada. Grave Reference Sec. Q. East half of lot 134.

Lieutenant Colonel The Revd. William Henry EMSLEY
Canadian Army Chaplains' Department.

The son of the late Joseph and Elizabeth Emsley, he died of pneumonia on the 15th October 1919 aged 69. The husband of Susie Emsley, of 143, Brock Street East, Oshawa, Ontario, he is buried in Whitevale Cemetery, Canada.

The Revd. Webster Henry Fanning HARRIS
Chaplain 4th Class
Canadian Army Chaplains' Department.
Attached 6th Brigade H.Q., Canadian Infantry.

The son of Robert Fanning Harris and Sarah Maria Longley Harris, he was born at St. Thomas, Ontario. He was the husband of Grace Harris, of Tuscola, Co. Michigan, U.S.A. He died on the 4th May 1917, aged 41, and is buried in Brookwood Military Cemetery, United Kingdom, Grave Reference III.A.8.

The Revd. George Leycester INGLES
Chaplain 4th Class Canadian Army Chaplains'
Department. Attached 3rd Battalion Canadian Infantry.
(Central Ontario Regiment).

The son of Charles Leycester Ingles and his wife, Frances Helen, of 408, Brunswick Avenue, Toronto, Ontario. He died on the 1st January 1915 aged 28, and is buried in Bulford Church Cemetery, United Kingdom, Grave Ref. I. 3. 2.

The Revd. Eric F. JOHNSTON
Chaplain Canadian Army Chaplains' Department.
Attached 2nd Canadian Division.

The son of Joshua Reynolds Johnston and Jennie Poole Johnston, of Carleton Place, Ontario, he died on the 18th November 1918 aged 29. He was the husband of E. F. Johnston, of 509 Palmerston Boulevard, Toronto. He is buried in Etaples Military Cemetery, France, Grave Reference XLV. A.3.

The Revd. Roy Joseph KAIN
Captain Canadian Army Chaplains' Department.

The son of John and Margaret Jane Kain, of Walkerton, Ontario, he died on the 17th October 1918 aged 27. He was the husband of L. H. Kain, of 1637 Washington Avenue, New York, U.S.A. He is buried in Walkertom Cemetery, Canada.

Major The Revd. Robert KER
Canadian Army Chaplains' Department.
Attached H.Q. Welland Canal Force.

The son of the late Robert and Eliza Ker, he died of sickness on the 21st February 1917 aged 75. He was the husband of the late Elizabeth Ker, and is buried in St. Catherine's (Victoria Lawn) Cemetery Canada, Grave Reference Family.

The Revd. Donald George MacPHAIL
Chaplain Canadian Army Chaplains' Department.
Attached 72nd Battalion Canadian Infantry.
(British Columbia Regiment).

The son of Donald and Christina MacPhail, of Perth, Ontario, he drowned from H.S. "Llandovery Castle" on the 27th June 1918 aged 55. He was the husband of Louisa B. MacPhail, of 35 King Street, West Kingston, Ontario, Canada. He is buried in the South-East corner of Lampaul Churchyard, Ile D'Ouessant, France. The H.S. "Llandovery Castle" was a requisitioned Union Castle liner and was an ambulance transport ship. She was bound from Halifax, Nova Scotia, for Liverpool, and was torpedoed at 9-30 p.m. 114 miles south west of the Fastnet Rock. There were 258 on board, including 94 Medical Officers and Nursing Sisters of the Canadian Medical Staff. She was displaying the Regulation Red Cross Lights. There were 24 survivors.

The Revd. John Doole MORROW
Captain Canadian Army Chaplains' Department.
Attached 185th Battalion, Canadian Infantry.

The son of Nancy Morrow, of 32 Barton Avenue, Toronto and the late Hugh Morrow, he died of sickness on the 28th April 1921 aged 47. He was the husband of Edith Lynette Morrow, of 410 Roxton Road, Toronto, Ontario. He is buried in Toronto (Prospect) Cemetery, Canada, Grave Reference Sec. 12. Lot 832.

The Revd. Charles A. SPARLING
Captain (Acting) Canadian Army Chaplains' Department.

The son of Charles Philip and Amelia Sparling, of 15 Edgar Avenue, Toronto, Ontario, he died of pneumonia on the 26th October 1918 aged 37. He was the husband of Mary Elizabeth Sparling, of 292 Bay Street, Hamilton, Ontario, and is buried in Hamilton Cemetery, Canada, Grave Reference Lot 649. Sec. M.6.

EAST AFRICAN ARMY'S CHAPLAINS' DEPARTMENT
WORLD WAR I

The Revd. Noel ALDRIDGE
Capt. Chaplain South African Chaplains' Department
Attached 5th Kaffrarian Rifles

The son of the late Charles Aldridge, F.R.I.B.A., of Birkenhead, he was born in 1879. He was educated at Birkenhead School from1892 to 1897. He studied at Liverpool University where he obtained a B.A. He served in the Boer War as a Sergeant in the Royal Engineers. He returned to England in 1902 and trained for the Priesthood at Lichfield Theological College and was Ordained in the same year. He returned to South Africa, and in 1906 he was Vicar of Rodepoort and of Cleveland in 1910. He was Commissioned on the 5th September 1914 and served in the German South West Africa Central Force leaving on the 14th June 1915. Mentioned in Despatches - London Gazette 22nd August 1918, he died on the 7th September 1916

From "Memorials of Old Birkonians 1914-1918"

When the war broke out he took an Army Chaplaincy and served through the campaign in German South-West Africa, being 'mentioned in Despatches.' He was worn out as the result of this campaign and would have come home, but it was important that 'St. George's Home' an orphanage of which he had been appointed 'Head' should be built. At this he worked as bricklayer, joiner, etc., and got everything in order; but three days before the chapel was to be opened he died, after five days' illness. His Bishop, who travelled up specially to be present at his funeral, wrote of him :- 'His death is the biggest blow which the diocese has received for many a long day, and scores of individuals, and I among them, will miss him as a friend more than they can say. . . . He had such very special gifts for the work which he was doing at St. George's Home - gifts, so far as my experience goes, such as you find extraordinarily seldom combined in one man. He was a genius with boys: he combined the sentiment and love of a mother with the sternness and discipline of a father; to his natural gifts for such work he had added, by sheer hard work and study, just that practical capacity for turning his hand to anything that had to be done, from putting up a building to soling a shoe or cooking a dinner, which stood him and his boys in such good stead. And he thought. I always felt about him that he was growing all the time; he was dead keen on becoming a real expert in his particular job, and he bent all his energies to that end. Very level headed and thoroughly sane, an old head on young shoulders, and with it all a humble heart and a very simple and childlike faith in our Blessed Lord.'

The Venerable W. E. A. CHADWICK
Chaplain East African Army's Chaplains' Department.
Archdeacon of Kavirando.

He studied at Trinity College, Dublin, obtaining a B.A. in 1897, and passing the Divinity Test in 1898. He was made a Deacon in 1898 and Ordained Priest by the Lord Bishop of London, in 1899. He served his Title as Curate of St. Matthew's, Fulham, from 1898 until 1900. He joined The Church Missionary Society (C.M.S.) as a Missionary and served at Bukedi 1901-02; Simgo 1903-05; Entebbe 1905-07; Bugala 1907-08; Entebbe 1909-1912; Kisumu 1912; Maseno 1914(last six months in Uganda); C.M.S. at Butere Mumias, Diocese of Uganda. He was on Furlough 1902-03, 1908-09, and 1913-14. Returning to Uganda in 1915, he became Archdeacon of Kavirando. Records show that he was a Despatch Rider with the Uganda Rifle Corps. He died in German East Africa while serving with the Military Labour Bureau (formerly Carrier Corps) on the 30th September 1917. Harry Fecitt recalls that "churchmen played a significant role in caring for the Africans who worked as carriers, especially the Bishop of Zanzibar". He is buried in Dar es Salaam War Cemetery, Tanzania, Grave Reference 4.B.10. and remembered on the Aldershot Memorial.

See *Uganda Volunteers and the War* by C. J. Phillips published in Kampala 1917. pp.51 & 59.

The Revd. Fr. DAWUDU
Chaplain 516 Nigerian Regiment W.A.A.F

A Roman Catholic Priest, he died on the 4th August 1917 and is remembered on the Ibadan Memorial

The Revd. John Frederick Christopher FIXSEN
United Mission to Central Africa. German East Africa.

The son of The Revd. John Frederick Fixsen, one time Vicar of Bucknell, with Buckton, Salop, he was born on the 17th January 1880 at Ugborough, Devon. Educated at Bradfield School, he studied at Pembroke College, Cambridge, where he obtained a B.A. in 1902 and an M.A. in 1905. He trained for the Priesthood at Cuddesdon College, Oxford in 1902 and was made a Deacon in 1903. Ordained Priest in 1904 by the Bishop of Peterborough, he was Curate of Kettering from 1903 until 1907 and Bucknell with Buckton until 1910. He joined the United Mission to Central Africa, at Luwatala, German East Africa from 1910 and was at Kigongoi, South East Africa, Tanga. in the Diocese of Zanzibar from 1913. He was interned in a POW Camp in German East Africa. Harry Lecitt states that "The British Churchmen who worked under the Bishop of Zanzibar on the mainland were in a bad position when war was declared. They were interned as enemy aliens". Survivors recall that despite severe privation he acted as Chaplain to those interred and held prisoner. He died, probably of typhoid, on the 26th December 1915. The Notice in The Times shows date of death as 25th December 1915. Details of this man are to be found in the records of Cuddesdon College, Oxford.

He was remembered on the Cuddesdon College, Oxford Memorial.

INDIAN ARMY'S CHAPLAINS' DEPARTMENT
WORLD WAR I

The Revd. James GANDAMALL
Assistant Chaplain Indian Army Chaplains' Department.

He died of pneumonia on the 10th October 1918 and is buried in Basra War Cemetery, Iraq, Grave Ref. I. P. 12. Exhaustive searches have failed to reveal any additional information.

NEW ZEALAND ARMY'S CHAPLAINS' DEPARTMENT
WORLD WAR I

The Revd. Alexander ALLEN
48144. Chaplain 4th Class
New Zealand Chaplains' Department.
Attached 4th Battalion 3rd New Zealand Rifle Brigade.

The son of Joseph and Annie Allen, and the husband of Eva Allen, of Wai-iti Avenue, Wai-iti Road, Timaru, New Zealand. He died on the 8th May 1918 aged 34. He is buried in Doullens Communal Cemetery Extension No.2, France, Grave Reference I. B. 32.

The Revd. Guy Spencer BRYAN - BROWN
41286 Chaplain 4th Class
New Zealand Chaplains' Department.
Canterbury Regiment 3rd Battalion 21st Reinforcements.

He was the second son of Grace Margaret Bryan-Brown (nee Nash), of Lydgate, Boar's Hill, Oxford, England, and the late Revd. Willoughby Bryan - Brown, former Vicar of St. Stephens, Eastbourne. He was born in 1885 at Amberley, Stroud, Gloucestershire. Educated at Tonbridge School, from 1899 to 1904, he was a Classical Exhibitioner at Downing College, Cambridge, where he obtained a B.A. 3rd Class Th. Trip in 1907, and an M.A. in 1911. After study at Ridley Hall, Cambridge, he was made a Deacon in 1909 by the Lord Bishop of London for St. Andrews. Ordained Priest by the Bishop of St. Andrews in 1911. From 1908 to 1913 he was Assistant Master at Trinity College, Glenalmond, Perthshire, in the Diocese of St. Andrews, and Chaplain to the College from 1911 to 1913. He went to New Zealand, and was Chaplain to Christ's College in the City and Diocese of Christchurch. He became a Chaplain to the Forces with the New Zealand Expeditionary Force, and was killed in action, on the 4th October 1917 aged 32. He is remembered on the Tyne Cot Memorial, Belgium, Reference N.Z. Apse, Panel 9, and in a stained glass window in Christ's College, Christchurch, New Zealand, and the Ridley Hall Memorial, Cambridge.

Captain The Revd. John Robert BURGIN
18/29 New Zealand Chaplains' Department.
3rd/4th Rifle Brigade.

The son of John and Arm Burgin, he was born on the 10th October 1869 at Long Bennington, Grantham, Lincolnshire, England. Educated at Grantham Church School, and at Nottingham, he was a Church Army Officer from 1889 to 1892; SPG Lay Missionary at Macloutsie, Matabeleland in 1892; CMS Lay Missionary with Bishop Tugwell of Hausaland from 1899 to 1901. He studied at Bishop Wilson Theological School, Douglas, Isle of Man in 1901, and was made a Deacon in 1903 by the Bishop of Lagos and Hausaland for the West Equatorial Africa Mission. Ordained Priest by the Bishop of Sodor and Man in 1904. Due to ill health he was Curate at Peel, Isle of Man, from 1903 to 1905; St. Georges, Douglas, Isle of Man from 1905 to 1906; Vicar of Partree, Co. Antrim, in the diocese of Connor 1906 to 1907;

St. Budeaux, Davenport, in the Diocese of Exeter 1907 to 1909, and was a Chaplain to the Forces. He went to Wellington, New Zealand, in March 1909, and held a Parochial Curacy in the District of Havelock, in the Diocese of Nelson, with permission to officiate in the Diocese of Wellington. He was Assistant Curate of St. Mary's Cathedral, Auckland, from 1910 to 1911; Member of the Church Army Mission of Help at Cambridge, Waikato in 1910; Vicar of Epsom, in the Diocese of Auckland from 1911 to 1912; Vicar of Asburton, in the Diocese of Christchurch from 1912 to 1915. He became a Chaplain to the Forces serving in Egypt in 1916, and then on the Western Front. In 1917, on returning to New Zealand, he was Hon. Assistant Curate at St. Mary's Cathedral, Auckland, and Chaplain to returning soldiers. In 1919 he was appointed Vicar of Onehunga, in the Diocese of Auckland. He was the husband of Henrietta Jane Burgin (nee Woolcombe), of 17 Arcadia Road, Epsom, Auckland. He died on the 2nd December 1920 of a heart attack, aged 51, having been gassed on the Somme. He is buried in Purewa Public Cemetery, Auckland, New Zealand, Grave Ref. Block A, Row 28, Grave 6.
(New Zealand records show his parents as William and Elizabeth)

Captain The Revd. Fr. Patrick DORE, MC
13/655. New Zealand Chaplains' Department.

The son of M. Dore, of Ballylionare, Newcastle West, Co. Limerick, Ireland, he died on the 15th July 1918 aged 33, and is buried in Foxton Cemetery, New Zealand.

The Revd. William GRANT
11/86. Chaplain (Major.) New Zealand
Chaplains' Department.
Attached Main Body Wellington Mounted Rifles. N.Z.E.F.

The son of the late Mr. and Mrs. George Grant, of Ormondville, he was born at Kirriemuir, Scotland. Mentioned in Despatches, he was the husband of Isabella Grant, of Lancaster Street, Karori, Wellington. He died on the 28th August 1915 aged 56. He is remembered on Hill 60 (New Zealand) Memorial, Turkey.

Lieut. Col. The Revd. John Aldred LUXFORD CMG
8/307A. New Zealand Chaplains' Department.

Born at Wellington, the son of Charles Edward and Elizabeth Ellen Luxford (nee Fairhall), he served in the South African Campaign (1902); Egypt, 1914 to 1915, and at Gallipoli. He was twice Mentioned in Despatches. The husband of Emma A. M. Luxford, of "Chunuk Bair", 2 Burwood Crescent, Remuera, Auckland. He died on the 28th January 1921 aged 66, and is buried in Waikaraka Park Cemetery, New Zealand, Grave Reference Area 1, Block H. Grave 128.

Captain The Revd. Cecil Alfred MALLETT
70779 New Zealand Chaplains' Department.

The son of Alfred Sidney and Emma Ann Mallett, he was born at Willesden Green, St. Marylebone, London on the 27th November 1880. Educated at Kentish Town High School, and Stroud Green Grammar School, he began work as an insurance clerk. He studied at the University of Durham, where he obtained a L.Th. in 1910, and then at St. Augustine's College, Canterbury. He was made a Deacon in 1910 and Ordained Priest by the Bishop of Rochester in 1911. He was Curate of Aylesford, Kent, from 1910 to 1912. He went to New Zealand and was Home Missioner at Ohura District, in the Diocese of Auckland to 1915, and Curate in Charge and subsequently Vicar, of Morrinsville. He became a Chaplain to the Forces in January 1918, and died of accidental injuries, following a fire, on the 30th September 1918 aged 37. He was the husband of May Mallett, who returned to England and resided at 60 Bexley Lane, Crayford, Kent, England. He is buried in Etaples Military Cemetery, France, Grave Reference XLVIII. A. 2.

The Revd. Fr. James Joseph McMENAMIN
6/1215. Chaplain New Zealand Chaplains' Department.
Attached 2nd Battalion Canterbury Regiment. N.Z.E.F.

He was killed in action on the 9th June 1917, and is buried in Nieppe Communal Cemetery, France, Grave Reference Cures' vault under Crucifix.

The Revd. Frederick RANDS
42884. Chaplain 4th Class New Zealand
Chaplains' Department.
Attached 1st Battalion Auckland Regiment. N.Z.E.F.

The son of Henry and Emma Rands, he died of sickness on the 14th February 1919 aged 35. He was the husband of Dorothy M. Rands, of Old Kaiwarra Road, Ngaio, Wellington, New Zealand, and is buried in Cologne Southern Cemetery, Germany, Grave Reference I. E. 11.

Captain The Revd. Charles Edward O'Hara TOBIN
18/4. New Zealand Chaplains' Department.

He was born at New Plymouth, and the husband of E. Tobin, of Hikurangi Maori College, Carterton. He died on the 20th March 1921 aged 42, and is buried in Masterton Cemetery, New Zealand, Grave Reference Plot 2782.

SOUTH AFRICAN ARMY'S CHAPLAINS' DEPARTMENT
WORLD WAR I

Captain The Revd. George Thornhill COOK
Chaplain South African Infantry 3rd Regiment.

He was the son of Mr. J. Thornhill Cook and Mrs. S. S. Cook of 36 St. Mark's Road, East London, Cape Province and believed to be a Methodist Minister. South African Records indicate that he was serving with the South African Field Ambulance at the time of his death. Correspondence with his executrix in 1920 claimed that he was serving with the 3rd South African Infantry. He was killed in action, in France, on the 11th July 1916 aged 41. He is remembered on the Thiepval Memorial Pier and Face 4 C. and the Aldershot Memorial.

The Revd. C. J. DAMBUSA
Chaplain South African Native Labour Corps

Born in 1868 he was a Presbyterian Minister and served in France, he died on the 24th May 1920.

The Revd. KONI LUHLONGWANA
(also known as Koni G. Hlongwana/Luhlongwane T.E.)
Chaplain 9580 "C" Company 5th Battalion
South African Native Labour Corps.

He drowned on the 21st February 1917 while on board the Troop Transport Mendi and is remembered on the Hollybrook Memorial Southampton. The Mendi was sailing from Cape Town bound for Le Harve. After leaving Plymouth in thick mist some 12 miles off St. Catherine's Point, Isle of Wight, she was in collision with the 11,000 ton liner SS Darro and sank with the loss of 607 Officers and men of the Native Battalion and 29 crew, almost one third of the names on the Memorial. Further details can be found in *African Voices from Two World Wars* - David Killingray

The Revd. MALAM GARDI
Chaplain Res/281.
Gold Coast Regiment, W.A.F.F.

Listed by the Commonwealth War Graves Commission as a Priest serving with South African Forces, he died on the 18th March 1920 and is remembered on the Kumasi Memorial, Ghana

The Revd. Wilfred Michael MOLTER
Chaplain 4th Class
South African Chaplains' Department.
Attached 1st South African Horse.

The husband of H. M. le Rout (formerly Molter), of Gibeon, South-West Africa, he died on the 24th October 1918, aged 33. He is buried in Karibib Cemetery, Namibia, Grave Ref. 132.

EPILOGUE

Many Chaplains survived having carried out their duties in similar fashion
to those recorded. Much of what they did is documented in other places.

The final words are those chosen by Rudyard Kipling who,
like thousands of others, mourned.
They are to be found on some CWGC headstones across the world.

Their Glory shall not be blotted out

Ecclesiasticus 44:13.

INDEX OF CHAPLAINS WHO DIED

ABBOTT William David;
died 3.12.18; buried Janval Cemetery, Dieppe, France.
ACTON Armar Edward;
died 4.11.17; buried Wimereux Communal Cemetery, France.
AINLEY Frederick William;
died 5.12.18; buried Terlincthun British Cemetery, Wimille, France.
AINLEY William Preston;
died 12.10.15;
ALDRIDGE Noel; East Africa.
died 7.9.16.
ALLEN Alexander; New Zealand.
died 8.5.18; buried Doullens Communal Cemetery Extension No.2, France.
ASH John;
died 7.9.17; buried Vlamertinghe New Military Cemetery, Belgium.
ASHTON Frederick William;
died 18.11.18; buried Sheffield City Road Cemetery.
AVENT Ernest;
died 25.08.20; buried Fulford Cemetery.

BAILE George William;
died 27.1.18; buried Etaples Cemetery, France.
BAINES Thomas Leo;
died 31.5.18; buried Aire Communal Cemetery, France.
BAIRD James;
died 13.2.19; buried Longuenesse (St. Omer) Souvenir Cemetery, France.
BARKER Edward Walter;
died 18.3.18; buried Achiet le Grand Communal Cemetery Extension, France.
BATES Albert Edward; Australian.
died 9.2.19; buried in Brookwood Military Cemetery, United Kingdom.
BEDALE Charles Lees;
died 8.3.19; buried Histon Road Cemetery, Cambridge, England.
BELCHER R H;
died 25.10.15; buried Lewes Cemetery.
BELL Charles Henry, MC;
died 23.8.18; buried Douchy-Les-Ayette British Cemetery, France.
BENNETT Arnold John, MC;
died 26.1.18; commemorated on Kantara War Memorial Cemetery, Egypt.
BERGIN Michael, MC; Australian.
died 12.10.17; buried Renninghelst Churchyard Extension, Belgium.
BERTINI Umberto Michael;
died 30.9.18; buried Farnborough Abbey RC Churchyard Cemetery, Hampshire, England.
BIRT Henry Norbert;
BISHOP George Bernard Hamilton;
died 27.5.18; buried Soissons Memorial Cemetery France.
BLACK William;
died 10.7.18; buried Terlincthun British Cemetery, Wimille, France.
BLACK William Duncan Thomson;
died 22.8.17; buried Brandhoek New Military Cemetery No 3, Vlamertinghe, Belgium.
BLAKEWAY Philip John Thomas;
died 16.6.15; buried Ismailia War Memorial Cemetery, Egypt.

BODDINGTON Vincent Coke;
died 13.3.17; buried St. Sebastian's Churchyard, Wokingham, Surrey, England.
BOTWOOD Edward Keighltey;
died 28.7.16; buried St. Giles Churchyard, Kilmington, Devon, England.
BROUGH James Stanley Bromfield;
died 11.11.18.
BROWN William;
died 10.3.19; buried Aldershot Military Cemetery, Surrey, England.
BRUCE John Kemp; Australian.
died 9.2.18; Hollybrook Memorial, Southampton, United Kingdom.
BRYAN-BROWN Guy Spencer; New Zealand.
died 4.10.17; Tyne Cot Memorial, Belgium.
BUCK Cyril Bernard Wilson;
died 29.9.18; buried Busigny Communal Cemetery Extension, France.
BURDESS Matthew Forster;
died 18.4.17; buried Villers-Faucon Communal Cemetery, France.
BURGIN John Robert; New Zealand.
died 2.12.20. buried Purewa Public Cemetery, Auckland, New Zealand.
BURNS Joseph Dobson;
died 7.6.18; buried Ebblinghem Military Cemetery, France.

CAPPELL James Leitch;
died 23.1.18; buried Ste Marie Cemetery, Le Havre, France.
CAREY Timothy;
died 27.2.19; buried Audruicq Churchyard and Extension, France.
CHADWICK Walter E A;
died 30.9.17; buried Dar Es Salaam War Cemetery, Tanzania (East Africa Chaplains Dept).
CHEESE William Gerard;
died 7.11.18; buried St. Sever Cemetery Extension, Rouen, France.
CLARKE Stephen;
died 4.10.17; commemorated on Tyne Cot Memorial, Belgium.
CLEAVER Frederick Canning;
died 17.6.17; buried Basra Cemetery, Iraq.
CLEVELAND Frederick Walter, MC;
died 11.10.18; buried St. Sever Cemetery Extension, Rouen, France.
COBHAM Elijah, MC;
died 19.9.17; buried Dar Es Salaam Cemetery, Tanzania.
COLBOURNE Richard Arthur Pell;
died 28.5.18; buried Dainville Cemetery, France.
COLLINS Herbert H. John;
died 9.4.17; buried Cabaret Rouge Cemetery, Souchez, France.
CONDIE George;
died 30.06.18; buried Cathcart Cemetery, Renfrewshire, Scotland.
COOK George Thornhill; South African.
died 11.6.19; Thiepval Memorial.
COOPER-MARSDIN Arthur;
died 16.8.18; buried Thanet.
CORBETT Frederick St. John;
died 14.03.19; buried Ruislip (St. Martin) Churchyard.
COWD ARTHUR Martin;
died 22.12.18; buried Mazargues Cemetery, France.

CRAVEN George Edward;
died 7.12.18; buried Mikra Cemetery, Kalamaria Greece.
CREIGHTON Oswin;
died 15.4.18; buried Choques Cemetery, France.
CROCHETIERE G. E. R.; Canadian.
died 2.4.18; buried Bailleulmont Communal Cemetery, France.

DALLAS William Loraine Seymour;
died 20.9.17; commemorated on Tyne Cot Memorial, Belgium.
DALY John James;
died 17.11.21; after demob.
DAMBUSA C. J.; South African.
died 24.5.20;
DAVIS William Henry, MC; Canadian.
died 9.4.18; buried Le Quesnel Communal Cemetery, France.
DAWUDU; East African.
died 4.8.1917; Ibadan Memorial.
DE VINE Hatton Bertram St. John;
died 27.4.16; buried Vermelles Cemetery, France.
DEEDES Arthur Gordon;
died 29.11.16; buried Brookwood Cemetery, England.
DEMPSEY John; Australian.
died 13.6.17; buried Cairo War Memorial Cemetery, Egypt.
DICKINSON Harry;
died 30.10.17; buried Passchendaele New Cemetery, Belgium.
DORE. Patrick, MC; New Zealand.
died 15.7.18; buried Foxton Cemetery, New Zealand.
DOUDNEY Charles Edmund;
died 16.10.15; buried Lijssenthoek Cemetery, Belgium.
DOYLE Denis;
died 17.8.16; buried Dive Copse Cemetery, France.
DOYLE William Joseph, MC;
died 17.8.17; commemorated on Tyne Cot Memorial, Belgium.
DRANSFIELD HERBERT;
died 1920.
DUGDALE Richard William, MC;
died 24.10.18; buried Caudry Cemetery, France.
DUNBAR William James; Australian.
died 7.11.17; buried Gaza War Cemetery, Israel.
DUNCAN Edward Francis, MC;
died 11.3.17; buried Faubourg D'Amiens Cemetery, Arras, France.
DUNSTAN Sidney;
died 16.7.18; buried Nottingham Road Cemetery, Mansfield, England.
DUVALL John Richard;
died 6.10.17; buried Sarigol Cemetery, Kriston Greece.

EAST Herbert Hinton;
died 5.8.17; commemorated on Menin Gate, Ypres, Belgium.
EDINGER Frank Harrison;
died 26.2.18; commemorated on Hollybrook Memorial, Southampton, England.
EDWARDS Evan;
died 27.2.18; buried Anfield Cemetery, Liverpool, England.
EGAN Pierce John;
died 6.4.16; buried Chatby Cemetery, Egypt.
ELLIOT John Charles;
died 5.10.20; buried Baslow (St. Anne) Churchyard.

ELLIOTT Joseph; Canadian.
died 12.12.19; buried London (Woodland) Cemetery, Canada.
EMSLEY William Henry; Canadian.
died 15.10.19; buried Whitevale Cemetery, Canada.
EVANS Geoffrey Maynard, MC;
died 11.8.17; buried Divisional Collecting Post Cemetery Extension, Boesinghe, Belgium.
EVANS Edward Williams;
died 10.2.19; buried Maker Churchyard Cemetery, Cornwall, England.
EYRE - POWELL John William Alcock;
died 16.4.18; commemorated on Tyne Cot Memorial, Belgium.

FALSIDE William James;
died 7.10.18; buried Faenza Communal Cemetery, Italy.
FINCH Henry Kingsley;
Medically Boarded 1916 Aldershot Memorial.
FINN William Joseph;
died 25.4.15; buried V Beach Cemetery, Gallipoli.
FISHER Oswald Garrow;
died 4.11.20; buried Baghdad North Gate War Cemetery, Iraq.
FITZGIBBON John J. MC;
died 18.9.18; buried Trefcon Cemetery, France.
FIXSEN John Frederick Christopher;
died 26.12.15;
FRASER Donald, DSO;
died 2.6.18; buried Couin New Cemetery, France.
FREESTONE William Herbert;
died 14.12.16; buried Mukra Cemetery, Kalamaria, Greece.
FULFORD Reginald Hardwick;
died 15.12.16; buried Basra Cemetery, Iraq.

GANDAMALL James; Indian Army.
died 10.10.18; buried Basra War Cemetery, Iraq.
GARRETT Charles Harold;
died 26.9.17; buried Brandhoek New Cemetery No 3, Vlamertinghe, Belgium.
GEARE William Duncan;
died 31.7.17; buried Vlamertinghe New Cemetery, Belgium.
GEDGE Basil Johnson;
died 25.4.17; buried Doiran Military Cemetery, Greece.
GIBBS Edward Reginald;
died 29.3.18; buried Boisieux an Mont Communal Cemetery, France.
GILLISON Andrew; Australian.
died 22.8.15; Special Memorial Embarkation Pier Cemetery, Turkey.
GOLLER Alfred Ernest; Australian.
died 29.9.18; buried in Templeux-le-Guerard British Cemetery, France.
GORDON Michael Patrick;
died 27.8.17; buried Coxyde Cemetery, Belgium.
GRANT William; New Zealand.
died 28.8.15; Hill 60 (New Zealand) Memorial, Turkey.
GREEN Ernest Newham;
died 26.3.16; buried Willesden New Cemetery, Middlesex, England.
GREEN Herbert, MC;
died 24.8.17; buried The Huts Cemetery, Belgium.
GREEN Hugh James Bernard;
died 8.12.18; buried Longuenesse Souvenir Cemetery, St. Omer, France.

GREER Richard Ussher;
died 23.6.15;
GRIFFITHS David Howell;
died 15.12.17; buried Usk (St. Mary Magdalene) Churchyard.
GROBEL Peter;
died 1.1.17; buried Boulogne Eastern Cemetery, France.
GUNSON Henry Edward;
died 23.8.18; buried Christ Church Portsdown, England.
GUTHRIE David Michall;
died 1.11.16; buried Varennes Cemetery, France.
GWYNN John;
died 12.10.15; buried Bethune Town Cemetery, France.

HALL Henry Armstrong, CBE;
died 12.05.21; buried Methley (St. Oswald) Churchyard.
HARBORD Frank Robert;
died 8.8.17; buried Brandhoek New Cemetery, Vlamertinghe, Belgium.
HARDING Wilfred John, MC;
died 31.10.17; commemorated on Tyne Cot Memorial, Belgium.
HARDY James Henry;
died 5.5.18; buried Nine Elms Cemetery, Poperinge, Belgium.
HARDY Theodore Bayley, VC DSO MC;
died 18.10.18; buried St. Sever Cemetery Extension, Rouen, France.
HARRIS Webster Henry Fanning; Canadian.
died 4.5.17; buried Brookwood Military Cemetery, United Kingdom.
HARTIGAN Jeremiah Austin;
died 16.7.16; buried Amara War Cemetery, Iraq.
HATFIELD Arthur Percival;
died 9.7.18; buried Amara War Cemetery, Iraq.
HAWDON Noel Elliot;
died 16.11.18; buried Terlincthun British Cemetery, Wimille, France.
HEADING William Henry;
died 21.11.18; buried Chatteris General Cemetery, Cambridgeshire, England.
HEATH Alfred;
died 30.6.18; buried Toutencourt Communal Cemetery, France.
HEGGIE David;
died 23.10.17; buried Curragh Military Cemetery, Co. Kildare, Ireland.
HENDERSON Robert Morley;
died 3.2.19; buried Belgrade Cemetery, Namur, Belgium.
HEWITT Frederick Whitmore;
died 27.9.15; buried Vermelles Cemetery, France.
HEWITT Sydney Rangeley, OBE;
died 16.2.19; buried Cologne Southern Cemetery, Germany.
HOARE Henry James;
died 5.8.17; buried in India.
HODDER Charles William Ackerman;
died 21.10.18; buried Richmond Cemetery, England.
HOLDEN Oswald Addenbrooke;
died 1.12.17; buried Fifteen Ravine Cemetery, Villers Plouich, France.
HOOD Charles Ivo Sinclair;
died 15.4.18; buried Lijssenthoek Cemetery, Belgium.
HOPKINS R. Wilson;
died 24.4.18; buried Lijssenthoek Cemetery, Belgium.
HOULSTON Edgar Charles;
died 4.5.17; buried Mazargues Cemetery, Marseille, France.

HOWELL Thomas;
died 1.12.17; buried Fifteen Ravine Cemetery, Villers Plouich, France.
HUNTER David de Venny; Australian.
died 28.9.17; buried Hooge Crater Cemetery, Belgium.
HUNTER Philip Needham;
died 14.3.19; buried Shorncliffe Cemetery, Kent, England.

INGLES George Leycester; Canadian.
died 1.1.15; buried Bulford Church Cemetery, United Kingdom.
INGLIS Rupert Edward;
died 18.9.16; commemorated on Thiepval Memorial, France.
IRELAND John Thomas Craig;
died 4.5.17; buried Savona Memorial Cemetery, Italy.

JEFFERYS Charles Thomas Claude;
died 20.11.18; buried St. James' Cemetery, Bath, England.
JENKINS David;
died 6.3.19; buried St. James' Church, Pyle, Glamorgan, Wales.
JOHNSON Ernest Edward;
died 1.12.18; buried Le Cateau Communal Cemetery, France.
JOHNSON-SMYTH Edward;
died 10.2.17; buried St. Sever Cemetery, Rouen, France.
JOHNSTON Eric F; Canadian.
died 18.11.18; buried Etaples Military Cemetery, France.
JONES Basil;
died 25.10.18; buried Ste Marie Cemetery, Le Havre, France.
JONES Thomas Glasfryn;
died 12.4.17; buried St. Ceitho's Cemetery, Llangeitho, Cardigan, Wales.
JONES William Edgar;
died 24.10.18; buried Roisel Communal Cemetery Extension, France.
JONES William Evans;
died 8.10.18; buried Prospect Hill Cemetery, Gouy, France.
JONES-ROBERTS Peter;
died 23.6.21; buried Bangor (Glanadda) Cemetery.
JUDD Alan Cecil, MC;
died 21.3.18; commemorated on Arras Memorial France.

KAIN Roy Joseph; Canadian.
died 17.10.18; buried Walkertom Cemetery, Canada.
KAVANAGH Bernard;
died 21.12.17; buried Jerusalem War Cemetery, Israel.
KAY William Henry, MC;
died 5.4.18; buried Mazingarbe Communal Cemetery Extension, France.
KELLIE John;
died 1.8.17; commemorated on Menin Gate, Ypres, Belgium.
KER Robert; Canadian.
died 21.2.17; buried in St. Catherine's (Victoria Lawn) Cemetery Canada.
KIRK James, MC;
died 1.4.18; buried Wimereux Communal Cemetery, France.
KIRWAN Robert Mansel;
died 23.05.16; buried Kensington (Hanwell) Cemetery.
KNAPP Simon Stock, DSO, MC;
died 1.8.17; buried Dozinghem Cemetery, Belgium.
KONI LUHLONGANA; South African.
died 21.2.17; Hollybrook Memorial.

LANGDON Cecil;
died 31.10.17; buried Gwalia Cemetery, Poperinge, Belgium.
LAWSON Henry Heaton;
died 24.3.18; buried Fouquescourt British Cemetery, France.
LEAKEY Herbert Nettleton;
died 27.7.17; buried Dar es Salaam Cemetery, Tanzania.
LEDBITTER Herbert Peter;
died 28.2.17; buried Le Treport Cemetery, France.
LEESON James Thomas;
died 23.4.17; buried Point-Du-Jour Cemetery, Athies, France.
LENDRUM James Herbert Reginald;
died 22.8.18; buried Bienvillers Cemetery, France.
LESTER Gerald James;
died 16.12.18; buried St. Sever Cemetery. Extension, Rouen, France.
LONGRIDGE Archibald Owen Carwithen;
died 12.10.18; buried Topsham Cemetery Devon, England.
LOOBY Patrick;
died 3.10.16; buried Poelcapelle Cemetery, Belgium.
LUXFORD John Aldred, CMG. New Zealand.
died 28.1.21; buried Waikaraka Park Cemetery, New Zealand.

MACE Alban Bodley;
died 3.10.16; buried Struma Cemetery, Greece.
MACGREGOR John Campbell;
died 4.11.16; buried Janval Cemetery, Dieppe, France.
MACPHAIL Donald George; Canadian.
died 27.6.18; buried Lampaul Churchyard, Ile D'Ouessant, France.
MAJOR Charles William Wykeham;
died 19.3.19; buried Cologne Southern Cemetery, Germany.
MALAM GARDI; Gold Coast / South African Forces.
died 18.3.20; Kumasi Memorial.
MALLETT Cecil Alfred; New Zealand.
died 30.9.18; buried Etaples Military Cemetery, France.
MARONA Charles Antonio;
died 28.02.15; buried Hurstpierrpoint (Holy Trinity) Churchyard.
MARTYN Cecil Radcliffe;
died 3.3.19; buried St. Sever Cemetery Extension, Rouen, France.
MATTHEWS Lewis Joseph;
died 25.5.16; buried Kensal Green RC Cemetery, England.
McAULIFFE Cornelius (Raphael);
died 6.10.16; buried St. Lawrence's Catholic Cemetery, Limerick, Ireland.
McDONNELL John Joseph;
died 9.4.18; buried Beuvry Communal Cemetery Extension, France.
McGINITY Henry Cuthbert;
died 8.11.18; buried Giavera British Arcade Cemetery, Italy.
McILVAINE John Joseph;
died 26.2.18; commemorated on Hollybrook Memorial, Southampton, England.
McMENAMIN James Joseph; New Zealand.
died 9.6.17; buried Nieppe Communal Cemetery, France.
McMURTRIE Stanley Gibson;
died 14.06.19; buried Egremont (St. John) Churchyard.
MAXTED Spencer Edward; Australian.
died19/20.7.16; buried in Rue-Petillon Military Cemetery, Fleurbaix, France.
MEISTER Charles Gustave Clark, MC;
died 18.4.18; buried La Clytte Military Cemetery, Belgium.
METTERS Alfred; Australian.
died 1.3.18; buried Adelaide (West Terrace) Cemetery.

MILLAR George;
died 26.8.17; buried Boulogne Eastern Cemetery, France.
MITCHELL Charles Wand;
died 3.5.17; buried Fauberg d'Amiens Cemetery, Arras, France.
MOLTER Wilfred Michael; South African.
died 24.10.1918; Karibib Cemetery, Namibia.
MONTAGU Walter Philip;
died 31.10.18; buried Awoingt Cemetery, France.
MONTEITH Robert John;
died 27.1.17; buried Ribecourt Cemetery, France.
MOORE Edgar Noel, MC;
died 5.1.18; buried Railway Dugouts Cemetery, Zillebeke, Belgium.
MORRISON Samuel;
died 24.7.20; buried Manchester Southern Cemetery, England.
MORROW John Doole; Canadian.
died 28.4.21; buried Toronto (Prospect) Cemetery, Canada.

NAIRN James White;
died December 1917.

O'CONOR William Owen;
died 24.1.19; buried Teheran War Cemetery, Iran.
O'DEA Lawrence;
died 4.11.17; buried Crawley Monastery Burial Ground, England.
O'MEEHAN Isodore James;
died 19.12.19; buried Amara War Cemetery, Iraq.
O'RORKE Benjamin Garniss, DSO;
died 25.12.18; buried Falmouth Cemetery, England.
O'SULLIVAN Donald Vincent;
died 5.7.16; buried Bouzincourt Communal Cemetery, France.
OGLE Wilfred Rathmell;
died 1916.
ONSLOW CARLTON William McNiell;
died 5.10.18; Aldershot Memorial.

PARDOE George Southey;
died 15.10.18; buried Jerusalem War Cemetery, Israel.
PEEL Hon. Maurice Berkeley, MC & Bar;
died 14.5.17; buried Queant Road Cemetery, France.
PENNEFATHER Somerset Edward;
died 29.08.17; buried Kensington (Hanwell) Cemetery.
PLUMMER Charles Benjamin;
died 12.3.17; buried Carnoy Cemetery, France.
PLUMPTRE Basil Pemberton, MC;
died 16.7.17; buried La Clytte Military Cemetery, Belgium.
POWLEY Walter Harry;
died 23.2.19; buried Abney Park Cemetery, Stoke Newington, England.
PRATT Arthur Morrell;
died 26.6.17; buried St. Sever Cemetery, Rouen, France.
PRENDERGAST Matthew Vincent;
died 16.9.18; buried Cairo War Memorial Cemetery.

RAINE Foster;
died 7.12.18; buried St. Martin's Churchyard Cemetery, Cornwall, England.
RANDS Frederick; New Zealand.
died 14.2.19; buried Cologne Southern Cemetery, Germany.
RANKINE William Henry;
died 11.7.19; buried Kirkmichael Parish Churchyard, Ayrshire.

RANKING George Harvey;
died 20.11 17; buried Hermies British Cemetery, France.
RAWNSLEY Hardwicke Drummond;
READ Eric Oswald;
died 3.10.18; buried Chapel Corner Cemetery, France.
REED Clifford Hugh, MC;
died 7.6.17; buried Oosttaverne Wood Cemetery, Belgium.
RICHARDS Walter H.;
died 10.02.20; buried Clynnog Fawr (St. Beuno) Churchyard.
ROBERTSON Charles, MC;
died 3.10.18; buried Mikra British Cemetery, Kalamara, Greece.
ROCHE Francis Cavendish;
died 14.11.15; commemorated on Chatby War Memorial Cemetery, Egypt.
RUCK-KEENE Benjamin Corrie;
died 26.9.17; buried Ypres Reservoir Cemetery, Belgium.
RYAN Michael;
died 1.11.16; Kirkee Memorial Cemetery, Poona, India.

SANDERS Samuel John Woodhouse;
died 1916.
SCHOOLING Cecil Herbert;
died 21.6.17; buried Lijssenthoek Cemetery, Belgium.
SHAW James;
SHINE James;
died 21.4.18; buried Boulogne Eastern Cemetery, France.
SHOVEL Thomas Jasper;
died 5.10.18; buried Louverval Cemetery, France.
SMITH Frederick Seaton;
died 15.11.18; buried Terlincthun British Cemetery, Wimille, France.
SMITH Peter George;
Medically Boarded, died 3.12.19.
SPARLING Charles A.; Canadian.
died 26.10.18; buried Hamilton Cemetery, Canada.
SPENCE Alexander, MC;
died 31.3.18; buried Roye New Cemetery, France.
SPINK Hubert Octavius;
died 9.8.16; buried Dive Copse Cemetery, France.
STAUNTON Harvey;
died 14.1.18; buried Baghdad (north gate) Cemetery, Iraq.
STEVENS Silas William;
died 23.10.15.
STEVENS William Johnstone; Australian.
died 15.11.17; buried Brookwood Military Cemetery, England.
STEWART James Robert;
died 2.1.16; buried Bethune Town Cemetery, France.
STEWART Robert Arthur;
died 3.11.17; buried St. Pol Communal Cemetery Extension, France.
STREETEN Basil Robert;
died 1.11.18; buried Don Communal Cemetery, Annoellin, France.
STRICKLAND Joseph;
died 15.7.17; buried Addolorata Cemetery, Malta.
STUART Alexander;
died 24.10.17; buried Ruyaulcourt Cemetery, France.
SULLINGS Stephen John;
died 21.11.15; buried Lodge Hill Cemetery, Birmingham, England.
SUTHERLAND Andrew Neil;
died 16.01.18; buried Glasgow Western Necropolis.

SWEET George Charles Walrond;
died 7.8.19; buried Holy Cross Cemetery, Sampford, Arundel, England.
SYDES Edward John.; Australian.
died 15.11.18; buried Kensal Green (St. Mary's), Roman Catholic Cemetery, England.

TAYLOR William;
died 19.10.16; buried Montrose (Sleepyhillock) Cemetery.
THORPE Thomas J.;
died 20.2.15.
TOBIN Charles Edward O'Hara; New Zealand.
died 20.3.21; buried Masterton Cemetery, New Zealand.
TOMKINS William Henry;
died 28.9.18; buried Cagnicourt Cemetery, France.
TREVOR Ernest Wilberforce;
died 14.11.16; buried Hamel Military Cemetery, France.
TUKE Francis Henry;
died 20.7.16; commemorated on Thiepval Memorial, France.

VERYARD Albert Thomas;
died 28.6.17; buried Roclincourt Cemetery, France.

WALLACE John James;
died 8.11.18; buried Awoingt Cemetery, France.
WATSON Charles;
died 22.7.18; buried Basra Cemetery, Iraq.
WATSON John Edmund Malone, MC;
died 10.4.18; buried Haverskerque Cemetery, France.
WATTERS John A;
died 7.11.18; buried Awoingt Cemetery, France.
WERE Cyril Narramore;
died 9.1.18; buried Outtersteene Communal Cemetery Extension, France.
WHITEFOORD Charles B;
died 30.5.18; buried Bagneux British Cemetery, France.
WILKS Walter Charles, MC;
died 4.10.17; buried Bard Cottage Cemetery, Belgium.
WOOD Harold William;
died 1.11.18; buried Terlincthun British Cemetery, Wimille, France.
WOODHOUSE Disney Charles;
died 6.10.16; buried Boulogne Eastern Cemetery, France.

Cemetery Location and Grave/Memorial Reference of
CHAPLAINS

Australia
ADELAIDE (WEST TERRACE) CEMETERY - South Australia.
METTERS, Alfred; Australian Army Chaplains' Department.
Gen.LN.6.14E/5E. (GRM/5*)

Belgium
BARD COTTAGE CEMETERY - Ieper, West-Vlaanderen.
WILKS, Walter Charles, M C; Army Chaplains' Department. V.A.1.

BELGRADE CEMETERY - Namur.
HENDERSON, Robert Morley; Army Chaplains' Department. B.3.

BRANDHOEK NEW MILITARY CEMETERY - Ieper, West-Vlaanderen.
HARBORD, Frank Robert; Army Chaplains' Department. A.1.

BRANDHOEK NEW MILITARY CEMETERY No.3 - Ieper, West-Vlaanderen.
BLACK, William Duncan Thomson; Army Chaplains' Department. II.A.18.
GARRETT, Charles Harold; Army Chaplains' Department. I.H.27.

COXYDE MILITARY CEMETERY - Koksijde, West-Vlaanderen.
GORDON, Michael Patrick; Army Chaplains' Department. III.C.13.

DIV. COLLECTING POST CEMETERY AND EXTENSION Ieper West-Vlaanderen.
EVANS, Geoffrey Maynard, MC; Army Chaplains' Department.II.E.12.

DOZINGHEM MILITARY CEMETERY - Poperinge, West-Vlaanderen.
KNAPP, Simon Stock, D S O, MC; Army Chaplains' Department. II.C.1.

GWALIA CEMETERY - Ieper, West-Vlaanderen.
LANGDON, Cecil; Army Chaplains' Department. II.E.11.

HOOGE CRATER CEMETERY - Ieper, West-Vlaanderen.
HUNTER, David De Venny; Australian Army Chaplains' Department. II.F.16.

LA CLYTTE MILITARY CEMETERY - Heuvelland, West-Vlaanderen.
MEISTER, Charles Gustave Clark, MC; Army Chaplains' Department. IV.E.1.
PLUMPTRE, Basil Pemberton, MC; Army Chaplains' Department. II.F.36.

LIJSSENTHOEK MILITARY CEMETERY - Poperinge, West-Vlaanderen.
DOUDNEY, Charles Edmund; Army Chaplains' Department. I.A.31.
HOOD, Charles Ivo Sinclair; Army Chaplains' Department. XXVI.FF.9.
HOPKINS, R Wilson; Army Chaplains' Department. XXXI.D.21.
SCHOOLING, Cecil Herbert; Army Chaplains' Department. XIII.A.21.

NINE ELMS BRITISH CEMETERY - Poperinge, West-Vlaanderen.
HARDY, James Henry; Army Chaplains' Department. XI.B.17.

OOSTTAVERNE WOOD CEMETERY - Heuvelland, West-Vlaanderen.
REED, Clifford Hugh, MC; Army Chaplains' Department. I.A.12.

PASSCHENDAELE NEW BRITISH CEMETERY - Zonnebeke, West-Vlaanderen.
DICKINSON, Harry; Army Chaplains' Department. Sp.Mem.5.

POELCAPELLE BRITISH CEMETERY - Langemark-Poelkapelle, West-V.
LOOBY, Patrick; Army Chaplains' Department. VI.E.13.

RAILWAY DUGOUTS BURIAL GROUND - Ieper, West-Vlaanderen.
MOORE, Edgar Noel, MC; Army Chaplains' Department. VII.V.5.

RENINGHELST CHURCHYARD EXTENSION - Poperinge, West-Vlaanderen.
BERGIN, Michael, MC; Australian Army Chaplains' Department 1.

THE HUTS CEMETERY - Ieper, West-Vlaanderen.
GREEN, Herbert, MC; Army Chaplains' Department. III.B.13.

TYNE COT MEMORIAL - Zonnebeke, West-Vlaanderen.
BRYAN-BROWN, Guy Spencer; New Zealand Apse, Panel 9.
CLARKE, Stephen; Army Chaplains' Department. Panel 160.
DALLAS, William Loraine Seymour; Army Chaplains' Department. Panel 160.
DOYLE, William Joseph , MC; Army Chaplains' Department. Panel 160.
EYRE-POWELL, John William Alcock; Army Chaplains' Department. Panel 160.
HARDING, Wilfrid John, MC; Army Chaplains' Department. Panel 160.

VLAMERTINGHE NEW MILITARY CEMETERY - Ieper, West-Vlaanderen.
ASH, John; Army Chaplains' Department. IX.H.6.
GEARE, William Duncan; Army Chaplains' Department. VI.A.1.

YPRES (MENIN GATE) MEMORIAL - Ieper, West-Vlaanderen.
EAST, Herbert Hinton; Army Chaplains' Department. Panel 56.
KELLIE, John; Army Chaplains' Department. Panel 56.

YPRES RESERVOIR CEMETERY - Ieper, West-Vlaanderen.
RUCK-KEENE, Benjamin Corrie; Army Chaplains' Department. I.F.37.

Canada
HAMILTON CEMETERY CANADA
SPARLING Charles A.; Canadian Army Chaplains' Department Lot 649 Sec. M.6.

LONDON (WOODLANDS) CEMETERY CANADA
ELLIOTT Joseph; Canadian Army Chaplains' Department Sec. Q East Lot 134.

ST. CATHERINE'S (VICTORIA LAWN) CEMETERY CANADA
KER Robert; Canadian Army Chaplains' Department, Family Grave.

TORONTO (PROSPECT) CEMETERY CANADA
MORROW John Doole; Canadian Army Chaplains' Department. Sec.12. Lot 832.

WALKERTOM CEMETERY CANADA
KAIN, Roy Joseph; Canadian Army Chaplains' Department.

WHITEVALE CEMETERY CANADA
EMSLEY William Henry; Canadian Army Chaplains' Department.

Egypt
ALEXANDRIA (CHATBY) MILITARY AND WAR MEMORIAL CEMETERY
EGAN, Pierce John; Army Chaplains' Department. Q.568.
ROCHE, Francis Cavendish; Army Chaplains' Department. J.2.

CAIRO WAR MEMORIAL CEMETERY
DEMPSEY, John; Australian Army Chaplains' Department. F.262.
PRENDERGAST, Mathew Vincent ; Army Chaplains' Department. M.179.

ISMAILIA WAR MEMORIAL CEMETERY
BLAKEWAY, Philip John Thomas; Army Chaplains' Department. A.108.

KANTARA WAR MEMORIAL CEMETERY
BENNETT, Arnold John, MC; Army Chaplains' Department. E.135.

France
ACHIET-LE-GRAND COMMUNAL CEMETERY EXTENSION - Pas de Calais.
BARKER, Edward John; Army Chaplains' Department. II.C.13.

AIRE COMMUNAL CEMETERY - Pas de Calais.
BAINES, Thomas Leo; Army Chaplains' Department. III.B.29.

ARRAS MEMORIAL - Pas de Calais.
JUDD, Alan Cecil, MC; Army Chaplains' Department. Panel 10.

AUDRUICQ CHURCHYARD AND EXTENSION - Pas de Calais.
CAREY, Timothy; Army Chaplains' Department. Near West end of Church.

AWOINGT BRITISH CEMETERY - Nord.
MONTAGU, Walter Philip; Army Chaplains' Department. III.A.1.
WALLACE, John James; Army Chaplains' Department. III.E.13.
WATTERS, John A.; Army Chaplains' Department. III.G.9.

BAGNEUX BRITISH CEMETERY, GEZAINCOURT - Somme.
WHITEFOORD, Charles B.; Army Chaplains' Department. II.E.23.

BAILLEULMONT COMMUNAL CEMETERY - Pas de Calais.
CROCHETIERE, G. E. R.; Canadian Army Chaplains' Department. Grave left of centre path between two French tombs.

BETHUNE TOWN CEMETERY - Pas de Calais.
GWYNN, John; Army Chaplains' Department. II.K.6.
STEWART, James Robert; Army Chaplains' Department. II.L.11.

BEUVRY COMMUNAL CEMETERY EXTENSION - Pas de Calais.
McDONNELL, John Joseph; Army Chaplains' Department. II.B.8.

BIENVILLERS MILITARY CEMETERY - Pas de Calais.
LENDRUM, James Herbert Reginald; Army Chaplains' Department. XIX.E.14.

BOISLEUX-AU-MONT COMMUNAL CEMETERY - Pas de Calais.
GIBBS, Edward Reginald; Army Chaplains' Department. 2.

BOULOGNE EASTERN CEMETERY - Pas de Calais.
GROBEL, Peter, Army Chaplains' Department. VII.A.12.
MILLAR, George; Army Chaplains' Department. VII.A.27.
SHINE, James; Army Chaplains' Department. VII.B.40.
WOODHOUSE, Disney Charles; Army Chaplains' Department. VII.A.5.

BOUZINCOURT COMMUNAL CEMETERY - Somme.
O'SULLIVAN, Donal Vincent; Army Chaplains' Department. Right of entrance to the Extension.

BUSIGNY COMMUNAL CEMETERY EXTENSION - Nord.
BUCK, Cyril Barnard Wilson; Army Chaplains' Department. V.C.6.

CABARET-ROUGE BRITISH CEMETERY, SOUCHEZ - Pas de Calais.
COLLINS, Herbert H. John; Army Chaplains' Department. XVII.K.10.

CAGNICOURT BRITISH CEMETERY - Pas de Calais.
TOMKINS, William Henry; Army Chaplains' Department. I.C.7.

CARNOY MILITARY CEMETERY - Somme.
PLUMMER, Charles Benjamin; Army Chaplains' Department. A.5.

CAUDRY BRITISH CEMETERY - Nord.
DUGDALE, Richard William, MC; Army Chaplains' Department. IV.G.22.

CHAPEL CORNER CEMETERY, SAUCHY-LESTREE - Pas de Calais.
READ, Eric Oswald; Army Chaplains' Department. C.3.

CHOCQUES MILITARY CEMETERY - Pas de Calais.
CREIGHTON, Oswin; Army Chaplains' Department. I.P.34.

COUIN NEW BRITISH CEMETERY - Pas de Calais.
FRASER, Donald, D S O; Army Chaplains' Department. A.2.

DAINVILLE BRITISH CEMETERY - Pas de Calais.
COLBORNE, Richard Arthur Pell; Army Chaplains' Department. I.D.1.

DIVE COPSE BRITISH CEMETERY - Somme.
DOYLE, Denis; Army Chaplains' Department. I.C.6.
SPINK, Hubert Octavius; Army Chaplains' Department. II.D.46.

DON COMMUNAL CEMETERY, ANNOEULLIN - Nord.
STREETEN, Basil Robert; Army Chaplains' Department. t I.A.27.

DOUCHY-LES-AYETTE BRITISH CEMETERY - Pas de Calais.
BELL, Charles Henry, MC; Army Chaplains' Department. II.G.10.

DOULLENS COMMUNAL CEMETERY EXTENSION No.2 - Somme.
ALLEN, Alexander; New Zealand Chaplains' Department. I.B.32.

EBBLINGHEM MILITARY CEMETERY - Nord.
BURNS, Joseph Dobson; Army Chaplains' Department. II.D.11.

ETAPLES MILITARY CEMETERY - Pas de Calais.
BAILE, George William; Army Chaplains' Department. XXVIII.E.10.
JOHNSTON, Eric F.; Canadian Army Chaplains' Department. XLV.A.3.
MALLETT Cecil Alfred; New Zealand Army Chaplains' Department. XLVIII.A.2.

FAUBOURG D'AMIENS CEMETERY, ARRAS - Pas de Calais.
DUNCAN, Edward Francis, MC; Army Chaplains' Department. II.F.8.
MITCHELL, Charles Wand; Army Chaplains' Department. IV.E.28.

FIFTEEN RAVINE BRITISH CEMETERY, VILLERS-PLOUICH - Nord.
HOLDEN, Oswald Addenbrooke; Army Chaplains' Department. IV.C.15.
HOWELL, Thomas; Army Chaplains' Department. IV.C.16.

FOUQUESCOURT BRITISH CEMETERY - Somme.
LAWSON, Henry Heaton; Army Chaplains' Department. Iii.A.1.

HAMEL MILITARY CEMETERY, BEAUMONT-HAMEL - Somme.
TREVOR, Ernest Wilberforce; Army Chaplains' Department. II.D.21.

HAVERSKERQUE BRITISH CEMETERY - Nord.
WATSON, John Edmund Malone, MC; Army Chaplains' Department. E.11.

HERMIES BRITISH CEMETERY - Pas de Calais.
RANKING, George Harvey; Army Chaplains' Department. F.3.

JANVAL CEMETERY, DIEPPE - Seine-Maritime.
ABBOTT, William David; Army Chaplains' Department. II.A.1.
CAMPBELL-MACGREGOR, John; Army Chaplains' Department. I.D.5.

LAMPAUL CHURCHYARD, ILE D'OUESSANT - Finistere.
MacPHAIL, Donald George; Canadian Army Chaplains' Department.
South-East corner.

LE CATEAU COMMUNAL CEMETERY - Nord.
JOHNSON, Ernest Edward; Army Chaplains' Department. I.32.

LE QUESNEL COMMUNAL CEMETERY - Somme.
DAVIS, William Henry, MC; Canadian Army Chaplains' Department.
1.

LE TREPORT MILITARY CEMETERY - Seine-Maritime.
LEDBITTER, Herbert Peter; Army Chaplains' Department. Plot 2.
Row O. Grave 3.

LONGUENESSE (ST. OMER) SOUVENIR CEMETERY - Pas de Calais.
BAIRD, James; Army Chaplains' Department. V.F.20.
GREEN, Hugh James Bernard; Army Chaplains' Department. V.E.75.

LOUVERVAL MILITARY CEMETERY, DOIGNIES - Nord.
SHOVEL, Thomas Jasper; Army Chaplains' Department. A.6.

MAZARGUES WAR CEMETERY, MARSEILLES - Bouches-du-Rhone.
COWD, Arthur Martin; Army Chaplains' Department. III.B.57.
HOULSTON, Edgar Charles; Army Chaplains' Department. III.A.18.

MAZINGARBE COMMUNAL CEMETERY EXTENSION - Pas de Calais.
KAY, William Henry, MC; Army Chaplains' Department. III.C.3.

NIEPPE COMMUNAL CEMETERY - Nord.
McMENAMIN, James Joseph; New Zealand Chaplains' Department.
Cures' vault under Crucifix.

OUTTERSTEENE COMMUNAL CEMETERY EXTENSION, BAILLEUL - Nord.
WERE, Cyril Narramore; Army Chaplains' Department. II.D.53.

POINT-DU-JOUR MILITARY CEMETERY, ATHIES - Pas de Calais.
LEESON, James Thomas; Army Chaplains' Department. II.G.14.

PROSPECT HILL CEMETERY, GOUY - Aisne.
JONES, William Evans; Army Chaplains' Department. IV.E.2.

QUEANT ROAD CEMETERY, BUISSY - Pas de Calais.
PEEL, The Hon. Maurice Berkeley, MC and Bar; Army Chaplains'
Department. V.A.31.

RIBECOURT BRITISH CEMETERY - Nord.
MONTEITH, Robert John; Army Chaplains' Department. I.D.11.

ROCLINCOURT MILITARY CEMETERY - Pas de Calais.
VERYARD, Albert Thomas; Army Chaplains' Department. II.C.9.

ROISEL COMMUNAL CEMETERY EXTENSION - Somme.
JONES, William Edgar; Army Chaplains' Department. II.D.25.

ROYE NEW BRITISH CEMETERY - Somme.
SPENCE, Alexander, MC; Army Chaplains' Department. IV.C.17.

RUE-PETILLON MILITARY CEMETERY, FLEURBAIX - Pas de Calais.
MAXTED, Spencer Edward; Australian Army Chaplains' Department.
I.K.2.

RUYAULCOURT MILITARY CEMETERY - Pas de Calais.
STUART, Alexander; Army Chaplains' Department. F.5.

SOISSONS MEMORIAL - Aisne.
BISHOP, George Bernard Hamilton; Army Chaplains' Department
E.135.

ST. POL COMMUNAL CEMETERY EXTENSION - Pas de Calais.
STEWART, Robert Arthur; Army Chaplains' Department. H.3.

ST. SEVER CEMETERY EXTENSION, ROUEN - Seine-Maritime.
CHEESE, William Gerard; Army Chaplains' Department. S.V.G.6.
CLEVELAND, Frederick Walter, MC; Army Chaplains' Department.
S.V.C.2.
HARDY, Theodore Bailey, VC, DSO, MC; Army Chaplains'
Department. S.V.J.1.
MARTYN, Cecil Radcliffe; Army Chaplains' Department. S.V.M.8.

ST. SEVER CEMETERY, ROUEN - Seine-Maritime.
JOHNSON-SMYTH, Edward; Army Chaplains' Department. B.4.11.
PRATT, Arthur Morrell, Army Chaplains' Department Officers,B.8.5.

STE. MARIE CEMETERY, LE HAVRE - Seine-Maritime.
CAPPELL, James Leitch; Army Chaplains' Department. Div.62.I.O.4.
JONES, Basil; Army Chaplains' Department. Div.62.V.N.2.

TEMPLEUX-LE-GUERARD BRITISH CEMETERY - Somme.
GOLLER, Alfred Ernest; Australian Army Chaplains' Department.
II.F.29.

TERLINCTHUN BRITISH CEMETERY, WIMILLE - Pas de Calais.
AINLEY, Frederick William; Army Chaplains' Department. XII.B.23.
BLACK, William; Army Chaplains' Department. I.E.36.
HAWDON, Noel Elliot; Army Chaplains' Department. XI.B.1.
SMITH, Fred Seaton; Army Chaplains' Department. XI.A.29.
WOOD, Harold William; Army Chaplains' Department. VI.F.45.

THIEPVAL MEMORIAL - Somme.
COOK George Thornhill; South African Chaplains' Department. Pier
and Face 4C.
INGLIS, Rupert Edward; Army Chaplains' Department. Pier and Face
4C.
TUKE, Francis Henry; Army Chaplains' Department. Pier and Face
4C.

TOUTENCOURT COMMUNAL CEMETERY - Somme.
HEATH, Alfred; Army Chaplains' Department. II.A.1.

TREFCON BRITISH CEMETERY, CAULAINCOURT - Aisne.
FITZGIBBON, John J., MC; Army Chaplains' Department. B.56.

VARENNES MILITARY CEMETERY - Somme.
GUTHRIE, David Michall; Army Chaplains' Department. I.C.34.

VERMELLES BRITISH CEMETERY - Pas de Calais.
DE VINE, Hatton Bertram St. John; Army Chaplains' Department.
II.G.29.
HEWITT, Frederick Whitmore; Army Chaplains' Department. I.G.31.

VILLERS-FAUCON COMMUNAL CEMETERY - Somme.
BURDESS, Matthew Forster; Army Chaplains' Department. D.50.

WIMEREUX COMMUNAL CEMETERY - Pas de Calais.
ACTON, Armar Edward; Army Chaplains' Department. IV.L.2.
KIRK, James, MC;, Army Chaplains' Department. IV.E.2.

Germany
COLOGNE SOUTHERN CEMETERY - Köln (Cologne), Nordrhein-
Westfal.
HEWITT, Sydney Rangeley, OBE; Army Chaplains' Department
IX.F.22.
MAJOR, Charles William Wykeham; Army Chaplains' Department.
IX.B.9.
RANDS, Frederick; New Zealand Chaplains' Department. I.E.11.

Ghana
KUMASI MEMORIAL
MALAM GARDI, Chaplain, Gold Coast Regiment, W.A.F.F.

Greece
DOIRAN MILITARY CEMETERY
GEDGE, Basil Johnson; Army Chaplains' Department. I.F.17.

MIKRA BRITISH CEMETERY, KALAMARIA
CRAVEN, George Edward; Army Chaplains' Department. 807.
FREESTONE, William Herbert; Army Chaplains' Department. 1891.
ROBERTSON, Charles, MC; Army Chaplains' Department. 421.

SARIGOL MILITARY CEMETERY, KRISTON
DUVALL, John Richard; Army Chaplains' Department. C.443.

STRUMA MILITARY CEMETERY
MACE, Alban Bodley; Army Chaplains' Department. II.H.I.

India
KIRKEE 1914 - 1918 MEMORIAL
RYAN, Michael; Army Chaplains' Department. Face 1.

Iran
TEHRAN WAR CEMETERY
O'CONOR, William Owen; Army Chaplains' Department. V.A.7.

Iraq
AMARA WAR CEMETERY
HARTIGAN, Jeremiah Austin; Army Chaplains' Department. IX.G.19.
HATFIELD, Arthur Percival; Army Chaplains' Department. XIV.C.14.
O'MEEHAN, Isidore James; Army Chaplains' Department. XII.E.3.

BAGHDAD (NORTH GATE) WAR CEMETERY
FISHER, Oswald Garrow; Army Chaplains' Department. VIII.J.9.
STAUNTON, Harvey; Army Chaplains' Department. XX.J.7.

BASRA MEMORIAL
FULFORD, Reginald Hardwick; Army Chaplains' Department. Panel 43.

BASRA WAR CEMETERY
CLEAVER, Frederick Canning; Army Chaplains' Department. II.B.12.
GANDAMALL, James; Assistant Chaplain, Indian Army Chaplains' Department. I.P.12.
WATSON, Charles; Army Chaplains' Department. IV.Q.8.

Ireland, Republic of
CURRAGH MILITARY CEMETERY - County Kildare.
HEGGIE, David; Army Chaplains' Department. 1250.

LIMERICK (ST. LAWRENCE'S) CATHOLIC CEMETERY - County Limerick.
McAULIFFE, Cornelius, (Raphae l); Army Chaplains' Department. 30861.

Israel
GAZA WAR CEMETERY
DUNBAR, William James; Australian Army Chaplains' Department. XII.E.3.

JERUSALEM WAR CEMETERY
KAVANAGH, Bernard; Army Chaplains' Department. Q.82.
PARDOE, George Southey; Army Chaplains' Department. R.106.

Italy
GIAVERA BRITISH ARCADE CEMETERY
McGINITY Henry Cuthbert; Army Chaplains' Department. Plot 5. Row C. Grave 11.

FAENZA COMMUNAL CEMETERY
FALSIDE, William James; Army Chaplains' Department. I.D.2.

SAVONA MEMORIAL
IRELAND, John Thomas Craig; Army Chaplains' Department.

Malta
ADDOLORATA CEMETERY
STRICKLAND, Joseph; Army Chaplains' Department. Ossuary of the Jesuit Fathers.

Namibia
KARIBIB CEMETERY
MOLTER, Wilfred Michael; South African Chaplains' Department.

New Zealand
FOXTON CEMETERY N.Z.
DORE Patrick, MC; New Zealand Army Chaplains' Department.

MASTERTON CEMETERY New Zealand.
TOBIN Charles Edward; New Zealand Army Chaplains' Department Plot 2782.

PUREWA PUBLIC CEMETERY AUCKLAND New Zealand.
BURGIN John Robert; New Zealand Army Chaplains' Department. A.28.6.

WAIKARAKA PARK CEMETERY New Zealand.
LUXFORD John Aldred, CMG; New Zealand Army Chaplains' Department Area 1.H.128.

Nigeria
IBADAN MEMORIAL
DAWUDU Chaplain W.A.A.F.

South Africa (Graves unknown)
ALDRIDGE Noel Chaplain South African Forces.
DAMBUSA C. J. Chaplain South African Native Labour Corps.

Tanzania
DAR ES SALAAM WAR CEMETERY
CHADWICK, Walter E. A.; East African Army's Chaplains' Department. 4.B.10.
COBHAM, Elijah, MC; Army Chaplains' Department 5.A.15.
LEAKEY, Herbert Nettleton; Army Chaplains' Department. 4.C.5.

Turkey
EMBARKATION PIER CEMETERY
GILLISON, Andrew; Australian Army Special Memorial B. 62.

HILL 60 (NEW ZEALAND) MEMORIAL
GRANT, William; New Zealand Chaplains' Department. 8.1.7.

V BEACH CEMETERY
FINN, William Joseph; Army Chaplains' Department. F.4.

United Kingdom
ABNEY PARK CEMETERY - London.
POWLEY, Walter Harry; Army Chaplains' Department. E.4.2.RN.17242.

ALDERSHOT MILITARY CEMETERY - Hampshire.
BROWN, William; Army Chaplains' Department. AG.395.

BANGOR (GLANADDA) CEMETERY - Caernarvonshire.
JONES-ROBERTS, Peter; Army Chaplains' Department. W.C.P.13.

BASLOW (ST. ANNE) CHURCHYARD - Derbyshire.
ELLIOTT, John Charles; Army Chaplains' Department. In South West part.

BATH (ST. JAMES'S) CEMETERY - Somerset.
JEFFERYS, Charles Thomas Claude; Army Chaplains' Department. Y.F.43.

BIRMINGHAM (LODGE HILL) CEMETERY - Warwickshire.
SULLINGS, Stephen John; Army Chaplains' Department. B10.I.143.

BROOKWOOD CEMETERY - Surrey.
DEEDES, Arthur Gordon; Army Chaplains' Department. V.178262.

BROOKWOOD MILITARY CEMETERY - Surrey.
BATES, Albert Edward; Australian Army Chaplains' Department. IV.K.8.
HARRIS, Webster Henry Fanning; Canadian Army Chaplains' Department. III.A.8.
STEVENS, William Johnstone; Australian Army Chaplains' Department. XI.B.18.

BULFORD CHURCH CEMETERY - Wiltshire.
INGLES, George Leycester; Canadian Army Chaplains' Department. I.3.2.

CAMBRIDGE (HISTON ROAD) CEMETERY - Cambridgeshire.
BEDALE, Charles Lees; Army Chaplains' Department. 24 .B.26.

CATHCART CEMETERY - Renfrewshire.
CONDIE, George; Army Chaplains' Department. Q.933.61.

CHATTERIS GENERAL CEMETERY - Cambridgeshire.
HEADING, William Henry; Army Chaplains' Department. B.640.

CLYNNOG FAWR (ST. BEUNO) CHURCHYARD - Caernarvonshire.
RICHARDS, W. H.; Army Chaplains' Department. West of St. Beuno's Chapel.

CRAWLEY MONASTERY BURIAL GROUND - Sussex.
O'DEA, Laurence; Army Chaplains' Department.

EGREMONT (ST. JOHN) CHURCHYARD. - Cheshire.
McMURTRIE, Stanley Gibson; Army Chaplains' Department. South.284.

FALMOUTH CEMETERY - Cornwall.
O'RORKE, Benjamin Garniss, DSO; Army Chaplains' Department. L.B.9.

FARNBOROUGH ABBEY ROMAN CATHOLIC CHURCHYARD - Hampshire.
BERTINI, Umberto Michael; Army Chaplains' Department. North side of Church.

FULFORD CEMETERY - Yorkshire.
AVENT, Ernest; Army Chaplains' Department.

GLASGOW WESTERN NECROPOLIS - Glasgow.
SUTHERLAND, Andrew Neil; Army Chaplains' Department. K.402.

HOLLYBROOK MEMORIAL, SOUTHAMPTON - Hampshire.
BRUCE, John Kemp; Australian Army Chaplains' Department.
EDINGER, Frank Harrison; Army Chaplains' Department.
KONI LUHLONGWAN; South African Native Labour Corps.
McILVAINE, John Joseph; Army Chaplains' Department.

HURSTPIERPOINT (HOLY TRINITY) CHURCHYARD - Sussex.
MARONA, Charles Antonio; Army Chaplains' Department.

KENSAL GREEN (ST. MARY'S) ROMAN CATHOLIC CEMETERY - London.
MATTHEWS, Lewis Joseph; Army Chaplains' Department. Cardinals.2650.
SYDES, Edward John; Australian Army Chaplains' Department. 2.3991.

KENSINGTON (HANWELL) CEMETERY - Middlesex.
KIRWAN, Robert Mansel; Army Chaplains' Department. 166.7 and 8.
PENNEFATHER, Somerset Edward; Army Chaplains' Department. 22.56.21and 222.

KILMINGTON (ST. GILES) CHURCHYARD - Devon.
BOTWOOD, Edward Keightley; Army Chaplains' Department. North of Church Tower.

KIRKMICHAEL PARISH CHURCHYARD, AYRSHIRE - Ayrshire.
RANKINE, William Henry; Army Chaplains' Department. At South-West corner of Church.

LEWES CEMETERY - Sussex.
BELCHER, Robert Henry; Army Chaplains' Department.

LIVERPOOL (ANFIELD) CEMETERY - Lancashire.
EDWARDS, Evan; Army Chaplains' Department. VI.U.1375.

LLANGEITHO (ST. CEITHO) CHURCHYARD - Cardiganshire.
JONES, Thomas Glasfryn; Army Chaplains' Department. New ground, North side.

MAKER (SS. MACRA, MARY AND JULIAN) CHURCHYARD - Cornwall.
EVANS, Edward Williams; Army Chaplains' Department. South of Church.

MANCHESTER SOUTHERN CEMETERY - Lancashire.
MORRISON, Samuel; Army Chaplains' Department. S.CE.4.

MANSFIELD (NOTTINGHAM ROAD) CEMETERY - Nottinghamshire.
DUNSTAN, Sidney; Army Chaplains' Department. A.3414.

METHLEY (ST. OSWALD) CHURCHYARD - Yorkshire.
HALL, Henry Armstrong, CBE; Army Chaplains' Department. In South-East part, near War Memorial.

MONTROSE (SLEEPYHILLOCK) CEMETERY - Angus.
TAYLOR, William; Army Chaplains' Department. D.2.51.

PORTSDOWN (CHRIST CHURCH) CHURCHYARD - Hampshire.
GUNSON, Henry Edward; Army Chaplains' Department.

PYLE (ST. JAMES) CHURCHYARD - Glamorganshire.
JENKINS, David; Army Chaplains' Department. In South-East part.

RICHMOND CEMETERY, SURREY - Surrey.
HODDER, Charles William Ackerman; Army Chaplains' Department. U.4566.

RUISLIP (ST. MARTIN) CHURCHYARD EXTENSION - Middlesex.
CORBETT, Frederick St. John; Army Chaplains' Department. I.75.

SAMPFORD ARUNDEL (HOLY CROSS) CHURCHYARD - Somerset.
SWEET, George Charles Walrond; Army Chaplains' Department.

SHEFFIELD (CITY ROAD) CEMETERY - Yorkshire.
ASHTON, Frederick William; Royal Air Force. Buried in Sheffield General Cemetery. Screen Wall Memorial.

SHORNCLIFFE MILITARY CEMETERY - Kent.
HUNTER, Philip Needham; Army Chaplains' Department. M.744.

ST. MARTIN'S CHURCHYARD - Isles of Scily Cornwall.
RAINE, Foster; Army Chaplains' Department.

TOPSHAM CEMETERY - Devon.
LONGRIDGE, Archibald Owen Carwithan; Army Chaplains' Department. 1.1684.

USK (ST. MARY MAGDALENE) CHURCHYARD - Monmouthshire.
GRIFFITHS, David Howell; Army Chaplains' Department. North-East of Church.

WILLESDEN NEW CEMETERY - Middlesex.
GREEN, Ernest Newham; Army Chaplains' Department. I.340.

WOKINGHAM (ST. SEBASTIAN) CHURCHYARD - Berkshire.
BODDINGTON, Vincent Coke; Army Chaplains' Department. Special Plot 23.

Denominations of Chaplains

(Not all those listed in the Directory appear here. It has not been possible to identify all of the denominations)

ANGLICAN
Comprising the Churches of England, Ireland and Wales and the Episcopal Church of Scotland:
ABBOTT, William David; ACTON, Armar Edward; AINLEY, Frederick William; AINLEY, William Preston; AVENT, Ernest; BAILIE, George William; BAIRD, James; BARKER, Edward Walter; BELCHER, R. H.; BELL, Charles Henry, MC; BENNETT, Arnold John, MC; BISHOP, George Bernard Hamilton; BLAKEWAY, Philip John Thomas; BODDINGTON, Vincent Coke; BOTWOOD, Edward Keightley; BROUGH, James Stanley Bromfield; BROWN, William; BUCK, Cyril Barnard Wilson; CAPPELL, James Leitch; CHEESE, William Gerard; CLEAVER, Frederick Canning; CLEVELAND, Frederick Walter, MC; COBHAM, Elijah, MC; COLBOURNE, Richard Arthur Pell; CORBETT, Frederick St. John; COOPER - MARSDIN, Arthur; CRAVEN, George Edward; CREIGHTON, Oswin; DALLAS, William Loraine Seymour; DEEDES, Arthur Gordon; DE VINE, Hatton Bertram St. John; DICKINSON, Harry; DOUDNEY, Charles Edmund; DRANSFIELD, Herbert; DUGDALE, Richard William, MC; DUNCAN, Edward Francis, MC; DUNSTAN, Sidney; DUVALL, John Richard; EAST, Herbert Hinton; EDINGER, Frank Harrison; EGAN, Pierce John; ELLIOT, John Charles; EVANS, Geoffrey Maynard, MC; EVANS, Edward Williams; EYRE - POWELL, John William Alcock; FINCH, Henry Kingsley; FISHER, Oswald Garrow; FREESTONE, William Herbert; FULFORD, Reginald Hardwick; GARRETT, Charles Harold; GEARE, William Duncan; GEDGE, Basil Johnson; GIBBS, Edward Reginald; GREEN, Ernest Newham; GREEN, Hugh James Bernard; GREER, Richard Ussher; GRIFFITHS, David Howell; GUNSON, Henry Edward; HALL, Henry Armstrong, CBE; HARBORD, Frank Robert; HARDY, Theodore Bayley, VC DSO MC; HATFIELD, Arthur Percival; HAWDON, Noel Elliot; HEATH, Alfred; HENDERSON, Robert Morley; HEWITT, Frederick Whitmore; HOARE, Henry James; HODDER, Charles William Ackerman; HOLDEN, Oswald Addenbrooke; HOOD, Charles Ivo Sinclair; HOULSTON, Edgar Charles; HUNTER, Philip Needham; INGLIS, Rupert Edward; JEFFERYS, Charles Thomas Claude; JENKINS, David; JOHNSON, Ernest Edward; JOHNSON-SMYTH, Edward; JONES, Basil; JONES, Thomas Glasfryn; JONES, William Edgar; JUDD, Alan Cecil, MC; KAY, William Henry, MC; KIRWAN, Robert Mansel; LANGDON, Cecil; LAWSON, Henry Heaton; LEAKEY, Herbert Nettleton; LEDBITTER, Herbert Peter; LENDRUM, James Herbert Reginald; LESTER, Gerald James; LONGRIDGE, Archibald Owen Carwithen; MACE, Alban Bodley; MAJOR, Charles William Wykeham; MARONA, Charles Antonio; MARTYN, Cecil Radcliffe; MCMURTRIE, Stanley Gibson; MEISTER, Charles Gustave Clark, MC; MITCHELL, Charles Wand; MOORE, Edgar Noel, MC; O'CONOR, William Owen; O'RORKE, Benjamin Garniss, DSO;

PARDOE, George Southey; PEEL, Hon. Maurice Berkeley, MC & Bar; PENNEFATHER, Somerset Edward; PLUMMER, Charles Benjamin; PLUMPTRE, Basil Pemberton, MC; PRATT, Arthur Morrell; RANKING, George Harvey; READ, Eric Oswald; ROCHE, Francis Cavendish; RUCK - KEENE, Benjamin Corrie; SCHOOLING, Cecil Herbert; SMITH, Frederick Seaton; SPENCE, Alexander, MC; SPINK, Hubert Octavius; STAUNTON, Harvey; STEWART, James Robert; STREETEN, Basil Robert; SWEET, George Charles Walrond; TREVOR, Ernest Wilberforce; TUKE, Francis Henry; WALLACE, John James; WATSON, John Edmund Malone, MC; WERE, Cyril Narramore; WOODHOUSE, Disney Charles;

Australia
BERGIN, Michael, MC; GOLLER, Alfred Ernest; MAXTED, Spencer Edward;

East Africa
ALDRIDGE, Noel; CHADWICK, Walter. E. A;

New Zealand
BRYAN - BROWN, Guy Spencer; BURGIN, John Robert; MALLETT, Cecil Alfred;

BAPTIST

FRASER, Donald, DSO; HEADING, William Henry; JONES, William Evans; TOMKINS, William Henry; VERYARD, Albert Thomas; WOOD, Harold William;

CHURCH OF SCOTLAND

BLACK, William; BLACK, William Duncan Thomson; CONDIE, George; HEGGIE, David; KELLIE, John; KIRK, James, MC; RANKINE, William Henry; ROBERTSON, Charles, MC; SMITH, Peter George; STUART, Alexander; TAYLOR, William;

CONGREGATIONALIST

BURNS, Joseph Dobson; EDWARDS, Evan; HARDY, James Henry; HOWELL, Thomas;

Australia
DEMPSEY, John;

South Africa
ONSLOW CARLTON, William McNiell;

METHODIST
Australia
DUNBAR, William James; HUNTER, David de Venny;

South Africa
COOK, George Thornhill;

PRESBYTERIAN
MORRISON, Samuel; STEWART, Robert Arthur;
Australia
BATES, Albert Edward.; BRUCE, John Kemp; GILLISON, Andrew; STEVENS, William Johnstone;
South Africa
KONI LUHLONGANA; DAMBUSA C. J.;

ROMAN CATHOLIC
BAINES, Thomas Leo; BERTINI, Umberto Michael; BIRT, Henry Norbert; BURDESS, Matthew Forster; CAREY, Timothy; CLARKE, Stephen; COLLINS, Herbert H. John; COWD, Arthur Martin; DOYLE, Denis; DOYLE, William Joseph, MC; FINN, William Joseph; FITZGIBBON, John J., MC; GORDON, Michael Patrick; GROBEL, Peter; GUTHRIE, David Michall; GWYNN, John; HARTIGAN, Jeremiah Austin; KAVANAGH, Bernard; KNAPP, Simon Stock, DSO MC; LEESON, James Thomas; LOOBY, Patrick; MATTHEWS, Lewis Joseph; McAULIFFE, Cornelius (Raphael); McDONNELL, John Joseph; McGINITY, Henry Cuthbert; McLLVAINE, John Joseph; MONTAGU, Walter Philip; MONTEITH, Robert John; O'DEA, Lawrence; O'MEEHAN, Isodore James; O'SULLIVAN, Donald Vincent; PRENDERGAST, Matthew Vincent; RYAN, Michael; SHINE, James; STRICKLAND, Joseph; WATSON, Charles; WATTERS, John A.; WHITEFOORD, Charles B.;
Australia
SYDES, Edward John.
Canada
CROCHETIERE, G. E. R.;
East Africa
DAWUDU;
Gold Coast
MALAM GARDI;
New Zealand
DORE, Patrick, MC; McMENAMIN, James Joseph;

SALVATION ARMY
POWLEY, Walter Harry;

UNITED FREE CHURCH OF SCOTLAND
FALSIDE, William James; IRELAND, John Thomas Craig; MACGREGOR, John Campbell; MILLAR, George; SUTHERLAND, Andrew Neil;

UNITED METHODIST
ASH, John; ASHTON, Frederick William; RAINE, Foster;

WESLEYAN
BEDALE, Charles Lees; DALY, John James; GREEN, Herbert, MC; HEWITT, Sydney Rangeley, OBE; HOPKINS, R. Wilson; JONES - ROBERTS, Peter; REED, Clifford Hugh, MC; RICHARDS, Walter H.; SHOVEL, Thomas Jasper; SULLINGS, Stephen John; THORPE, Thomas J.; WILKS, Walter Charles, MC;

Theological Colleges attended by Chaplains
(Not all those listed in the Directory appear here)

Australian College of Theology
MAXTED, Spencer Edward.

Bala - Bangor Baptist College
EDWARDS, Evan; JONES, William Evans.

Bishop's College Cheshunt
EVANS, Geoffrey Maynard, MC; RUCK-KEENE, Benjamin Corrie.

Bishop's College Lennox
MITCHELL, Charles Wand.

Bishop's Hostel Farnham
CREIGHTON, Oswin; DUGDALE, William, MC; HOULSTON, Edgar Charles;
RANKING, George Harvey; SWEET, George Charles Walrond; WERE, Cyril Narramore.

Bristol Baptist College
WOOD, Harold William.

Chichester Theological College
MARONA, Charles Antonio.

C.M.S. College Islington
HOARE, Henry James.

Cuddesdon College Oxford
BUCK, Cyril Bernard Wilson; DEEDES, Arthur Gordon; FIXSEN, John Frederick Christopher; GEDGE, Basil Johnson; GIBBS, Edward Reginald; HENDERSON, Robert Morley; HOOD, Charles Ivo Sinclair; O'CONOR, William Owen.

Dorchester Missionary College
DUNSTAN, Sidney.

Edinburgh Theological College
CAPPELL, James Leitch; MEISTER, Charles Gustave Clark, MC.

Ely Theological College
BLAKEWAY, Philip John Thomas; DUVALL, John Richard; INGLIS, Rupert Edward; JONES, William Edgar; LANGDON, Cecil; LONGRIDGE, Archibald Owen Carwithen.

English College Rome
BURDESS, Matthew Forster.

Kelham (Society of the Sacred Mission) Newark
LEDBITTER, Herbert Peter.

Kings College London
BAIRD, James; EDINGER, Frank Harrison; GREEN, Ernest Newham; HALL, Henry Armstrong, CBE; EDINGER, Frank Harrison; HEATH, Alfred; MAJOR, Charles William Wykeham; MARONA, Charles Antonio; WALLACE, John James.

Leeds Clergy School
AVENT, Ernest; BROUGH, James Stanley Bromfield; GEARE, William Duncan.

Lichfield Theological College
ABBOTT, William David; ALDRIDGE, Noel; BROWN, William; CLEVELAND, Frederick Walter, MC (Also at Mirfield); GREEN, Hugh James Bernard.

London College of Divinity
AINLEY, Frederick William.

Nottingham Institute
BURNS, Joseph Dobson.

Metropolitan Baptist College
FRASER, Donald, DSO; TOMKINS, William Henry; VERYARD, Albert Thomas.

Mirfield (House of the Resurrection)
CLEVELAND, Frederick Walter, MC. (Also at Lichfield); FREESTONE, William Henry.

New College Edinburgh
IRELAND, John Thomas Craig; STUART, Alexander.

Richmond College
GREEN, Herbert, MC.

Ridley Hall Cambridge
BARKER, Edward Walter; BRYAN-BROWN, Guy Spencer; COBHAM, Elijah, MC; DE VINE, Hatton Bertram St. John; DOUDNEY, Charles Edmund; ELLIOTT, John Charles; HEWITT, Frederick Whitmore; PLUMPTRE, Basil Pemberton, MC; WOODHOUSE, Disney Charles.

Ripon College
CRAVEN, George Edward; HARDING, Wilfrid John, MC; LAWSON, Henry Heaton; LEAKEY, Herbert Nettleton.

Sarum College Salisbury
BENNETT, Arnold John, MC; HEWITT, Frederick Whitmore.

Scots College Rome
COWD, Arthur Martin.

St. Aidan's College Birkenhead
CLEAVER, Frederick Canning; SPINK, Hubert Octavious.

St. Chad's Hostel, Regina Canada
EAST, Herbert Hinton.

St. Edmunds College Ware
CAREY, Timothy; COLLINS, Herbert H. John; KNAPP, Simon Stock, DSO. MC.

St. Michael's College Aberdare
JONES, Thomas Glasfryn.

Ushaw Seminary Durham
BAINES, Thomas Leo; BURDESS, Matthew Forster. (also English College, Rome); FINN, William Joseph; WATSON, Charles.

Wells Theological College
ACTON, Armar Edward; BELL, Charles Henry, MC; DALLAS, William Loraine Seymour; FINCH, Henry Kingsley; HAWDON, Noel Elliot; MACE, Alban Bodley; PEEL, Hon. Maurice Berkeley, MC and Bar; SCHOOLING, Cecil Herbert; STREETEN, Basil Robert; TREVOR, Ernest Wilberforce.

Wycliffe Hall Oxford
JONES, Basil; O'RORKE, Benjamin Garniss, DSO; PLUMPTRE, Basil Pemberton, MC.

Universities attended by Chaplains
(Not all those listed in the Directory appear here)

Aberdeen University
PENNEFATHER, Somerset Edward.

Cambridge University
AINLEY, William Preston; Jesus College.
AVENT, Ernest; Gonville and Caius College.
BARKER, Edward Walter; Bedford and Queen's College.
BELL, Charles Henry, MC; Christ College.
BODDINGTON, Vincent Coke; St. John's College.
BOTWOOD, Edward Keightley; Queen's College.
BROUGH, James Stanley Bromfield; Emmanuel College.
BRYAN - BROWN, Guy Spencer; Downing College.
CHEESE, William Gerard; St. John's College.
COBHAM, Elijah, MC; Emmanuel College.
COOPER - MARSDIN, Arthur; Jesus College (See Directory).
DE VINE, Hatton Bertram St. John; Jesus College.
DOUDNEY, Charles Edmund; Corpus Christi College.
DUVALL, John Richard; Selwyn College.
ELLIOT, John Charles; Queen's College.
FINCH, Henry Kingsley; St. John's College.
FULFORD, Reginald Hardwick.
GEARE, William Duncan; Queen's College.
GEDGE, Basil Johnson; Selwyn College.
HARDING, Wilfrid John, MC;
HAWDON, Noel Elliot; Jesus College.
HEWITT, Frederick Whitmore; Corpus Christi College.
LANGDON, Cecil; Selwyn College.
LEAKEY, Herbert Nettleton;
LONGRIDGE, Archibald Owen Carwithen; Trinity College.
McMURTRIE, Stanley Gibson; St. Catherine's College.
MITCHELL, Charles Wand; Emmanuel College.
PLUMPTRE, Basil Pemberton, MC; Emmanuel College.
PRATT, Arthur Morrell; Queen's College.
READ, Eric Oswald; Corpus Christi College.
SANDERS, Samuel John Woodward; St. John's College.
SCHOOLING, Cecil Herbert; Pembroke College.
STAUNTON, Harvey; Selwyn College.
STEVENS, Silas William; St. John's College.
TUKE, Francis Henry; Trinity College.
WOODHOUSE, Disney Charles; Clare College.

Cardiff University College
HOWELL Thomas;

Dublin (Trinity College)
ACTON, Armar Edward; BAILIE, George William; CHADWICK, Walter E. A.; CORBETT, Frederick St. John; DUNCAN, Edward Francis, MC; EGAN, Pierce John; EYRE-POWELL, John William Alcock; FISHER, Oswald Garrow; GREER, Richard Usher; JOHNSON-SMYTH, Edward; O'CONOR, William Owen; PENNEFATHER, Somerset Edward; ROCHE, Francis Cavendish; SPENCE, Alexander, MC; WATSON, John Edmund Malone, MC;

Durham University
BAIRD, James; St. John's Hall.
BISHOP, George Bernard Hamilton; St. Chad's Hall.
CLEAVER, Frederick Canning;
CLEVELAND, Frederick Walter, MC;
DICKINSON, Harry; Hatfield Hall.

EVANS, Edward Williams; University College.
GARRETT, Charles Harold; St. Chad's Hall.
GRIFFITHS, David Howell;
HALL, Henry Armstrong, CBE; University College.
HATFIELD, Arthur Percival; Hatfield Hall.
HOARE, Henry James;
JEFFERYS, Charles Thomas Claude; St. Chad's Hall.
JENKINS, David; University College.
JOHNSON, Ernest Edward; Hatfield Hall.
LESTER, Gerald James; Hatfield Hall.
MALLETT, Cecil Alfred;
MARTYN, Cecil Radcliffe; Hatfield Hall.
PENNEFATHER, Somerset Edward;

Edinburgh University
HEGGIE, David; IRELAND, John Thomas Craig; KELLIE, John; KIRK, James, MC; MEISTER, Charles Gustave Clark, MC; MILLAR, George; RANKINE, William Henry; ROBERTSON, Charles, MC;

Glasgow University
BLACK, William Duncan Thomson; CAPPELL, James Leitch; CONDIE, George; FALSIDE, William James; KELLIE, John; MACGREGOR, John Campbell; SMITH, Peter George; SUTHERLAND, Andrew Neil; TAYLOR, William.

Lampeter St. Deiniol's College
JONES, Basil; JONES, Thomas Glasfryn; JONES, William Edgar; SMITH, Frederick Seaton.

Liverpool University
ALDRIDGE, Noel.

London University
BELCHER, Robert Henry; BIRT, Henry Norbert; EDINGER, Frank Harrison; GREEN, Ernest Newham; HARDY, Theodore Bayley, VC DSO MC; HEATH, Alfred; KAY, William Henry, MC; LENDRUM, James Herbert Reginald; MAJOR, Charles William Wykeham.

Manchester University
LAWSON, Henry Heaton; MARONA, Charles Antonio; WALLACE, John James.

Melbourne (Australia) Trinity College
MAXTED, Spencer Edward.

Oxford University
BLAKEWAY, Philip John Thomas; Magdalene College.
BUCK, Cyril Barnard Wilson; Trinity College.
COLBOURNE, Richard Arthur Pell; Worcester College.
CRAVEN, George Edward; Queen's College.
CREIGHTON, Oswin; Keble College.
DALLAS, William Loraine Seymour; St. Edmund's Hall.
DEEDES, Arthur Gordon;
DUGDALE, Richard William, MC; Corpus Christi College.
FREESTONE, William Herbert;
GIBBS, Edward Reginald; Keble College.
GREEN, Hugh James Bernard; St. Stephen's House.
GUNSON, Henry Edward; St. Edmund's Hall.
HENDERSON, Robert Morley;
HOLDEN, Oswald Addenbrooke; Exeter College.
HOOD, Charles Ivo Sinclair; Magdalene College.
HOULSTON, Edgar Charles; St. Edmund's Hall.
INGLIS, Rupert Edward;
JUDD, Alan Cecil, MC; Exeter College.
KIRWAN, Robert Mansel; Keble College.
MACE, Alban Bodley; Queen's College.
MOORE, Edgar Noel, MC; Exeter College.
OGLE, Wilfred Rathmell; Trinity College.
O'RORKE, Benjamin Garniss, DSO; Exeter College.
PARDOE, George Southey; University College.
PEEL, Hon. Maurice Berkeley, MC and Bar; New College.
RANKING, George Harvey; New College.
RUCK - KEENE, Benjamin Corrie; Keble College.
SWEET, George Charles Walrond;
TREVOR, Ernest Wilberforce;
WERE, Cyril Narramore; Christ Church.
WHITEFOORD, Charles B; Merton College.

St. Andrews University
KIRK, James, MC.

Sydney (Australia) University
STEWART, James Robert;

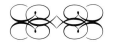

ACKNOWLEDGEMENTS

I am extremely grateful to those who volunteered information and provided data.

Mr. David Blake B.A. (Hones), M.A. A.M.A. Curator of the Museum of Army Chaplaincy.

The Revd. Canon John Barton, MBE, M.A.

The Revd. Fr. Peter Dwyer M.A.

The Revd. Julian Gray.

The Revd. Canon Paul Hardy.

The Revd. Maurice G. Hewett B.A.

The Revd. Dr. Peter J. Howson B.Sc., M.A., M.B.A., Ph.D.

The Revd. John Porter.

The Revd. H. W. White B.A.

Fr. Paul Casey, Diocese of Kilmore.

Fr. Ignatius Fennessy, Franciscan Library, Dun Mhuire, Killiney, Co. Dublin.

Fr. James Hodkinson, Society of Jesus, British Province.

Fr. Michael Hughes, Archivist, OMI, St. Anne's, Inchicore, Dublin.

Fr. Fabian McCormack, OCD, Carmelite Priory, Kensington.

Fr. Fergus O'Donoghue, Society of Jesus, Irish Province.

Fr. Nicholas Schofield, Archivist, Archdiocese of Westminster.

Fr. Geoffrey Scott, Douai Abbey.

Dom Paul Stonham, Abbot of Belmont, Hereford.

Dom Nicholas, Downside Abbey.

Muriel Adams.

Paul Baillie.

Mr. R. G. Bowlcs.

Anne Clarke, YMCA Archives, University of Birmingham.

John B. Davies, Archivist, Cuddesdon College, Oxford.

Mr. Duncan, grandson of Revd. E. F. Duncan, MC.

Tony Durkin, Archivist, Diocese of Hexham and Newcastle.

Harry Fecitt, MBE.

Peter Forsaith, Wesleyan Centre Oxford.

Stan Grosvenor.

Mr. H. G. Holden.

Kay Day, RC Bishopric of the Forces.

Dr. Julian Lock, Archivist, Regent Park, Baptist College, Oxford.

Mrs. P. A. Masters.

Alistair MacGregor, Hatfield College, Durham.

Alan K. McMillan, Presbyterian Church of Ireland.

Historical Society.

Alison Murray, Archivist, Church of Scotland.

Peter Seed, Director of Estates and Faculties, Ushaw College, Durham.

David Smallwood, Archivist, RC Diocese of Middlesbrough.

Ron Thew.

Margaret Thompson, B.A., URC Historic Society, Cambridge.

Dr. Meg Whittle, Archivist, Archdiocese of Liverpool.

Commonwealth War Graves Commission.

Directory of Anglican Clergy based in New Zealand.

Durham University Library.

Guildhall Library, London.

Kings School, Ely.

Lambeth Palace Library.

Middlesbrough Reference Library.

Ridley Hall Cambridge.

Rugby Football Union Archives, Twickenham.

John Ryland's Library, University of Manchester.

Salvation Army International Archives.

Sarum College.

APPENDIX

ARMY AND NAVY OFFICIATING MINISTERS 1915.

The Baptist Union of Great Britain and Ireland and the Congregational Union of England and Wales act together in securing the appointment of Army and Navy officiating ministers. A further agreement sanctioned by the war Office, has now been come to under which we act also on behalf of the Primitive Methodists and the United Methodists. The letters following the names indicate therefore whether Baptist, Congregationalist, Primitive Methodist, or United Methodist, and unless otherwise designated the troops of the four Denominations; at the place named are served by the minister named, p, stands for Presbyterian; w, stands for Wesleyan; c.f. stands for Chaplain to the Forces.

CHAPLAINS ACCEPTED FOR THE FRONT.

Rev. J. R. Ackroyd, B.D.C.F.
Rev. J. J. L. Clayton, C. F.
Rev. J. Firth, C. F.

Rev. T. Jones, C. F.
Rev. T. N. Tattersail, C. F.
Rev. E. L. Watson, C. F.

CHAPLIANS IN HOME CAMPS AND OFFICIATING MINISTERS AT INSTITUTES OR HUTS.

Rev. W. C. Charteris. C. F.
Rev. F. G. Kemp. C. F. Aldershot. South camp (Institute shortly to be erected) North camp (Hut shortly to be erected).
Rev. H. C. Mander, C. F. Swansea (3rd Welsh field Ambulance, R.A.M.C.) T.F.
Rev. Evan Mathias. C. F. Hastings.
Rev. C. S. Rose. Salisbury Plain - Sutton Veney and Corton (Institute).
Rev. J. Seelay, C. F. Woolwich.
Rev. C. H. Shave, C. F. Salisbury Plain Codford (Institute).
Rev. M. Stacey, C. F. Salisbury Plain Bulford and Durrington (Institute shortly to be erected).
Rev. J. Wallett. C. F. Purfleet..

Ministers appointed to pastoral oversight in the Army and Navy

Belfast. B. and C.	W. J. Davey. C. Army.
Bodmin. B. and C.	J. P. Southwell. C. Army.
Bradford. B. and C.	J. R. Davies. B. Army.
Brecon. B. and C.	D. Owen Griffiths. B. Army.
Bristol. B. and C.	E. C. Griffin. B. Army.
Cardiff. B.	C. Griffiths. B. Army and Navy.
Cardiff. C.	W. C. Parry. C. Army and Navy.
Carrickfergus. B. and C.	James. Lyon. C. Army.
Caterham. B. and C.	S. Milledge. C. Army.
Chatham. C.	J. E. Williams. C. Army and Navy.
Chatham. B.	H. F. Gower. B. Army and Navy.
Chatham. B.	W. W. Blocksldge. B. (Deputy) Army and Navy.
Chester. B. and C.	J. J. Hargreaves. B. Army.
Colchester. B. and C.	K. L. Parry. B,Sc., C. Army.
Cork. B. and C.	F. W. Gracey. B. Army.
Dartmouth. B. and C.	E. Elliot. C. Navy.
Deal. C. and P.	T. G. Prosser. C. Army and Navy.
Deal. B.	W. L. Mackenzie. B. Army and Navy.
Derby. B. and C.	W. A. Richards. B. Army.
Devizes. B. and C.	J. Day. B. Army.

Dorchester. B. C. and P.	R. S. Holmes. C. Army.
Dover. C.	F. P. Basden. C. Army and Navy.
Dover. B.	W. Holyoak. B. Army and Navy.
Dublin. B. and C.	J. W. Pearce. B. Army.
Exeter. B. and C.	G. Frankling Owen. B. Army.
Gosport. B.	E. W. Berry. B. Army and Navy.
Gosport. C	E. W. Franks. M.A. C. Navy
Gravesend. B. and C	Geo. Sneesby. B. Army.
Grimsby. B. and C.	A. E. Owen-Jones. B. Navy.
Halifax. B. and C.	Alec Charlton. B. Army.
Harwich. B. C.	E. E.Greening.(Dovercourt) C. Army and Navy (Shotley and ships at Felixstowe and Harwich) B. C.
Holyhead. B. C.	J. Hawen Rees. C. Navy.
Home Division. B. and C. (including Wellinton, Chelsea, Knightsbridge, and Pirbright Barracks)	W. E. Wells. B. Army.
Hounslow B. and C. (also for Congregational. Baptist and Presbyterian Boys at Royal Military School of Music, Kneller Hall, Hounslow).	L. J. McCrea. C. Army.
Hythe School of Musketry. B. and C.	J. Solon Rees. C. Army.
Liverpool (Seaforth). B. C	S. R. Jenkins. B.A., C. Army.Lowestoft.
Gunboats putting into Port at. B. and C.	A. Vaughan Thomas. A.T.S.B. Navy.
Milford haven. C.	D. Garro-Jones. C. Navy.
Milford Haven. B.	E. Y. Tidman. B. Navy.
Newcastle upon Tyne. B. C.	T. J. Whitman. B. Army.
Newhaven. B. C. P. M. and U.M.	J. Curson. C. Army.
Newport (Mon) B. and C.	A. T. Jones. B. Army.
Newquay, Cornwall. B. and C.	J. F. Archer. B. Army and Navy.
Oxford. B. and C.	J. Dann. B. Army.
Pembroke Docks. B.	F. A. Hogbin. B. Army and Navy.
Pembroke Docks. C.	J. E. Griffiths. C. Army and Navy.
Plymouth. B. and C.	F. W. Dunster. B. Army and Navy.
Portland. B. C. and P.	S. V. Wylie. C. Army and Navy.
Portsmouth and Hilsea. C.	J. Watkins Davies. C. Army and Navy.
Portsmouth and Hilsea. B.	E. J. Woodall. B. Army and Navy.
Preston. B. and C.	W. J. Loader. B. D. B. Army.
Queenstown, Ireland. B. C. and P	Y. A. Cotter M.A. P. Navy.
Reading. B. and C.	W. J. Phillips. B. Army.
Ross-on-Wye. B. and C.	J. W. Kettle. B. Army.
Salisbury Plain (Park house camp) B.C.P. M. and U. M.	C. F. Parry. P.M. Army.
Salisbury Plain (Rollestone. Bustard. Fargo and West Down Camps). B. C.	W. S. Wyle. B. Army.
Salisbury Plain (Tidworth). B.C.P. M. and U.M.	T. W. Hancox. P.M. Army.
Sandgate (Shorncliffs).	C.A. Wilson. B.A. C. Army.
Sheerness. B. and C.	Arthur E. Bradford. B. Navy.

Swansea. B. and C. 6th Glamorgan
Welsh Regt. Territorial Force   D. Howell Thomas. C. Army.
Taunton (Military Depot)
B. and C.   J. H. Cox. C. Army.
Torquay. B. and C.   J. Charteris Johnson. C. Navy.
Warwick. Budbrooke
Barracks. B.and C.   C. Harold Dodd. M.A., C. Army.
Weedon. B. and C.   C. Army.
Weymouth. B. and C.   W. Lawson Forster. C. Army.
Winchester. B. and C.   A. G. Edgerton. B. Army.
Windsor. B. and C.   G. Felix Williams. C. Army.
York and Strensall
Camp B. and C.   J. Brighting. C. Army.

Gibraltar. W. B. and C.   A. B. Sackatt. W. Army and Navy.
South China. B. and C.   J. Kirk Maconachie
   The Manse Hong Kong. C. Army and
   Navy.
St. Helena. B. and C.   H. G. Wood. B. Army and Navy.
India:-
Agre. B. C. W.   G. A. Smith. B. Army.
Bombay B. and C.   A. E. Hubbard. B. Navy.
Dinapore. B. C. W.   H. Dyche. B. Army.
Kasauli and District. B. C. P.   C. H. Williams. B. Army.
Correspondents.   W. R. Le Queane. C. Calcutta.
   G. E. Phillips. C. Bangalore.
   H. Anderson. B. Calcutta.
   T. W. Norledge. B. Calcutta.

APPOINTED SINCE THE OUTBREAK OF WAR AUGUST 1914.

Aldershot - Beacon Hill
and Hinderland.   W. K. Burford. C. Army.
   Assisted by A. Snape. C. Army.
Borbon and Headley.   Bentley Neal. C. Army.
Bramshott, Liphook
and Longmoor.   J. C. Sweet. U. M. Army.
Witley.   J. E. Gilbert. P. M. Army.
Alton.   H. G. Lewis. B. A. C. Army.
Ashton-under-Lyne.   A. N. Geary. B. Army.
Avonmouth.   John Morgan. C. Army.
Barrow-in-Furness.   Wm. Walker. B. Army.
Bessels Green District
(Sevenoaks)   G. H. Harris. B. Army.

THE UNITED NAVY AND ARMY BOARD.

The Baptist Union of Great Britain and Ireland, the Congregational union of England and Wales, the Primitive Methodist Denomination and the United Methodists Denomination, have constituted a United Board and act together in securing the appointment of Navy and Army Chaplains, and "Officiating Clergymen." And also in watching over the rights and interests of the members of these Denominations in the Army and Navy. The letters following the names indicate therefore, whether Baptist, Congregationalist, Primitive Methodist, or United Methodist; P. stands for Presbyterians, and W. for Wesleyans.

CHAPLAINS TO THE FORCES.
1 BAPTISTS.

Bray, Rev. A. E.   Kemp, Rev. F. G., S.C.F.
Charteris, Rev. W. G.   Mander, Rev. H. C.
Clifford, Rev. E. O., B.A.   Morgan, Rev. D. J.

Dawson, Rev. J. T.   Morse, Rev. D. G.
Fraser, Rev. Donald.   Owen, Rev. W. G.
Gower, Rev. H. F.   Patterson, Rev. D. Tait.
Hart, Rev. T. W.   Pearce, Rev. J. H., M.A.
Harte, Rev. G. W.   Rice, Rev. G. M.
Harvey, Rev. J. Lamb.   Roberts, Rev. F. Waldo.
Hiley, Rev. D. J.   Rose, Rev. C. S.
Hoare, Rev. H. G., B.A.   Seeley, Rev. J.
Hogbin, Rev. F. A   Snelgrove, Rev. R. M.
Holme, Rev. Ralph.   Stearn, Rev. C. H. B.A., R.D.
Hughes, Rev. L. G.   Tattersall, Rev. T. N.
Humphrey, Rev. F.   Walker, Rev. J. R.
Jackman, Rev. J. H.   Walkey, Rev. F. J.
Jones, Rev. A. E. Owen   Watson, Rev. E. L.,S.C.F.
Jones, Rev. Hugh.   Wilkinson, Rev. S. H.
Jones, Rev. R. E.   Wood, Rev. Clifford.
Jones, Rev. S. J.
Jones, Rev. T.

2 CONGREGATIONALISTS.

Adams, Rev. J.   Mathias, Rev. E.
Ballard, Rev. F. H.   Maxwell, Rev. A. R.
Bartlett, Rev. R.   Ormerod, Rev. J. C., M.A.
Berry, Rev. R. W.   Patten, Rev. J. A., M.A.
Bevan, Rev. J., M.A.   Pickthall, Rev. J., M.A., B.D.
Bevan, Rev. J.   Rawcliffe, Rev. E. B.
Bohn, Rev. J. C. A.   Shave, Rev. C. H.
Clayton, Rev. J. J. L.   Shepherd, Rev. J., B.A.
Coates, Rev. W. J., B.D.   Skilton, Rev. E.
Edwards, Rev. J., B.A.   Stacey, Rev. M.
Evans, Rev. J., B.A.   Stevenson, Rev. J. E.
Farrington, Rev. A.   Tweedie, Rev. E.
Gamble, Rev. H. J., B.A.   Uffen, Rev. B.
Giffin, Rev. J. W.   Weir, Rev. E. J.
Hughes, Rev. R. W.   Wheeler, Rev. F. H.
Jenkins, Rev, E., M.A.   Williams, Rev. R. Paris.
Jones, Rev. E., M.A. B.D.   Winder, Rev. C. A.
Kaye, Rev. T. B.

3 PRIMITIVE METHODISTS.

Bellew, Rev. W. E.   Horne, Rev. E. J. de
Dalafield, Rev. S. George.   Kendall, Rev. George.
Emmitt, Rev. Ernest. S.   Lowe, Rev. Albert.
Firth, Rev. J.   Sands, Rev. Thomas.
Fisher, Rev. Phillip. J.   Scott, Rev. G. Tulip.
Gilbert, Rev. J. E.   Smith, Rev. E. W.
Grayson, Rev. J. Watson.   Standing, Rev. George.
Hancox, Rev. T. W.   Wearmouth, Rev. R. F.
Heward, Rev. T. B.

4 UNITED METHODISTS.

Allen, Rev. Herbert. D.   Langley, Rev. J. Ernest.
Bowyer, Rev. A. E.   locket, Rev. A. C.
Clarke, Rev. T. E.   Minnear, Rev. G. E.
Davey, Rev, J. Penry.   Rhodes, Rev. W. P.
Fairfax, Rev. Frank.   Wallett, Rev. Joseph.
Field, Rev. William.   Walters, Rev. G. F.
Hinchcliffe, Rev. Harry.   Wooldridge, Rev. R. H.
Jeffries, Rev. W. H.

Aberdeen.	G. C. Milne. C. Army.
Hospitals.	S. G. Woodrow. B. Army.
Abergele, Kinmel Camp and St. Asaph (Welsh).	W. G. Owen. C.F., B. Army.
	E. Jones. M.A., B.D., C. Army.
Aldeburgh.	E. Davies. B. Army.
Aldeshot.	F. G. Kemp.S.C.F., B. Army.
Beacon Hill, Frensham, Grayshott and Hindhead.	W. K. Burford. C. Army.
	assisted by A. Snape.
Bordon and Headley.	Bentley Neal. C. Army.
Bramshott, Liphook and Longmore.	J. C. Sweet. U.M. army.
	W. Jollans. U.M. Army.
Witley.	H. M. Hull. P.M. Army.
Alton.	H. G. Lewis. C. Army.
Annan.	G. Smisson. C. Army.
Ashburton.	F. E. Harker. C. Army.
Ashford Kent.	W. R. Chesterton. B. Army.
Ashton - in - Markerfield.	W. Harris. B.A., B.D.,C. Army.
Ashton - under - Lyne.	A. N. Geary. B. Army.
Avonmouth.	J. Morgan. C. Army.
Aylsham.	J. Read. B. Army.
Ayr.	R. McQueen. C. Army.
Baddesley.	E. F. M. Yokes. B. Army.
Baldock.	G. F. Sears. C. Army.
Barbon (Military Hospital)	H. C. Over. C. Army.
Barrow - in - Furness.	T. H. Barlow. P.M. Army.
Basingstoke.	R. Mackintosh. C. Army.
Bath Midsomer Norton.	F. Bell. P.M. Army.
Beccles.	W. E. Davies. C. Army.
Bedale, Yorkshire.	W. Skelson. P.M. Army.
Bedford.	G. H. R. Laslett. B. Army.
Belfast.	W. J. Davey. C. Army.
Belvedere.	H. S. Webb. C. Army.
Berkhamsted	
Berwick.	J. Ramsey. P.M. Army.
Beverley, Westwood Camp.	W. D. Reid. M.A., B. D., C. Army
Bexhill.	J. Osborne. M.A., C. Army.
Birmingham. & District. Troops in Training at -	
Sutton Park, Witton & Aston.	D. L. Jones. B.A.,B.D., C. Army.
Thorpe St. Barracks, Great Brook St. Barracks.	D. C. Cooper. P.M. Army.
Stoney Lane Barracks. Taunton Road.	
Collede Road.	R. C. Lemin. B. Army.
Smethwick. and Hospitals.	H. Singleton. B. Army.
Dudley Road. and Queen's.	A. H. Robins. U.M. Army.
Rubery. Highbury and Kings Heath.	T. Towers. C. Army.
University Buildings, Selly Park and General.	F. A. Rees. B. Army.
Stourbridge Section, 1st Southern Hospital.	K. Garthwaite. U.M. Army.
Birtley.	W. E. Farndale. P. M. Army.
Blackheath.	
31st Welsh Division.	R. J. French. B. Army.
Blackpool.	J. Fox. B. Army.

Blandford.	G. Evans. B.D., C. Navy and Army.
Blandford Camp.	A. W. Weford. P.M. Army.
Blyth.	W. Holryde. U.M. Army.
Bodmin.	J. P. Southwell. C. Army.
Bombay.	A. E. Hubbard. B. Navy Army.
Bournmouth.	H. A. Tree. B. Army.
Hospitals	F. W. Harper. P.m. Army.
Bovington.	G. R. Trussell. P.M. Army.
Bradford.	F. Hobson. B. Army.
Field House Hospital.	T. O. Ransford. B. Army.
Infirmary Hospital.	V. T. Pomeroy. B.A., C. Army.
St. Luke's Hospital.	J. J. Reeves. P.M. Army.
Bradford.	J. R. Davies. B. Army.
Brading.	W. F. Clarkson. B.A., C.
Braintree.	G. A. Price. P.M. Army.
Brasted and Westerham.	J. Smith. B. Army.
Brecon.	D. O. Griffiths. B. Army.
Brentwood.	W. Legerton. C. Army.
Bridlington.	W. C. Balmer. U.M. Army.
Brighouse.	L. Beaumont.. C. Army.
Brighton and Hove.	H. R. Williamson. C. Army.
Brighton Barracks.	F. J. Gould. C. Army.
Hospital.	W. A. Hammond. P.M55
Bristol.	F.G.Benskin, M.A.,B. Army
	Senior Officiating clergyman.
	R.C. Grifin, B. Army.
	F. J. Ellis, U.M. Army.
	T. S. Macey, B.A.,C. Army.
	J. Trebilco, C. Army.
	B. J. Gibbon, B. Army.
	J. T. Davies, C. Army.
Buckhaven.	D. M. Simpson, B. Army.
Buckingham.	A. Cannon, C.
Buntingford.	J. R. Jones, C. Army.
Burgess Hill.	W. C. Chisholm, C. Army.
Burnham.	J. I. Wensley, B.A.,B.D.,B. Army.
Burslem. (Raywood Hospital)	F. H. Edwards, P. M. Army.
Bury.	F. Wheatcroft ,C. Army.
Bury Infirmary Hospital.	J. A. Kershaw, P.M. Army.
Bury St. Edmunds.	A. J. Brown, C. Army.
Buxton.	R. M. Moffat, M.A., C. Army.
Calne, Bowood Park.	F. A. Ingham, P.M. Army.
Cambridge.	M. E. Aubrey, M.A.,B. Army.
Camberwell.	J. Allardyce, C. Army.
Canterbury.	J. Lewis, B. Army.
Cardiff, B.	C. Griffiths, B. Navy and Army.
Cardiff, C.	W. C.Parry, C. Navy and Army.
Cardiff, C. (Welsh speaking)	H. M.Hughes. B.A., C. Army.
Cardiff Hospitals.	J. Williams, B. Army.
	J. H. Walker,C. Army.
	W. E.Chivers, U.M. Army.
	J. L. Williamson, P.M. Army.
	C. Joshua, B. Army.
	D. R. Jones, M.A., C. Army.
	C. Pye, U.M. Army.
Carlisle, B. and C.	E. Booth, C. Army.
Carlisle, P.M. and U.M.	W .R. Etherington, P.M. Army.
Carrickfergus.	J. Lyon, C. Army.
Caterham.,	S. Milledge, C. Army.
Charlton.	
Chatham Garrison.	J. E. Williams, C. Navy.

	H. F. Gower, C. and B. Army.
Chelmsford.	J. W. Everingham, P.M. Army.
Cheltenham.	S. S. Shrubsole, B.D., C. Army.
Chester. B. and C.	J. J. Hargreaves, B. Army.
Chester. P.M. and U.M.	F. W. Henshall, P.M. Army.
Chester - le - Street.	E. Hall. C. Army.
Chipstead and Bessels	
Green District.	G.H. Harris, B. Army.
Christchurch.	H. Coley, C. Army.
Cinderford.	A. T. Matthews, B. Army.
Cirencester.	A. Warcup, P.M. Army.
Cleethorpes.	W. J. Ward, P.M. Army.
Colchester. B. and C.	L. K. Parry, B.SC., C. Army.
Colchester. P.M. and U.M.	T. Banks, P.M. Army.
Colwyn Bay, English C.	T. Lloyd, C. Army.
Colwyn Bay, English B.	D. Griffiths, B. Army.
Cork.	F. W. Gracey, B. Army.
Cosham.	F. Batten, B. Army.
Cottingham.	T. L. Moore, C. Army.
Cramlington.	J. J. Cook, P.M. Army.
Crowborough Camps.	A .C. Tarbolton, C. Army.
Crystal Palace.	W. J. Shergold, C. Navy.
Crystal Palace. P.M. and U.M.	W. R. Bird, P.M.
Cuckfield.	S. Maddock, C. Army.
Curragh.	J. W. Pearce, B. Army.
Darlington. B. and C.	H. H. Thompson, B. Army.
Darlington. P.M. and U.M.	W. Barton, P.M. Army.
Dartmouth.	H. U. Hobbs, B. Navy.
Deal. C. and P.	T. O. Prosser, C. Navy and Army.
Deal. B.	W. L. Mackenzie, Navy and Army.
Deal. P.M. and U.M.	D. E. J. Simpson, P.M. Army.
Deptford.	H. L. Hurn, C. Army.
Derby. B. and C.	W .A. Richards, B. Army.
Derby. P.M. and U.M.	J. A. Taylor, P.M. Army.
Devizes.	J. Day, B. Army.
Devonport B. and C.	F. W. Dunster, B. Navy and Army.
Devonport. P.M. and U.M.	A. J. Conibear, U.M. Navy.
Doncaster. B. and C.	C. B. Combe, B. Army.
Doncaster. P.M. and U.M.	G. E. Rudram, P.M. Army.
Dorchester.	R. S. Holmes, C. Army.
Dorking.	T. R. Grantham, C. Army.
Dover. C.	F. P. Basden, C. Navy and Army.
Dover. B.	W. Holyoak, B. Navy and Army.
Dover. P.M. and U.M.	W. W. Goldstraw, P.M. Army.
Dovercourt and Harwich,	
B. and C.	E. E. Greening, C. Navy and Army.
Dovercourt and Harwich,	
P.M. and U.M.	J. Wellings, P.M. Navy and Army.
Downham (Norfolk)	G. Eayrs, F.R.Hist.S., U.M. Army.
Driffield.	E. Rogers, U.M. Army.
Dublin.	J. W. Pearce, B. Army.
Dunfermline.	W. S. Stein, M.A., C. Army.
Dunmow.	W. H. Pace B.D. C. Army.
Dunstable.	T. L. Page, P.M. Army.
Eastbourne.	T. S. East, P.M. Army.
East Dereham.	H. R. Didcock, P.M. Army.
East Ham, (East Ham	
Battery of the R.F.A.)	A. Salmon, C. Army.
Eastleigh.	W. F. Grey, B. Army.
Eastleigh (Clearing Hostpital)	D. Tran, C. Army.

Edinburgh. Easter Road,	
Albion Road, Olympia,	
Shrub Hill and Kings Park.	A. Griffiths, B. Army.
The Castle, Forrest Road,	
Heriot School, Infirmary	
Street.	A. D. Martin, C. Army.
Gillespie's School,	
Bruntsfield and Warrender	
Park Schools.	H. M. Scott, C. Army.
Preston Street School,	
Nelson's Works,	
Livingstone Hall.	G. R. Russell, P.M. Army.
Dalmeny Street,	
Wellington Place,	
Leith Fort Granton.	A. D. Lewis, B. Army.
London Street,	
East Claremont Street,	
Brandon Terrace.	G. Donald, C. Army.
Craiglockart and Redford.	G. Harper, B. Army.
Ellesmere.	H. Parry, C. Army.
Englefield Green, Hospital.	A. E. Snashall, C. Army.
Epsom Hospital.	A. M. Chirgwin, B.A., C. Army.
Euston Thetford.	F. G. Starling, P.M. Army.
Ewell Hospital.	A. M. Chirgwin, B.A., C. Army.
Exeter.	G. F. Owen, B. Army.
Knightshayes Court Hospital.	H. B. Case, B. Army.
Exmouth.	A. Thompson, B.A., C. Army.
Fakenham.	A. E. H. Tucker, P.M. Army.
Falmouth. B. and C.	W. V. Robinson, B.A., B. Army.
Falmouth. P.M. and U.M.	H. P. Ellis, C.M. Army.
St. Anthony. B. and C.	H. G. Steer, C. Army.
Felixstowe.	F. T. Astbury, C. Army.
Feltham and Hanworth.	H. E. Hewitt, C. Army.
Fenny Stratford.	B. Williams, B. Army.
Filey.	G. P. Maynard, P.M. Army.
Fleet, Hants.	B. Broadbent, B. Army.
Fleetwood.	A. Bailey, J.P., C. Army.
Folkestone.	J.C. Carlile, B. Army.
Frome.	J. S. Paige, B. Army.
Gainsborough.	A. Baldwin, P.M. Army.
Gateshead.	E. Ratcliffe. U.M. Army.
Gibraltar.	A.B. Sackett, W. Army and Navy.
Glasgow.	Wm. Glover, P.M. Army.
Mary Hill and Burnhouse.	J. W. Derry, C. Army.
Springburn City Hall.	A. J. Westlake, B. army.
Godalming.	F. W. Collyer. C. Army.
Gosforth, Northumberland	
War Hospital.	G. W. Wilson, U.M. Army.
Gosport.	E. W. Barry, B. Navy and Army.
	E. W. Franks, M.A., C. Navy.
Govan.	P. Smith, Navy.
Grantham.	W. G. Summers, C. Army.
Gravesend. B. and C.	Geo. Sneesby, B. Army.
Gravesend. P.M. and U.M.	G. S. Read, P.M. Army.
Graylingwell Hospital.	C. H. Spivey, P.M. Army.
Great Harwood,	
Whalley Hospital.	A. Peel, M.A., C. Army.
Great Malvern.	W. J. Povey, M.A., B. Army.
Great Yarmouth.	G. McLuckie, B.A., Army.
Grimsby.	T. B. Hainsworth, B. Army.
	T. Cook, P.M. Army.

Guernsey.	J. Gard, B. Army.	Lewes.	J. P. Morris. B. Army.
Halesworth.	W. H. Hore, C. Army.	Leyburn Wensley Park.	J. Poynton. C. Army.
Halifax. B.and C.	Alec Charlton, B. Army.	Lichfield.	D. Sheen. C. Army.
Halifax. P.M. and U.M.	J. Dodd, P.M. Army.	Limerick.	H. E. Spelman. B. Army.
Haltwhistle.	J. E. Leuty, P.M. Army.	Lincoln Woodhall	
Hamilton.	F. C. Taylor, M.A., B.D., P.M. Army.	Spa Hospital.	J. L. Brooks. C. Army.
Harpenden.	L. E. Dowsett, C. Army.	Lincoln Hospitals.	W. Walker. B. Army.
Harrogate.	W. M. Barwell, M.A., C. Army.		(Mr) T. J. Withers. B. Army.
Hartlepool.	F. Humble, P.M. Army.		G. Barrett. C. Army.
Hartlepool West.	W. Heath, C. Army.		W. Lee. M.A., P.M. Army.
Harwich and Dovercourt.		Liverpool & District Camps.	T. R. Dann. B. Senior Officiating
B. and C.	E. E. Greening, C. Navy.		Clergyman.
Harwich and Dovercourt.		Aigburth.	E. Richards. U.M. Army.
P.M. and U.M.	J. Wellings, P.M. Navy.	Sniggery, Hightown	
Haslingden Hospital.	J. W. Nairn, C. Army.	and Crosby Battery.	T. H. Martin. M.A., C. Army.
Haverfordwest.		Moor Lane Thornton.	W. A. R. Collins. P.M. Army.
B. and C. Welsh.	E. Lawrence, B. army.	Seaforth and Litherland.	S. R. Jenkins. B.A., C. Army.
Helmsley.	G. Freeman, P.M. Army.	Wirral Peninsula Hospitals.	W. H. Jefferson. C. Army.
Hemel Hempstead and		Fazakerley	J. H. Ferguson. M.A., C. Army.
Boxmoor.	F. Neal, B. Army.	Alde Hey.	A. Pickles. M.A., C. Army.
Henley on Thames.	S. T. Tucker, C. Army.	Highfield Infirmary.	H. Golding. C. Army.
Hertford.	H. R. Cripps, B. Army.	Venice Street Council School	C. F. Hill. U.M. Army.
Haydon Couston and		Sherlock Street Council	
Haveringland Camps.	J. A. Ashworth, P.M. Army.	School.	F. W. Nicholson. C. Army.
Heytesbury.	F. Vardon, C. Army.	Westminster Road	
High Wycombe	H. C. Gaut, C. Army.	Council School.	P. Nume. P.M. Army.
Hitchin.	B. Army.	Royal Infirmary.	J. H. Burkitt. U.M. Army.
Holbeach.	A. C. Cawdron, B. Army.	Stanley Hospital	Albert Jones. B.A., B.D., C. Army.
Holyhead.	J. H. Rees, C. Navy.	Northern Hospital.	J. F. Shearer. B. Army.
Holywood.	W. J. Davey, C. Army.	Southern Hospital.	W. Barlow. P.M. Army.
Home Division.	W. E. Wells, B. Army.	Woolton.	J.S . Thompson. C. Army.
Horsham.	A. Waugh, B. Army.	Longmoor Lane	
Hounslow. B. and C.	L. J. McCrea, C. Army.	Council School.	A. Jones. C. Army.
Hounslow. P.M. and U.M.	C. Spooner, P.M. Army.	Hill Road Infirmary.	B. Army.
Hull.	A. Walliker, P.M. Army.	Llandrindod Wells.	J. Jones. B.sc. B. Army.
Huntingdon.	J. McAuslane, B. Army.	Llandudno (English).	J. Raymond. B. Army.
Hursley Park and Baddesley.	E. F. M. Vokes, B. Army.	Llandudno. B. P.M.	
Hythe.	F. Hirst, C. Army.	and U.M. (Welsh).	D. Davies. B. Army
Ipswich.	F. C. France, P.M. Army.	London Hospitals.	(see end of list)
Isle of Wight;		Longton.	C. W. Hall. C. Army.
Sandown & Sandguard Fort.	M. Johnson, C. Army.	Lostwithiel.	E. H. Smith. U.M. Army.
Parkhurst.	T. Letcher, U.M. Army.	Loughborough.	R. F. Handford. B. army.
Brading.	W F. Clarkson, B.A., C. Army.	Louth.	H. A. Hunt. B. Army.
Freshwater.	F. J. Jenkins, U.M. Army.	Lowestoft.	A. R.Barnes. U.M. Navy.
Jarrow on Tyne.	G. W. King, P.M. Army.	Lowestoft.	G. Hancock. P.M. Army.
Jersey.	W. C. Walters, C. Army.	Luton. B. and C.	G. R. Hern. B. Army.
Kettering.	C. Deeble, C. Army.	Luton. P.M. and U.M.	E. E. Jobling. P.M. Army.
Kidderminster.	E. D. Bainbridge, C. Army.	Lytham.	F. J. Layton. C. Army.
Kirkby Lonsdale.	H. C. Over, C. Army.	Maldon.	T. H. Alexander. C. Army.
Lancaster.	J. M. Brown, P.M. Army.	Manchester District.	J. Heath. Army. Senior Officiating
Lee, London.	E.O. Evans, C. Army.		Clergyman.
Leicester, Glen Parva.	W. S. Leach, P.M. Army.	Manchester and	
Royal Infirmary Hospital.	A. James, C. Army.	Salford Hospitals.	S. G. Walker. C. Army.
5th Northern Hospital.	D.H. Jenkins, B. Army.		R. Reid. C. Army.
North Evington		Old Trafford Hospital.	A. H. Hawkins. B. Army.
Military Hospital.	W. Leicester, U.M. Army.		E. L. Davis. U.M. Army.
Desford Convalescent Home.	E. A. martin, B. Army.	Seymour Park.	
Gilroes Convalescent Home.	R. Veitch, M.A., C. Army.	Military Hospital.	A. H. Hawkins. B. Army.
Leiston.	W. J. R. Petherick, C. Army.	Manchester P.M and U.M.	A. L. Humphreys. M.A., P.M. Army.
Levenshulme.		Manchester Heaton Park	
Manchester Hospital.	C. Musk, C. Army.	B. and C.	H. Gardner. C. Army.

Mansfield Clipstone Camp.	C. F. Gill. P.M. Army.
Margate.	J. J. knight. B. Army.
Martham.	W. H. Lawson. P.M. Army.
Matlock.	J. H. Taylor. P.M. Army.
Melton Constable.	A. E. Tucker. P.M. Army.
Middlesbrough.	F. W. Atkin. P.M. Army.
Milford Haven.	D. Garro-Jones. C. Navy.
	E. V. Tidman. B. Navy.
Mill Hill Barracks.	W. H. Harwood. C. Army.
Milton under Wychwood.	
Brueon Abbey Hospital.	G .A. Griffith. B. Army.
Monmouth.	F. C. Tucker. B. Army.
Morecambe.	M. de J. Lark. U.M. Army.
Morpeth.	J. C. Sutcliffe. P.M. Army.
Newark.	J. D. Burns. C. Army.
Newbury.	C. V. Pike. B. Army.
Newcastle on Tyne. B. & C.	T. J.Whitman. B. Army.
Newcastle on Tyne. P.M. U.M.	T. Cooper. U,M. Army.
Newcastle on Tyne.	
(Heaton, Shieldfield, Byker,	
St. Peters, Walker, Walkergate,	
and Wallsend) B. and C.	W. Clover. C. Army.
Newhaven.	S. F. Sullivan. B.D., C. Army.
Newmarket.	S. M. Hayward. B.A., C. Army.
Newport (Mon).	A. T. Jones. B. Army.
Hospital.	E. Walrond-Skinner. C. Army.
Newport Pagnell.	A. Seys Howell. C. Army.
Newquay.	J. F. Archer. B. Navy and Army.
Northampton. B.	E. J. Thynne. B. Army.
Northampton. C.	E. M. Stanley. M.A., C. Army.
Northampton. P.M. and U.M.	A. Beavan. P.M. Army.
North Shields.	C. Stanley. B. Army.
North Walsham.	F. W. Walter. C. Army.
Norwich and Hospitals. C.	J. J. Brooker. C. Army.
Norwich and Hospitals.	
P.M and U.M.	A. Bromley. U.M. Army.
Norwich and Hospitals. B.	J. G. Edwards.B.A., B. Army.
Nottingham.	A. R. Henderson. M.A., C. Army.
Nottingham Beeston.	R. C. Ford. M.A., B. Army.
Nottingham Bulwell.	A. M. Roberts. B. Army.
Ongar.	G. F. White. C. Army.
Oswestry Park Hill Camp.	
and Drenewydd.	J. J.Poynter. C. Army.
Otley.	C. T. Rae. M.A., B.D., C. Army.
Oxford. B. and C.	J. Dann. B. Army.
Oxford. P.M and U.M.	J. W. Fish. P.M. Army.
Paignton.	G. W. Warwick. B. Army.
Peebles.	J. Dewar. B. Army.
Pembroke Dock. C.	J. E. Griffiths. C. Navy and Army.
Pembroke Dock. P.M. & U.M.	G. Freezer. P.M. Army.
Petersfield.	T. L. Hutson. C. Army.
Pirbright and Home Division.	W. E. Wells. B. Army.
Plymouth.	Wilson Eccles. P.M. Army.
Pontefract.	J. W. Cotton. P.M. Army.
Pontypool.	J. B. Ashton. B. Army.
Portobello.	D. M. Walker. B. Army.
Portland.	S. V. Wylie. C. Navy and Army.
Portmadoc.	E. M. Rowlands. B. Army.
Portslade.	T. Whitehouse. C. Army.
Portsmouth. B.	E. J. Woodall. B. Navy and Army.
Portsmouth. P.M. and U.M.	E. Genner. U.M. Navy and Army.
Portsmouth. C.	J. W. Davies. C. Navy and Army.
Prees Heath.	A. U. Moffatt. C. Army.
Prescot.	E. Baguley. C. Army.
Prestatyn.	B. Williams. C. Army.
Preston.	A. Crage. U.M. Army.
Princes Risborough.	J. Naighbour. B. Army.
Purfleet.	J. E. Caswell. B. Army.
Queenborough.	C. Army.
Queenstown Ireland.	V. A. Cotter. M.A., P. Navy.
Ramsgate.	T. Hancocks. B. Army.
Rayleigh.	T. W. Mason. C. Army.
Reading.	J. A. Sutherland. B. Army.
Redcar.	A. Barrett. C. Army.
Redhill.	W. A.H. Legg. M.A., C. Army.
Reigate.	C. B. Jutson. C. Army.
Retford. Babworth Park.	H. F. Croft. C. Army.
Rhyl.	E. T. Davies. B. Army.
Richmond Park.	A. Johnstone. C. Army.
Richmond Military Hospital.	H. Warde. M.A., B. Army.
Richmond, Yorks.	
Hipswell Camp.	R. Lewis C. Army.
Scotton Camp.	B. Drewery. P.M. Army.
Ripon.	R. W. Johnson. C. Army.
Rochester. B.	G. A. Miller. B. Army.
Rochester. C.	J. Kingdon. C. Army.
Rochford.	H. Bevan. C. Army.
Rock Ferry and Birkenhead.	W. H. Jefferson. C. Army.
Romford. Hare Hall Camp.	E. Rusling. B. Army.
Romsey and District.	E. F. M. Yokes. B. Army.
Ross - on - Wye.	J. W. kettle. B. Army.
Rosyth and District.	D. M. Walker. B. Navy and Army.
Rothbury.	J. Simpson. C. Army.
St. Albans.	E. J. Debnam. B. Army.
St. Annes-on-the-Sea.	P. B. W. Cowie. M.A., B. Army.
St. Helena.	H. G. Wood. B. Navy and Army.
St. Neots.	J. Whale. C. Army.
Salisbury Plain. Bulford.	
Durrington.	M. Stacey. C.F., C. Army.
Codford.	C. H. Shave. C.F., C.
	Assisted by W. Daniel. C. Army.
Fovant.	C. J. Farr. C. Army.
Rollestone, Fargo and	
West Camps.	W. S. Wyle. B. Army.
Lark Hill.	H. C. Miller. C. Army.
Sutton Veny.	Edward. E. Hayward. M.A., B. Army.
Saltash and St. Stephen.	G. McFadyean. B. Army.
Saltburn by the Sea.	A. Antrobus. C. Army.
Sandgate, (Shorncliffe) C.	A. Wilson. B.A., C. Army.
Sandgate, (Shorncliffe) B.	J. C. Carlile. B. Army.
Scarborough.	W. T. Cole. P.M. Army.
Seaford. C.	Hugh Parry. C. Army
Seaford. B.	R. M. Hunter. B. Army.
Seaham Harbour.	W. M. Wilkinson. U.M. Army.
Seaton Delaval District	J. G. Soulsby. P.M. Army.
Sevenoaks and Riverhead.	C. J. Clarke. C. Army.
Shaftsbury.	H. Lancaster. P.M. Army.
Sheerness.	Arthur E. Bradford. B. Navy and Army.
Sheffield.	J. Redhead. P.M. Army.
Dore Masonic Hall Hospital.	J. J. Frewing. C. Army.
Base Hospital.	H. J. Watts. U.M. Army.
Wadsley Asylum Hospital.	G. C. Holt. C. Army.

Carter Knowle Hospital.	J. R. Tranmer. P.M. Army.
Fir Vale Hospital.	G. Carver. U.M. Army.
Graystones Council	
School Hospital.	F. W. B. Weeks. C. Army.
Western Road School	
Hospital.	F. D. Tranter. B. Army.
Royal Hospital.	M. J. Ffrence. C. Army.
Lodge Moor Hospital.	J. Jones Vaughan. C. Army.
Winter-street Hospital.	E. Lewis. B. Army.
Sherringham.	F. S. Page. U.M. Army.
Shoeburyness.	W. Tingle. P.M. Army.
Shoreham. B and C	E. Gregory. C. Army.
Shoreham. P.M. and U.M.	G. Wood. P.M. Army.
Shrewsbury.	W. J. Farrow. B.A., B.D., C. Army.
Skipton.	L. H. Gaunt. M.A., C. Army.
Slough.	T. Cousens. B. Army.
Snodland.	J. Reese Jones. C. Army.
Southampton.	H. T. Spencer. M.A., M.Sc., C. Army.
Netley Hospital.	F. W. Duncombe. B. Army.
Southport.	J. T. Barkby. P.M. Army.
South China. B.and C.	J. K. Maconachie. C. Army.
South Shields.	E. Smith. B. Army.
Southwold.	J. L. Buddell. M.A., C. Army.
Stafford, Penkridge Bank.	G. J. Johnson. B. Army.
Brocton and Tixall Camps.	F. S. foster. U.M. Army.
Staines.	H. T. Donaldson. B.A., C. Army.
Stockport.:--	
Greek Street Hospital.	H. Twyford. U.M. Army.
Stepping Hill Hospital.	J. H. Halstead. C. Army.
St. George's Hill Hospital.	W. H. Thomas. B. Army.
Hollywood Park Hospital.	D. W. Roberts. C. Army.
Vernon Park Hospital.	W. Dewdney. U.M. Army.
Stourport Hospitals.	A. Gibson. C. Army.
Streatham.	M. Caldwell. B. Army.
Sunderland, West End	
and Hendon,	
Monkwearmouth.	G. Fawcett. P.M. Army.
(including Roker & Fulwell)	W. Turton. C. Army.
Sutton, Red Cross Hospital.	E. P. Powell. M.A., C. Army.
Swainton.	G. T. Fawcett. P.M. Army.
Swanage.	G. H. Clother. C. Army.
Swansea.	J. T. Rhys. C. Army.
Gorseinon.	D. H. Thomas. C. Army.
Swindon. Draycott Camp.	P. M. Richardson. P.M. Army.
Tadworth Camp.	
County of London.	
Epsom & Ewell Hospitals.	A. M Chirgwin. B.A., C. Army.
Taplow Hospital.	T. F. Lewis. C. Army.
Taunton.	J. H. Cox. C. Army.
Tavistock.	D. E. Davies. B.A., C. Army.
Teignmouth.	S. J. Thorpe. B. Army.
Thame Hospital.	C. Army.
Tollesbury	W. B. Anstey. C. Army.
Tonbridge, (Kent).	J. H. Allen. C. Army.
Topsham.	J. Hallett. C. Army.
Torquay.	J. C. Johnson. C. Army and Navy.
Tower of London.	J. Adams. C.F., C. Army.
Tring.	C. Pearce. B. Army.
Trowbridge.	R. V. Pryce. M.A., LL.B.. C. Army.
Tumbridge Wells.	E. A. Dowsett. C. Army.
Upwey, Bincombe Park.	J. Le Pia. C. Army.

Walton on the Naze.	W. Harrison C. Army.
Wereham.	S. W. Allen C. Army.
Warminster Camp.	F. Smith B.A., B.sc., B. Army.
Warrington.	
Lord Derby War Hospital.	J. Davidson. C. Army.
Watford.	T. P. Lansdowne. C. Army.
Weedon.	A. M. Lewin. C. Army.
Weeton Camp.	J. S. Langley. C. Army.
Wendover.	
Halton Park Camp.	J. H. Packham. P.M. Army.
Westcliff on Sea.	A. D. Belden. B.D., C. Army.
Westerham and Brasted.	J. Smith B. Army.
Westgate on Sea.	E. P. Perry. C. Army.
Westminster.	G. Campbell Morgan. D.D., C. Army.
	Deputy Mr A.E. Marsh. C.
Weston - Super - Mare.	G. S. Johnson. B. Army.
Weybridge.	
(Brooklands. Barham.	
St. George's Hill, Caens'	
Hill & Erin Lodge Hospitals)	E. Hitchcock. C. Army.
Weymouth and District;-	
Bovington.	G. R. Trussell. P.M. Army.
Upway.	J. Le. Pla. C. Army.
Wyke Regis.	J. E. Sunderland. P.M. Army.
Weymouth, West Ham	
and Nothe.	W. L. Forster. C. Army.
Whitchurch.	A. U. Moffatt. C. Army.
Whitley Bay.	F. H. Capey. U.M. Army.
Willesden Green.	G. W. Keesey. C. Army.
Wimbledon.	J. Beeby. C. Army.
Wimborne.	E. J. Sainsbury. C. Army.
Winchester. B. C.	A. G. Edgerton. B. Army.
Winchester. P.M. and U.M	W. J. Hammersley. P.M. Army.
Windsor.	G. F. Williams. C. Army.
Wingham.	H. J. Bayley. C. Army.
Witham.	D. M. Picton. C. Army.
Woking, Inkererman Camp.	W. H. Tebbit. B. Army.
Woodcote Park	
Convalescent Hospital.	A. M.Chirgwin. B.A., C. Army.
Woolwich.	J. Seeley. C.F., B. Army.
Wood Green	
(Alexander Palace).	J. Stevens. D.D., C. Army.
Worksop.	G. C. Lambert. M.A., B.D., C. Army.
Wrexham.	L. Morris. B. Army.
Wymondham (Norfolk).	E. Russell. C. Army.
Yeovil.	J. J. Hodson. M.A., P.M. Army.
York. B. and C.	J. Brighting. C. Army.
York. P.M. and U.M	T .A. Brown. P.M. Army.

LONDON HOSPITALS.

Balham, Weir Hospital	H. H. Carlisle. M.A., C.
Bermondsey, Princess Louise Home.	G. S. Morgan. C.
Bethnal Green.	H. Parrott. P.M.
Brondesbury Park. R. C. Mission.	H. J. Andews. B.
Brixton, Camberwell. Myatt's Field. St. Gabriel's College, 1st London General Hospital.	W. P. Hodge. P.
Charing Cross.	W. A. Clyde. B.
Charlton, Dodson's Relief.	R. S. Jones. C.
Chelsea, (Lady Mountgarret's) Baroness de Goldsmith's.	W. A. Clyde. C.
St. Mark's College.	J. Adams. C.F. C.
Chiswick, Devon Nook.	C. W. Sykes. C.
Clapton, Lower, Clifden Road. (City of London Military Hospital).	D. Lindsay. B.
	H. Harries. M.A., C.
	J. K. Ellwood. P.M.
Cricklewood. St. Peter's.	H. J. Andrews. B.
Croydon War Hospital ;- Ecclesbourne Road Schools. Stamford Road Schools. Ingram Road Schools. Davison Road Schools. Crescent Schools.	A. J. Reid. B.
Infirmary.	J. W. Ewing. M.A., D.D., B.
Denmark Hill (4th London General Hospital).	J. Adams. C.F., C.
Dollis Hill. St. Andrew's R.C.	H. J. Andrews. B.
East Dulwich Military Hospital.	M. R. Kirkpatrick. C.
Edmonton Military Hospital.	C. Garrett. B.
Endell Street Military Hospital.	T. Phillips. B.A., B.
	F. C. Spurr. B.
	J. Adams. C.F., C.
	T. H. Lodge. P.M.
Fulham Military Hospital.	
Hammersmith, West London Military Hospital.	C. W. Skyes. C.
Hampstead Military Hospital.	E. Shillito. M.A., C.
Mount Vernon.	P. T. Thomson. M.A., B.

New End.	A. A. Bourne. C.
Hendon V. A. Hospital.	W. J. Lawrence. C.
Italian Hospital.	W. Charter Piggott. C.
Kingsland Road Relief Hospital.	E. Williams. B.
	C. F. Williams. C.
King George's Hospital Stamford Street.	J. Adams. C.F., C.
Lewisham Military Hospital.	J. Eames. M.A., C.
London Bridge, Fishmongers Hall.	T. Phillips. B.A., B.
Middlesex.	W. Carter Piggott. C.
Mile End Military Hospital.	E. Hamson. C.
Queen Alexandra's Hospital.	J. Adams.C.F., C.
Richmond Military Hospital.	H. Warde. M.A., B.
St. Thomas's.	H. Kenward. C.
Tooting Military Hospital.	C. Williams. C.
Tottenham Prince of Wales.	T. Warren. C.
Twickenham Military Hospital.	J. Sayer. B.
Uxbridge Military Hospital.	F. L. R. Lowe.
C.Wandsworth 3rd London General Hospital.	J. N. Britton. B.
	W. L. Lee. C.
	W. T. Dyke. C.
	A. J. Payne. B.
	G. H. Butt. P.M.
Wandsworth (Welsh-speaking soldiers)	D. Tyler Davies. Calv. Meth.
Wandsworth Bolingbroke Hospital.	G. S. Hull. B.
Willesden St. Mark's Institute.	H. J. Andrews. B.
V. A. Hospital. St. Matthews Institute.	
Winchmore Hill Roseneath.	N. Richards. B.D., C.
Gibraltar, W. B. and C.	A. B. Sackett. W. Army and Navy.
South China, B. and C.	J. Kirk Maconachie. C. Army and Navy. The Manse Hong Kong.
St. Helena B. and C.	H. G. Wood. B. Army and Navy.

India:-

Agra. B.C., W.	G. A. Smith. B. Army.
Bombay. B. and C.	A. E. Hubbard. B. Navy.
Dinapore. B.C., W.	H. Dyche. B. Army.
Kasauli and District. B.C., U.M., P.M., and P.	C. H. Williams. B. Army.

SUMMARY OF CHANGES IN THE BRITISH ISLES 1915.

NEW SETTLEMENTS

Name.	Place.	College.
Anderson, James Dalgleish.	Blyth.	Lancashire.
Atkins, Charles Leslie.	Rothwell.	Western.
Beer, W. Haddon.	Winslow.	Nottingham.
Bell, John Henry.	Brill.	Co. Un. Exam.
Bennett, James.	Goodwick.	Carmarthen.
Blandford, Frank. B.A.,	Southampton, Bitterne Park.	Western.
Booth, Charles Hall.	Ripponden.	Nottingham.
Bowen, D. Edgar.M.A., B.D.	Hereford, England.	Lancashire.
Burgoine, Norman.	Alsager.	Nottingham.
Constable, William Abbott, M.A.,	Halifax, Ovenden.	Bradford United.
Darrell, John William.	Barnsley.	Co. Un. Exam.
Davies, Albert George.	Halifax, Mixenden.	Nottingham.
Davies, Benjamin Palmerston.	Saron, Birchgrove.	Brecon.
Davies, F. H.	Bethesda, Talybout.	Manchester, Owens.
Davies, J.G. B.A., B.D.	Llantwit Major Bethesda Fro.	Bala-Bangor.
Evans, Henry Havelock. M. A.,	Godalming (Asst).	New.
Goodman, Frederick.	Wellingborough.	Nottingham.
Griffiths, Rees. M.A., B.D.	Llanelly Park.	New.
Griffiths, Rhys.	Llanbradach and Ystradmynach.	Carmarthen.
Jones, Ernest.	Stubbins.	Lancashire.
Jones, Simon Marion.	Gwersylit.	Bala-Bangor.
Lawson, Harry G.	Clacton-on-Sea.	Nottingham.
Lawson, S. McEwan. M.A., B.D.	Beckenham.	Lancashire.
Moreton, C. Oscar.	Oakham.	Hackney.
Partington, Howard M.A.,	Ulverston.	Lancashire.
Philips, Urias. B.A.,	Godrerhos and Saron Crynant.	Brecon.
Potts, John.	Dalton-in-Furness.	Nottingham.
Richards, David.	Treorchy.	Carmarthen.
Roberts, M. Damford.	Weymouth, Hope.	Western.
Simpson, Andrew Ferguson. M.A.,	Thurso.	Scottish Cong, Hall.
Spooner, Perrin James. B.D.	Hastings, Roberton Street (Asst).	Hackney.
Stock, Herbert.	Liverpool, Crescent.	Hackney.
Thompson, Carlton. M.A.,	Stamford.	Bradford United.
Tissier, Alfred John Le.	Ottery-St-Mary.	Western.
Weir, John Eric.	Army Chaplain.	Western.
Whitfield, John Noel Burridge. M.A.,	Oxford, Cowley Road.	Mansfield.
Williams, Keyworth Lloyd.	Treforest.	New College.
Williams, Richard Henry.	Corwen.	Bala-Bangor.

ENTERED CONGREGATIONL MINISTRY FROM OTHER DENOMINATIONS

Atkinson, George Duncan.	Belfast Rugby Avenue.	Irish Methodist Ministry.
Cookson, Richard Henry.	West Smethwick.	Primitive Church of America.